Augustus Jessopp

Random Roaming

And other Papers

Augustus Jessopp

Random Roaming
And other Papers

ISBN/EAN: 9783744678018

Printed in Europe, USA, Canada, Australia, Japan

Cover: Foto ©Thomas Meinert / pixelio.de

More available books at **www.hansebooks.com**

RANDOM ROAMING

Faithfully yours

Augustus Jessopp

RANDOM ROAMING

And Other Papers

BY

AUGUSTUS JESSOPP, D.D.

Rector of Scarning,
Formerly Head Master of King Edward VI. School, Norwich

" Life piled on life
Were all too little, and of one to me
Little remains : but every hour is saveu
From that eternal silence, something more,
A bringer of new things."

WITH PORTRAIT

London

T. FISHER UNWIN

PATERNOSTER SQUARE

MDCCCXCIV

Preface.

❧

IT must always be a question, for a writer who has once
put on record his serious convictions on subjects which
have long occupied his thoughts, how far he is at liberty
to alter the form in which those convictions were originally
published to the world. A work of art does not admit of
being tinkered at indefinitely; it has an interest as a
record of the artist's effort to express his thoughts under
such influences of times and circumstances as can never
recur. As the world goes round the lights and shadows
change; as the world moves on our point of view must
needs be other than it was. We see "with larger other
eyes."

It is so in pictorial art—it is so in Literary art also.
Therefore in republishing the papers in this volume, I
have made only such changes as are mere corrections of
misstatements or oversights; in some few instances I
have omitted a sentence which seemed to me ill-worded,

unkind, or obscure. In the main, however, the volume expresses pretty faithfully the opinions which I held two or three years ago and the conclusions which seemed to me deducible from that measure of knowledge which was accessible to me and to others at the time I wrote.

But the pace at which we live and the indefatigable energy of explorers in every department of Scientific or Historic research is so bewildering, that he must be a bold man indeed who will hope to keep abreast of that band of alert and brilliant pioneers who are in the van of the army of progress. The very first paper in this volume is already behind the times. The existence of a Christian Church which I with some hesitation ventured to think might be found at Silchester, has actually been proved by the excavations on the spot ; and the guess of yesterday has passed into one of the certainties of to-day. So with such hints and suggestions as I have ventured to throw out with regard to the pre-historic roads of East Anglia—the significance of the few remaining tumuli along their lines, and the probability of our finding many more evidences of the commerce and civilisation of our remote progenitors than we have yet discovered. It can be but a few years before we shall have largely increased our certainties upon such questions, and every contributor to the common stock of Knowledge must be left behind by those who start from the point which he reached before them. Even the most learned find it hard to keep their books up to date ; *their labours become absorbed by those they teach ; they cannot choose but pass the lamp on to other hands and submit with what grace they may to be superseded.*

Of course there are great men whose work must last. It is difficult to believe that the day will ever come when Gibbon will not be read by old and young ; difficult, too, to imagine that the magnificent researches of General Pitt Rivers or of Sir John Evans could ever be regarded as ephemeral, or cease to be the recognised landmarks *by the help of which others must steer their course. But the rank and file—who trudge along the track as they are led, and count it glorious to follow at a distance the leaders who give the word of command—they have their day and cease to be, illustrating too aptly the provoking theory, that*

> *" The final cause of Nature's laws*
> *Is to grow obsolete."*

For myself I have had a certain purpose in writing on Historical and Archæological subjects. I have found so much delight in such studies, they have made the common objects by the wayside so full of interest, and brought me into such close and mysterious relations with the generations behind us that, from very craving for sympathy, I have felt impelled to bring others under the spell of that same fascination which has not only added to the happiness of my life, but has, I believe, added to my usefulness in the duties of my calling. But I have never pretended to *be anything more than an eager learner, always asking questions of the past, and desiring to awaken in others an intelligent curiosity. My readers may very easily get far beyond me, but in the meantime—*Fungar vice cotis. *Even so unpretentious a thing as a whetstone serves its purpose if men will deign to use it.*

The last two papers attempt to deal with two crying needs of the present; and the first of them may seem to have little or nothing to do with the past. Nor has it, except in one respect. The provisions which our forefathers made on so liberal a scale for the maintenance of a body of men who should be the religious teachers of the nation and something more, are proving inadequate for the maintenance of the clergy now. The immense increase of our population is bringing about many changes in our attitude and sentiments towards one another in view of the fierce struggle for a livelihood. There is a growing conviction that the young and strong should have the work of the world committed to them, and that the old should be laid on the shelf as soon as may be. In more industries than one the " old hands " are rudely reminded that they have had their innings, and that it is time that they should make way for their juniors. I am told that even in the clerical profession it is becoming increasingly difficult for those who have passed middle life to obtain employment. The fact, if it be a fact, is significant. But if this is the direction in which we are all moving, what is to become of the ageing and the aged among the clergy who have never had more than a bare subsistence and much less than the " living wage " which the working men in other walks of life are sternly claiming as their due ? I can see no remedy but the one I have ventured to sketch out. It seems to me that among the clergy some form of compulsory insurance against death and old age must be resorted to in the near future—that it is inevitable, I cannot doubt. Those who have done me the honour of reading my essays on The Church and the Villages *and that one entitled* Quis Custodiet,[1] *will see that this paper on* Clergy Pensions *follows as a sequel to those earlier attempts to deal with some ecclesiastical problems of the day.*

The last paper I most earnestly commend to the attention of those who belong to the wealthy classes and who have a real desire to devote a portion of their wealth to add to the comfort and happiness of the needy and the stricken. Never a week passes by without an announcement appearing in the newspapers that some benevolent person has given thousands for promoting the well-being of the poor in our towns. God forbid that I should say one word which could imply that I regard such munificence as other than noble and sure to carry a blessing with it. But this I do venture to say, that we are in our time so mastered by the pressure of the masses, *so awed*

---

[1] *" Trials of a Country Parson," pp.* 97, 143.

by the clamours of the thronging multitudes in our crowded cities, that we have no ears to hear the faint crying of the feeble and sore broken, the widows and the aged in our country villages who pine and wither and weep and die off in pathetic silence, and whom it would be so very easy to comfort and cheer and make happy, if only there were some active pity and wise help provided for them.

One of the many miserable results of all our agricultural depression and of the wild talk of agrarian empirics is that even Philanthropists appear to have given up all thought of lightening the lot of our village poor. The poor, I say, for the able-bodied are quite able to take care of themselves. As long as men have votes you may depend upon it they will not be allowed to starve. But our aged poor are in evil case indeed. They are handed over to the tender mercies of the law, and the law decrees that half-a-crown a week and a stone of flour shall be the measure of help afforded to our aged couples worn out with a lifetime of labour on the land. This is the pittance from which they are expected to provide them-selves with food and raiment and house rent and fuel, though coal may be at famine prices and the blanket be ten years old. And this is called outdoor relief forsooth ! The alternative lies between accepting it without daring to murmur, or of selling their wedding-rings and their last rags and all the rickety little furniture that reminds them of happier days, and then to totter into the Workhouse at last—to pine and whimper and perish and be shovelled into the pauper's grave.

That grim expression relief *has a certain suggestiveness attached to it, however. Observe it is not called* support *or* maintenance. *It seems that the law does not pretend to maintain the poor, they are only to be* relieved *; the assumption being that the poor creatures must not look to the guardians to keep them alive. Indeed their case would be desperate if it were so. They would perish by the hundred—perish by famine and cold and nakedness—if there were not some little charity still left in the world. But the resources of those in our country villages who could not bear—who would not dare—to see their suffering neighbours slowly die of want, are steadily falling short. Money is rapidly going away from the country and passing into the towns and their suburbs. We in the villages are all getting more and more straitened year by year. It makes our hearts almost die in us sometimes when we reflect that our resources are diminishing while the claims upon our common humanity are growing and growing. Meanwhile our labourers can never get rid of the sight of poverty in its most appealing shape—of poverty helpless and hopeless—poverty which they know to be undeserved. Week by week they are haunted by that little gathering of feeble old men and women watching hungrily for the coming of the relieving officer, and in terror lest*

their allowance should have been stopped by "the board."
Do you wonder that, with these spectres fronting them,
the labourers say to themselves, "This is what we must
come to in our turn!" or that they are the victims of a
scowling discontent which makes them impatient for any
change which may upset all things that are?

Homes for the poor and needy, for the worn out and broken
down in our country villages—homes that they may call
their own, and where they may still enjoy the blessings of
quiet and keep together their little household gods, and
hope to hand them on—homes which their children and
their children's children may help to make bright and
glad and winsome, without a thought that the aged are
dependents upon the young, who may be having a hard
struggle for themselves — such homes the law and the
state can never provide; they must come from philanthro-
pists who are not ambitious of doing things in the grand
style, who have no desire to sound a trumpet before them
on the one hand nor to do good by deputy and send a big
cheque to some Society on the other. Such philanthropists
will have to take trouble, and make inquiries, and use
their judgment, and be on their guard against overmuch
haste in maturing their plans. And what they give, they
must give with the gentle, warm, loving, living, not
with the cold, bloodless, and often very cruel, dead hand.

ONE WORD MORE.

I desire to offer my most hearty thanks to those many known and unknown friends who have responded so liberally to the appeal I made in my last volume. By their help I have been enabled to carry out some much-needed structural repairs in the fabric of the Church of this parish. If the aggregate of subscriptions, so far, has not yet risen to half the estimate which I had the temerity to name, few will wonder. But it will surprise many to learn that that aggregate has already exceeded the sum total of profits accruing to me from the sale of the four volumes which I have published during the last seven years. The world is very prone to exaggerate the gains of authorship; but who shall say how much may be drawn from the generous sympathy and kindness of those who are always on the watch to help a friend in need? I am almost tempted to believe that the " begging-letter imposture" must be the most successful kind of authorship! Nevertheless, my readers need not be afraid of my habitually resorting to this method. I am in no danger of forgetting the real worth of those priceless expressions of confidence and regard which have come to me from every quarter of the globe.

CONTENTS.

I.

RANDOM ROAMING.

ENJOYING the happy privilege of living where the air is of the purest and the water of the best, I am in the habit of deriding those who assume that it is one of the necessities of life that a man should have an annual " change." Our fathers were not restless peripatetics, yet they were wise in their generation— wise and virtuous ; they lived their lives in a dogged, robust, and useful manner; they did not live in vain ; they did not pretend that they were subject to periodical attacks of lassitude ; they did not pose as overstrained workers ; they did not lackadaisically sigh for rest. We are of different stuff. We pretend, one and all, that we need change of scene and holidays. It is the fashion of the time and no more.

Confess that it is a mere fashion, and I am prepared
to grant that it is a pleasant fashion ; but ask me to
allow that going to the end of the earth is positively
required by the average Briton because the average
Briton is an overworked animal, and I protest
against the hypocrisy of such an assumption, and
obstinately assert that I, for one, am not overworked,
and decline to move until you withdraw your plea
of necessity, which I hold to be untenable and in-
sincere.

And yet I confess I love seeing strange places, and
visiting half-forgotten places that have always something new to teach, and I know too well how *borné*
any one becomes who never stirs from home. Only
don't talk to me of the advantage of "change of
air." For to such as we, any change of air is a change
for the worse.

We had been reading Professor Burrows' charm-
ing book about the Cinque Ports, and a hankering
came upon me to go and see the old towns with my
own eyes. So we made a beautiful plan, and we
mapped it out day by day, and we had it all set
down in black and white, and we were going to spend
nineteen days in researches of the most interesting
and instructive kind. Canterbury was to be our
base, and all the coast from Reculver to Beachy
Head our land of pilgrimage. What were we

not going to do and to see! Let it be confessed
at once that our plans came to nothing: we
did not even get to Dover, and we did not see
Dungeness.

Alack! How beautiful plans do fade into nothing-
ness! Something happens—and something happened
with us. I have the great happiness of knowing
two large-hearted brethren. Twins they are and
never parted—great-hearted brethren, and broad-
browed, strong and clear of brain, right manly and
gentle and generous, and of widest sympathies, and
their names are Walt and Vult. Perhaps you have
read of two such brethren in Jean Paul's perplexing
story. I am afraid young men do not read Richter
now. Young men now are not in the mood for anything sentimental—they "like incident," so they
tell me, and they "never heard of Walt and Vult."
Richter's pair of brothers are dead, and have been
dead for some two generations at least. But the
brothers Walt and Vult who are my dear friends, are
alive now; and long may they live to make the
world better and happier by their influence!

One morning, just as we were preparing to carry
out that carefully considered plan of ours, came a
letter from Walt and Vult, saying peremptorily,
"We desire to see you, friend. Redeem your
promise and let us know the Lady Shepherd [these

were their very words], and we will show you something of Sussex." It is pitiful to think of such
weakness as we exhibited ; but it seemed that some
occult force was acting on us, a wilfulness stronger
than our own wills prevailed, and actually next
morning—yes, within twenty-four hours—we had
thrown up all our plans and had started off without
helm or compass, surrendering ourselves to the
brothers Walt and Vult. When the train stopped,
lo ! we were at about the most prosaic town in the
island of Great Britain ; and the name of that town
is Brighton.

Until some ten years ago I had a bigoted aversion
to the very name of Brighton—nay, a rancorous and
vindictive hatred of the place. At four years old I
had the measles—blame me not, ye critics ! I had
no option in the matter—I took the measles, or,
rather, the measles took me ; and being weakened
by the malady, I was sent down to Brighton with
my nurse—a very wicked woman—who had strict
orders to give me baths in the sea. There was a
wickeder woman than she, and that last woman
derided me again and again, and resolutely plunged
me in the brine. Dr. Johnson once observed that
he never wished to meet a fool in heaven. What
would he have said to meeting a bathing-woman in
the Islands of the Blest ?

The recollection of that sea-bathing gave me a fierce repugnance to Brighton for well-nigh forty years, until one day accident took me there, and I found the place better than I had expected—I had no longer any dread of meeting that bathing-woman on the shore. Now, as I grasped the hands of Walt and Vult, I felt that no great harm could come to me; I acquiesced in the situation, and was almost glad. Having arrived at Brighton, it remained to make the best of our opportunities. We realised at once that we had begun our holiday.

Wise men take a holiday with two ends in view, just as they take their meat and drink; and those ends are pleasure and profit. For myself, my notion of holiday-making is the getting of a maximum of new information and new impressions at the cost of a minimum of discomfort and fatigue. That means, that when I set out on a ramble I take it as easily as I can, and I keep my eyes and my ears open. It is all very well for young men to set out like Tartarin, bent on staggering across the crevasses and floundering over the snow. We middle-aged folk have got beyond that.

> Stout Cortez, when with eagle eyes
> He stared at the Pacific, and all his men
> Look'd at each other with a wild surmise
> Silent, upon a peak of Darien,

did not find his soul satisfied with staring; he
saw an old world behind him and a new world
before.

I know not how it is, but some of us in this age
find ourselves possessed by an insatiable yearning
not to speculate upon the future, but to get into
touch with the past. Brighton has no past worth
mentioning, yet it has something to boast of which
the casual visitor rarely hears of, rarely visits. It
has in its Museum perhaps the most complete, and
certainly the most exquisite collection of chalk fossils
in the world, and also a unique collection of pottery
and porcelain. Both one and the other were made
by the brothers Walt and Vult, or rather by brother
Vult—the other brother not objecting. That unique
collection of pottery was " made to illustrate the
principle, or rather in development of the notion,
that the history of a country may be traced in its
homely pottery." I will not presume to describe it ;
but this I do venture to assert, that he who goes to
Brighton without spending an hour or two in looking
at those mugs and plates, and cups and saucers, and
chimney ornaments, and pondering upon their significance, is not a man to be envied, in fact, he is a
man to be pitied, as all men are who, having a good
chance of learning a new lesson, throw that chance
away. But if there is not much to see at Brighton,

there is a great deal to see *from* Brighton, and for a week or so Brighton was our *base*. And what a joycus *base* it was! The talk was a perpetual feast after a day's expedition—Walt and Vult cutting in and in with noble entanglements, sometimes the whimsical brother taking the lead, sometimes the deep voice of the other vibrating with emotion, rising with enthusiasm, loud with indignation at some mention of treachery or wrong. And there was prattle of children too, such sweet prattle, and so clearly articulate withal. And there was so much to look at—such hoards of wonders in every corner, and such stories to tell! The treasures of that house are not guarded by grim lions suggesting terror and laceration, but by sculptured dogs, emblems of faithful love and nobleness.

"Cinque Ports?" said brother Vult. "We will go to Newhaven to-morrow, Newhaven supplanted one of the Cinque Ports." Not quite that; but one of the *members* of the Cinque Ports. Seaford sent two representatives to Parliament in 1300, and for centuries had contributed its quota of ships to the Royal Navy; but before the 16th century had come to an end, the river Ouse, which in its exit to the sea had made Seaford harbour, was forced by the movement of the shingle to find for itself another channel, and a new port arose which assumed the

name of Newhaven, where the traffic to Dieppe now
goes on with ever-increasing briskness.

That there could be anything at Newhaven which
was worth going to see was new to me. But where
in this England of ours can you find a place that is
not worth a visit or that has not something to make a
man find out how very ignorant he is and help him
to go home the better for his day's journey? We
had to stop at Lewes on the way. Lewes is a place
of renown, but its glory is departed. Here William
de Warenne, the great Conqueror's doughty brother-
in-arms and first Earl of Surrey, kept his state after
his fashion, and here it seems he lies buried. Of
the castle I forbear to speak. As to the glorious
priory which the great Earl and Gundrada his wife
founded here to the glory of God and for the further-
ance of devotion ¡and the contemplative life—the
greater portion of it lies buried under the railroad.
Only fragments remain. The range of conventual
buildings presented a frontage of about 400 feet, the
church was 25 feet longer than Chichester Cathedral,
90 feet longer than the Conqueror's church which he
built for his Abbey of Battle, and exactly the same
length from end to end as Lichfield Cathedral. The
foundation of this priory was an event in English
history, and the story is worth the reading. Read
it, if you can, in Mr. Hope's paper in the *Journal of*

the Archæological Institute, and there you will find all that is ever likely to be known about the fortunes of the house, its origin, its rise, its growth, and its fall. It was the first house of the Cluniac order set up in England. About these Cluniacs there is much to tell, but who will tell it to us? rather, perhaps, it may be asked, who will listen if one should try and tell it? But when your guide-book informs you that this house at Lewes continued to be the only Cluniac priory in England for the next 150 years after its foundation; do as I did to that guide-book, and put a big note of admiration in the margin of the volume.

Opposite the castle, on the other side of the railway, there stands a mound, clearly artificial; and the tradition goes that the monks of Lewes erected on the top of it a cross, and at certain seasons went in procession by an encircling path up to the top, and that there were stations here and there where special prayers were offered. I thought of that frightful mound in the city of Mexico and the bloody rites that were carried on there, and I thought of some other parallels; and then of the old Winchester practice of "keeping hills"—only abolished the other day—and I asked myself, can it be that here we have the site of some prehistoric *cultus*, and that here, ages ago, the conquering cross was planted upon

that opprobious hill
Where, for the noise of drums and timbrels loud,
The children cried unheard that passed through fire
To that grim idol?

But Lewes was only on the way: we were bound
for Newhaven. Despise not Newhaven, my brethren.
It may yet have a future—it certainly has a past.
Despise nothing: *le mépris est le masque où s'abrite la
nullité,* and very few of us can be "splendidly null."

Said brother Vult, "You must go and see the
church." Said brother Walt, "We cannot bear you
company: we cannot away with Philistines, clerical
or other—you must go alone." In some perplexity
I obeyed. That church is worth a visit—emphati-
cally worth it, for the wondrous little Norman apse
and the beauty of its situation, and for something
more. There is a tombstone there, and on it an
epitaph. It is in memory of an old parishioner who
was, it seems, of a jovial turn, and of whom it is
recorded that *he knew his Hudibras by heart.* Distinctly Christian in its tone that epitaph can hardly
be said to be; yet its concluding line is not without
a lesson worth remembering, for it says of the dead
to the living—

Be better, wiser, laugh more if you can.[1]

_____

[1] In view of the many perils that threaten the monuments of

When I got back to my friends, brother Walt
looked gravely at me ; then it all came out. That
clerical Philistine had actually attempted to remove
that tombstone and utterly abolish it, merely because
it did not express his views. The brethren Walt
and Vult said "No," and they stopped that
Philistine.

See where we are, and what we are coming to!
That any man who is a tenant-for-life of his benefice
should have the power—of course he has not the
right, but that doesn't matter—to cart away any
monument, inside or outside "his" church, on
which there may be expressions at variance with his

the dead, I think it prudent to print this curious inscription.
Here it is :

To the memory of THOMAS TIPPER, *who departed this life*
May the 14th, 1785, aged 54 years.

> Reader with kind regret the grave survey,
> Nor heedless pass where Tipper's ashes lay.
> Honest he was, ingenuous, blunt and kind,
> And dared to do what few dare—speak his mind.
> Philosophy and history well he knew,
> Was versed in physic and in surgery too.
> The best old Stingo he both brewed and sold,
> Nor did one knavish act to gain his gold.
> He played through life a varied comic part
> And knew immortal Hudibras by heart.
> Reader in real truth such was the man,
> Be better, wiser, laugh more if you can.

views—is that to be tolerated ?   Yes, it *is* tolerated, and it is done on the sly every year.   Think of what might happen any day, if some wild-eyed fanatic should take it into his head to sweep away every monument in brass or marble or alabaster, on which he found the horrid legend, *Cujus animæ propicietur deus ;* or that other legend, *Orate pro anima x* or *y !* When will a voice be lifted up against this shame— a voice that can make itself heard ?

That night I forgot all about the Cinque Ports, I dreamt only of wicked tombstones ; and visions rose of an infinite procession of monuments passing in long array from world to world, reaching beyond the realms of this solar system of ours, and I could not read the writing upon them ; and a whisper came to me which said : " Is not our little, our very, very little planet full of sepulchres, whose story such as thou are trying to read, and trying all in vain ? "

*   *   *   *   *

There were five great castles in Sussex—to wit, Arundel, Bramber, Knapp, Hastings, and Lewes, and to these we may add Chichester—of which anon. " To-morrow," said the brethren, " we will go to Bramber." Thither we went. People go up the Rhine and chatter about the castles on the river

banks. They are toys to our Sussex castles. Every
one of those five I have named was the home of an
English chieftain for *centuries* before the mound on
which it stood was crested with a wall of masonry
or crowned with a keep after the Norman pattern.
What we now call Bramber Castle is only the ruined
keep of the great fortress which was constructed to
guard the pass, four miles long by half-a-mile wide,
through which the Adur makes its way to the sea at
Shoreham. The platform rose 120 feet above the
river, and was scarped down the sides so as to form
a rounded area 560 feet north and south by 280 feet
east and west. The ditch at the counterscarp level
was 100 feet broad. Before the invention of gunpowder the place must have been practically impregnable by assault. Who threw up this mighty
earthwork? Who and when? The Normans found
it where it is. It was a *castle* when William landed,
and Earl Guerd was its lord in the Confessor's time.
There are, however, no signs of the Romans having
meddled with it or cared for it, though the raised
causeway that crosses the valley, formerly flooded
by the sea, marks the course of a Roman road. It
is probable that the stronghold at Bramber was the
work of the English, as Professor Freeman tells us
we must call those people who came swarming into
this island when the Romans could hold it no

longer. The Normans soon occupied the place, and William de Braose received it among his other possessions and built there the great keep with its huge walls of masonry nine feet thick, of which but a fragment remains. In 1644 Captain Temple stood a siege there, fighting for the king. When the parliamentary forces got possession of it they blew up the place with gunpowder and left it as we see it now.

*   *   *   *   *

I have noticed that when a man of average intelligence once begins to yield to the fascination of ancient castles and earthworks, it is all over with him. I do verily believe that every stupendous earthwork in Dorsetshire, and every barrow in Wiltshire, and every great castle in Sussex, is haunted, haunted with myriads of pixies, and syrens, and gnomes, the ghosts of the men who raised those wonders. The unwary creature of flesh and blood goes among these tricksy spirits at his peril. He is like Endymion, enamoured of the moon. Cynthia shone upon Endymion with a gleam of promise— distinct but distant—she was so very far away. Oh! how he yearned to know her better!

The dark ages of England end, say, with the coming of Augustine. They stretch *back*, who shall say how far? into an illimitable past, ages before the time when Abraham migrated from Ur of the Chaldees. More light has been thrown upon these ages than is usually believed. Great men have lived —are living—among us who have here and there lifted the veil; men of genius, gifted with something more than " scientific imagination "—men who know how to pursue research and how to teach. We, the small men, feel we are no more than fumblers, but a delicious intoxication seizes us when we stand on the haunted and enchanted ground : the gnomes come round us, and a wild passion for fumbling takes possession of us—we cry with Ajax, foiled and darkened—

ἐν δὲ φάει καὶ ὄλεσσον ἐπεί νύ τοι εὐαδεν οὕτως.

I confess that the sight of Bramber drove me mad. Arundel I knew—Lewes had quickened my pulse— a complication of Roman fever and castle mania with kindred disasters had clutched me. Nothing was to be done but to confess myself very ill and make the best of it.

Next day we found ourselves at the Devil's Dyke —apparently one of those enormous works which the Britons (not English this time, if you please) began to construct before the Christian era, but for some reason or other, never finished. Below them stretched the vast forest of Anderida, north and west and east ; behind them were their homes. They had an eye for coignes of vantage; they knew how to turn to account the physical features which were favourable for defence ; the organisation of labour among them had been brought to astonishing perfection; but this island of ours was divided into a number of petty kingdoms, and Rome was One.

What room for speculating and surmising as one stands on that plateau ; as one looks down into that tremendous fissure made by the action of water issuing from the chalk ; as one thinks of that strip of coast, say only from Dorchester to Dover, swarming with rich and busy towns " made ready for the spoil," while yonder over at Boulogne—even then called Portus Britannicus—there was assembling that immense invading host, at least 50,000 strong, which was soon to cross the Channel ; this time not to be beaten back, as had happened nearly a century before.

*   *   *   *   *

" Are there any remains of the castle of Chichester ? " I asked. " Not one stone left upon another," was the reply. But the resistless masters of the world had been there, and thither next went we. From end to end of that Sussex coast we find the deep impress of Roman feet, the dent of the Roman heel, the imperishable work of the Roman hands. The very ocean shrank back before them. Nowhere in Britain has the coastline undergone such change as here. Once it seems that the tides came up to those massive walls· which the legionaries raised to guard the city then called Regnum—a city which doubtless had been growing for ages with its great earthworks, its port crowded with ships, its temple or temples, such as they were, its warriors, its merchants, its courtiers, its statesmen, its party of home rulers and its other party of liberal-conservatives, just as men live now, *mutatis mutandis*.

Was it here that King Cogidubnus bore sway?— he who so soon made his peace with the awful ones, and whom the gild of the masons and carpenters of Chichester immortalised in that stone which they set up when the king gave them leave to build their temple to the goddess of wisdom and the great god of the sea, they finding the funds and a Roman settler giving them the land? That eloquent inscription may be seen at Goodwood now. The date of it? Well! the experts incline to think it may have been set up during the first twenty years of the Roman occupation. If they are right, it follows as a moral certainty that Cogidubnus, the wary and politic, must have dined with Vespasian and his son when they were learning the arts of war during those long years in England, little Titus in petticoats,

3

never having heard as yet of Palestine, or having
any dream of setting up that arch of his at Rome,
where, bitten into the marble, there still front you
the "seven candlesticks" and those other spoils
that came from the holy hill of *Zion*. My thoughts
were so full of Rome—I had, in fact, so "gone over
to Rome" by this time, and I was so baffled in my
vain attempt to make out what the castle of Chichester could have been like—though the mound, or part
of it on which Roger de Montgomery built his keep,
stands still, *en evidence*—that I was in a bad humour
when my friendly and most hospitable guide took
me to the cathedral. Chichester seemed to me,
in that ill temper of mine, a poky place. Oh,
friend of the deathless verse! why should'st thou
cry to us—

> ". . . prepare
> You lovers to know Love a thing of moods :
> Not like hard life, of laws."

It is not love alone that is a thing of moods—all our
conscious life is but a thing of moods; and lifting
up my eyes to that cathedral spire, and hearing from
an old verger, "the old spire didn't *fall*, sir; it *sunk
down*, and I saw it sink, and it couldn't help it, poor
thing, when they took away the great screen that in
a manner had kept it up for hundreds and hundreds
of years "—I was wroth, and fumed, and held my

peace in sullen silence ; but I thought, " Oh, these restorers ! "

In this perverse mood of mine it seemed to me that the most *interesting* object in Chichester was St. Mary's Hospital—the ancient *Domus Dei.* One man has risen up to write its " story." I will not do him the wrong, nor do myself the wrong, of trying to make short work of that most instructive narrative.[1] I cannot dwell upon that subject now, for life is short and art is long. But, whosoever you be that make a pilgrimage to Chichester, be sure you go and pay a visit to St. Mary's Hospital, and try and learn something about the gentle work that has been done there in a quiet unpretentious way while the generations have succeeded one another, and give your vote with mine that these places may have some reverence shown them. I might almost plead for pity, for they cannot help themselves when the plunderers are strong.

*　　　*　　　*　　　*　　　*

" I think you will not do much at the Cinque Ports this time," said brother Vult. " He ought to do something better than that," said brother Walt ;

[1] See " The Story of the ' Domus Dei ' of Chichester," . . . by the Ven. Archdeacon H. P. Wright, . . . Parker & Co., 1885. With it compare the author's other volumes on the Domus Dei at Portsmouth and on that at Stamford.

"it is the duty of every Englishman to make a pilgrimage to Pevensey." With characteristic docility we obeyed, nothing loth, and we found ourselves at Pevensey. Pevensey is a modern name. They tell us it means Peofn's Island, and that some 1,500 years ago a certain Peofn won it and held it. In earlier ages it was known as Anderida or Andredecester, and by some such name it was called when Julius Cæsar landed near it in 55 B.C. Then, it seems, there was a stronghold or fortress on this same rising ground, and the sea came up to it in long waves crawling at spring tides over the great estuary, and barely covering the wide expanse of slime where the water was too shallow to allow the Roman transports to do anything but run aground. A century or so later the legions took it as their own, and turned it into the chief fortress of the " Saxon shore." Four centuries later the wretched Britons, left to defend themselves as best they could, and hard pressed by the new swarms of " Saxon " invaders, took refuge behind those tremendous walls, and they fought with desperate valour. Desperate indeed! Standing out from the mists of legend and tradition which hang about the story of that dark time, a single tale of slaughter has come down to us that could not pass away from men's memories. It has to do with Pevensey, or, as the chronicler calls it, Andredecester. It was in the year 491 A.D.

In that year, says one, "began the kingdom of Sussex, which Ælla held right forcefully for long. . . . With a huge host he beset Andredecester, a city of most strong defences. There the Britons were gathered like bees, and day by day and night by night they beat back their beseigers. . . . But then at last, exhausted by long famine, they were all devoured by the edge of the sword, they with their women and their little ones, insomuch that not one single one escaped ; and the foreigners destroyed that city, which was never afterwards rebuilt. Yet the place, as the site of a once most noble city, is shown to those that pass it by—a place of desolation."

I love to turn to Henry of Huntingdon for more reasons than one ; but chiefly because he was a country parson, and no monk, nor even a canon. To be sure he exercised archidiaconal functions, but that's another thing : he was a country parson for all that. Nevertheless the Rev. Henry was wrong in saying, "locus tantum *ostenditur* desolatus." It is one of those slips of the pen which are frequent when a writer is quoting from some older document at his elbow. If he had written *ostendebatur* he would have been right. For Pevensey, as we have seen, was not left desolate for long; and when Peofn, whoever he was, got his island, with its Roman walls and citadel, he found it something very different from a dilapidated ruin, and it seems that it continued to be a place to have and to hold against all comers.   Ah! but that depends upon the comers. Just a week before I saw this place I had sauntered into the Chapter House of Westminster Abbey, and there on the counterfeit presentment of the Bayeaux tapestry which may be seen there, I read out, " Mare transivit et venit ad Pevensel." Who was it that came? William, Duke of Normandy, bastard son of that grim and frantic man whom they called— and called rightly, it seems—Robert the Devil. What things had come to pass in those eleven hundred years since the scared Britons hereabouts had shrunk back dismayed at the sight of Cæsar's fleet—more than eight hundred ships, he tells us, were visible at one time—abandoning the fort which they dared not attempt to hold, and falling back for refuge upon the high ground behind them. Something of the same sort happened now again. Read all about it, if you will, in the monumental history of the Norman Conquest, written once and for ever.

It was not long before Pevensey became once more a place of strength. It was besieged again and again. In 1101 Henry I. assembled his

army here when his brother, Duke Robert, was
preparing for another invasion; and the Duke had
to look out for a different landing-place. In 1309
it was a neglected ruin. Shortly afterwards it
was looked to by Edward II. In 1399 Lady
Pelham held it against all the force that Sussex,
Kent, and Surrey could bring against her. Twenty
years later, Queen Joanna, widow of Henry IV.,
was shut up in Pevensey—they said she was a
witch—another of the Pelhams keeping guard over
her. What need to go on? The place is bewildering with its crowd of memories. As I looked down
from these walls I seemed to hear the low ripple
lapping below me, Roman and Saxon and Norman
navies riding at anchor in the bay, and all the
air throbbing with the shock of battle; and then
came upon me that fine saying of Professor Maitland—" the map of England, that most wonderful
of all palimpsests!"

From Pevensey to Herstmonceux. "What a
falling-off was there, my countrymen!" A mere
architectural freak of the 15th century, a very
splendid freak, I admit—a splendid example of what
may be done in bricks and mortar. As such it is
worth a visit, but it is horribly modern! It was
built with money that came from across the Channel,
as I gather. For Sir James Fiennes, the first Lord

Say and Sele, got his reward for the part he played when the battle of Agincourt was fought; and honours—which in those days meant wealth and huge increase of income—were showered upon him, and he built this most pretentious palace, which his posterity found too vast to live in—the family was over-housed. What care I for a ruin that is hardly more than 400 years old? It is a place for picnics, and not a bad place neither. " Who keeps up the gardens and grounds ? " quoth I to the damsel who took my shilling. " We do, sir. We hire it all and make what we can ! "

What a picture Watteau could have made of a *fête champêtre* in that courtyard! Now we are expected to buy photographs, photographs, photographs; of which about one in a hundred remotely suggests a picture. At Herstmonceux the ground-plan hanging up in the gate-house is worth all the photographs.

Having made our pilgrimage to Pevensey, it followed as a matter of course that we should go to Battle. The Duke of Cleveland was there, and the visit was a disappointment. A youth took us round —a party of some twenty or so; and all that he told us was wrong—a mere jumble got up by rote, after having invented his absurdities out of his head. He irritated me! The man was a kind of embodied whooping-cough, and would not let me look about me. He went on *hacking* out his nonsense till it was quite unbearable. Suddenly I broke forth into irrepressible laughter, for clearly, distinctly, there came upon me the memory of a showman at Horn fair, whose historic diorama I peeped through in my childhood, and paid a penny for the sight. I hear the fellow now : " The parting of Hector and Andromashee ! Him to the right ; her to the left ! And you see the grand effect which the sun, the moon, and the stars has upon the face of the waters ! " For sixpence you may buy a very fair little account of Battle Abbey. What excuse is there for that young man not getting up his lesson from that ?

To have listened to the historian of the Conquest acting as showman upon that terrace, as I believe he once did, and as I am sure he could, would have been an event in one's life, even though the great man had, metaphorically, stamped upon one's toes with his iron heel and hammered his fad of "Senlac" into one with the heavy mallet of stubborn reiteration. But when our little guide put himself into position and in a shrill falsetto cried aloud, " There Harold set up his standard," he waved his hand and boxed the compass after a fashion, looking round on this side and on that with a generous impartiality and with incomparably less decision than Mr. Bird-

o'-Freedom Sawin when—peremptorily bidden by
his dark-skinned lord and master to show him the
Polestar, he—

"Pickt out a middlin' shiney one and told him that was it."

Somehow we were not in the mood to go into
heroics at Battle. The rain came down, and we
said, "We'll come here another day!" So we will
when that other fever comes upon us which is sure
to come, and we have to prowl among nunneries
and priories and abbeys. Next day we found ourselves at Hastings; no Walt and Vult to guide and
order us, and no delightful home to come back to at
eventime, with all its light and leading, and those
merry children to romp with, if only an abominable
catarrh had not forbidden the playing of the noble
game of Great Ogre!

At this point once more I am impelled to utter my
protest against the cant of the professional traveller,
who is never tired of running down our English
hotels and crying up those on the other side of the
Channel. For comfort, for reasonable charges, for
cleanliness, and obligingness [a most convenient
word]—for scrupulous honesty from the dignified
lady behind the window down to the boots—for all
that goes to make a caravansery a traveller's joy,
commend me to our English hotels.

We were roamers, as you have seen, and very random rovers. We hardly knew when we laid our heads upon the pillow where we should go next ; but Hastings is still a Cinque Port (though we had quite cooled down upon that subject by this time), and Hastings boasts of its castle, and up to it we climbed. Standing inside the inner ward of what I must call the old fortress, I felt as I never felt before how helpless any one is who, without a competent knowledge of the dynamics of geology, attempts to read the riddles of the past. No wise man need be ashamed of his ignorance of most things; and if a specialist is arrogant and supercilious, that bumptious specialist is not a wise man. But it is vexatious to approach a specialist with a problem which you have not knowledge enough to state in correct terms; and at the edge of that cliff which overlooks the sea, I fretted myself with a desire to know how the rock got to be there and how it had acquired the shape it presents now. If there had been a competent geologist in sight I would have humbly taken him by the button ; but there was none, and as I continued "nagging" at the matter all day long, the very wife of my bosom snubbed me at last, saying severely, " How foolish you are ! If you *could* hire a geologist he would only tell you that you did not know enough to have the thing explained to you ! "

At Hastings, as elsewhere along this romantic
land of Sussex, we are driven back again in thought
to the dark ages. There is, to be sure, no sign of
Roman handiwork; but almost beyond a doubt the
great earthworks, on part of which the castle ruin
stands, were thrown up by those same Britons of
whom we have heard before, and thrown up long
before the Christian era. Nay, it may be before
King Servius built his walls round Rome.

When Aulus Plautius made his landing in A.D. 43,
he does not seem to have troubled himself about the
Regni and their Sussex kingdom. They seem to have
submitted to the inevitable when the tide of conquest, that kept moving westward, placed them in a
perilous isolation; and the vast forest of Anderida,
thirty miles deep, was between them and the northern world. The sea-board they could hardly now
presume to think of calling their own. But four
centuries pass, and the English—you *may* call them
so if it makes you happy—came in, swarm after
swarm. We have heard of them and of their doings
at Pevensey; and a generation or so later we find
them at Hastings—comfortably settled there too, and
coining money. Brother Vult can show you their
coins, as he can show you the coins of Commius,
Cæsar's friend, gold coins minted perhaps at this
very Hastings in the century before wise men from

the far East came following the star that led them
to the manger at Bethlehem, what time bad Herod
trembled for his throne and slew the little ones. Did
that mint continue all through those centuries ? or
was it only one of those queer revivals which history
is for ever startling us with ? Be it as it may,
Hastings continued to coin money for another
500 years, from the 7th century down to the
time of Henry I. at least, as the numismatists
assure us ; and they can give us proof positive of
that which they assert. The mound, at an angle of
the inner ward of the castle, is beyond doubt an
English work ; and when great William pushed on
from Pevensey to Hastings in quest of food for his
host he must have set eyes upon that mound, doubtless loftier then than now, perhaps crowned with a
formidable stockade. The ruined castle, with its
collegiate church, has of course a history. Becket,
the martyred Primate, was Dean of Hastings long
years before he was Primate, and William of Wyke-
ham was one of the canons of this church, which I
suppose may be taken to mean that some part of the
revenues of the Hastings house went to build the
college of Winchester. If you are lucky enough to
be able to buy Professor Freeman's "History of the
Reign of William Rufus," you are sure to find a
great deal there about Hastings : not that I have

read the book, for I am not one of the lucky ones—
but because in the nature of things it *must* be there.

We had started from home intending to spend a
week at Canterbury. That was out of the question
now, but yet we could not leave it quite unvisited.
So at Canterbury we found ourselves. There is no
place or city in these British Islands that can for
a moment be compared with Canterbury in the
memories that it recalls—the heroic and romantic
associations that are inseparably connected with it ;
the splendour of its present and its past; the
magnificent succession of great men who lie there
entombed; the almost unbroken continuity of its
history. The chronicle of London read side by side
with the memorials of Canterbury is a dull, prosaic,
humdrum record, tame, commonplace, and rather
vulgar.

There is only one man living who *knows* Canterbury
—the all unpaid but not now unhonoured seneschal
of the Cathedral, Dr. Sheppard. It is melancholy
to reflect how much recondite lore, which can never
be amassed again by any single man, must pass
away when this grand enthusiast joins the majority.
Books have been written by the score, and many of
them good books too ; but what are books to the
living teacher's words ?

The vergers of our cathedrals, as a rule, are

excellent showmen ; they are loyal to the glorious
buildings in which they pass their days ; they get up
their lessons well; but at Canterbury they are far
superior to the average of their class. They seem to
be notably intelligent, modestly inquiring, curiously
on the alert to pick up any hint or any new piece of
information, as if they expected to be learners even
to the end. The truth is, they are conscious of the
presence among them of a master for whom they
entertain unbounded reverence. All that men know,
he knows it—what he knows not is not knowledge.
Submitting myself humbly to this guide, philosopher,
and friend, through a great vista of light and shadow
there passed before me, all in living reality, a long
drama whose successive scenes were presented with
surpassing vividness. But who could *keep hold* of it
all ? A kind of despair came upon me as I listened
and as the pageantry moved on before my very eyes.

Those two days were days of sheer bewilderment,
and what I heard and what I learnt and what I
dreamt was sometimes present, and sometimes it was
as if it had been, and sometimes as if it belonged to
another world—a world not realised. In sheer per-
plexity, when I found myself alone and tried to
bring back only a little, a very little, of what the
gifted seer had been bringing before me, I threw
myself back into the days when there was no

Canterbury, and actually a sense of relief came upon
me when the symptoms of my Roman fever returned.
For Christian Canterbury you may go to that beautiful prose poem by our great prose poet, and in
following Dean Stanley's " Memorials " you will find
enough to make the " mother of all the bishoprics "
a place to sojourn in and find a joy in for many
delightful days.

But there was a time when there was no Canterbury—I mean when it was a very different place,
and called by a very different name. If, as seems
the fact, Cæsar's first landing-place was somewhere
in Pevensey Bay, it was a strategic mistake, and he
learnt his lesson from it. When he came next, it
seems that it was in Kent, not Sussex, that he
landed. In those days there was a British road
that crossed the Stour by a ford, and at this point
there stood an ancient British " city " which went
by the name of Durovernum. There is some reason
for believing that even before the Christian era—it
may be centuries before—the place had been the
seat of some now forgotten form of worship—a
sacred city, in fact, where men offered sacrifices and
had their mystic rites, and after their fashion praised
and prayed. The Danejon is undoubtedly a British
work, and round about it there might still be noted,
two centuries ago, other mounds or barrows which

may have been the sepulchres of dead ancestors, or may have been such "high places" as we read of again and again in the most ancient records. By and by, when the Romans had won the land, at least three great roads converged at Durovernum issuing from the three mighty fortresses on the coast—Richborough, Dover, and Lymne, for we will call them by their modern names. Durovernum itself was but a kind of outpost or depôt, from which the road ran straight as a line to London. At that outpost some of the greatest of the world's great ones halted or sojourned. Cæsar, on his march to the westward; Claudius, a century later, as he pushed forward to win the laurels that had been plucked for him by another; and, in the same year, or the next, Vespasian, needy then, and bent on plunder, a rising general thirty-four years old, and with him Titus, his little son, born just three years before. When Agricola accomplished that memorable circumnavigation of the island in A.D. 84, Richborough, some twelve miles from Durovernum, was his landing-place too; and when, as we are told he did, Agricola put his soldiers into winter quarters, do you think he did not ride into Durovernum to inspect the "statio" through which he must have passed many a time before?

When, at the beginning of the 4th century, the

4

Emperor Constantius Chlorus was organising his last campaign against the Picts, *his* son, the great Constantine, joined him at Boulogne, and together they sailed across the channel, and together they must needs have taken the road through Durovernum ; and through it again the son must have hastened to take possession of the empire after his father's death at York (July, A.D. 306).

Before the century came to an end, the swarms of Saxons and Angles had poured in upon the Kentish people, and a cry arose for help ;. for the legions, it seems, were not as they had been, and the discipline of the army in Britain was weakened by continual drafts to supply the lack of men in the other provinces of the empire. For the last time Rome found a really able general to send to Britain, in the person of Theodosius, and at Richborough he too landed in 367 A.D., and with him came *his* son Theodosius, afterwards emperor ; and on the road to London— can it have been under the very walls of Durovernum ?—they smote the heathen with a great slaughter, and rid the land of them for a little while. I say he smote the heathen, for father and son were both Christians, and the son is he in whose days Christianity became in effect the established religion of the Roman Empire. Is it anything less than probable that in that very church which two

centuries later Ethelbert gave to Augustine—that
church which Bede expressly says had been built in
old times, after the ancient fashion of the Roman
Christians—Theodosius himself may have offered
up his prayers to the God of battles as he made
ready for the onslaught ? Think of it ! The south-
western tower of Canterbury actually stands upon a
portion of the Roman wall; and that old Roman
church remains to this day the *core*, if I may say so,
of the most magnificent and the most inspiring of
England's great cathedrals. In the meantime, however, Durovernum had got to be called by another
name—it was now known as " Cantwarabyrig "—
the stronghold of the men of Kent, peradventure
memorable as the place where these Kentish men
made another of those last desperate stands, and
where the end was the same as at Pevensey—a
wholesale and remorseless slaughter.

" Who can understand his errors ? " says the
Psalmist. I confess I cannot account for mine.
When I ought to have been leaving all these Roman
emperors and their heathen surroundings quite out
of view and out of remembrance, and only thinking
of Canterbury as the holy place of Christian saints
and sages, I must needs go on talking about the ages
further back, as if I were a pagan or a Heathen
Chinee ! But what could I do ? For two days had

I been sitting at the feet of a great master, trying
to follow him as he poured forth from his vast
treasure-house of knowledge that stream of romantic
truth—so much more romantic and entrancing than
any fiction; and it was as if I had been blinded by
excess of light, as if I must needs retire into the
darkness for a while if so be there might be any
hope of attaining to clear vision of anything again.

*   *   *   *   *

From Canterbury to Portsmouth—that was our
next move. We found ourselves in another world.
It is not the ecclesiastical world; but Portsmouth,
too, has its splendid traditions, and heroes have
gone forth from thence at whose names nations
have trembled, and tyrants, as they heard them,
gnashed their teeth with rage that was all idle.
If here again we should be inclined to transport
ourselves to Roman days, they tell me that even
at Portsmouth we should find traces of their audacious engineering enterprises : but I know not—I
know not.

While we rowed about that wonderful harbour—
rowed, observe! just as the old admirals did—as
Nelson did—not panting and puffing and fuming
and smoking in a rickety steam-launch, as if we had
been in an ignorant hurry and only wanted to get
done with it—as we rowed leisurely along, our boat-

man, familiar with every mast and every buoy, and
garrulously saving us even the trouble of asking
questions, we were perfectly sure that the lotus-
eaters had never known such conscious bliss as
ours. They chaunted querulously; we were silent.

In that delicious October sunshine, with never a
breath to disturb the quiet air, and never a ruffle on
the gently heaving water, we gave ourselves up to
the impressions of the moment. Imagination, even
while we rowed bareheaded under the *Victory's* bows,
refused to rise to the occasion: she claimed, and
she took, a holiday.

An attitude of somewhat haughty modernism
characterises Portsmouth. There people have little
taste for retrospection; all that has been is worth
thinking of only so far as it may have led up to what
is and what shall be. As to the great ironclads, and
the monster guns, and the vast dockyard, *et hoc genus
omne*, there is no need to speak of them; but there
are two modern buildings, the one civil, the other
ecclesiastical, which no visitor of Portsmouth should
leave without inspecting. There are many public
edifices elsewhere which are larger and more pretentious; but for its admirable and carefully considered plan, its splended site, its superb façade, and
the surprisingly small cost at which it has been
completed in a short four years, the Town Hall of

Portsmouth may be safely pronounced to be the
most successful municipal building erected in England during our time. And make what deductions
you please for a tower which is a *fiasco*, and a
chancel which needs much lengthening, the evil
spirit of detraction will be startled out of you if you
find yourself one Sunday morning standing up to
praise God with the immense congregation; the
grandeur and magnificence of all the surroundings
will impress you with the conviction that, take it all
in all, Portsea Church is among the stateliest of our
19th century churches; and you will think that
man is to be envied to whom that great church
owes so much of its splendour. Men like he may
try in their modesty to conceal their names, but
gratitude and pride in such a glorious possession as
this will not suffer those who now gather within its
walls to keep his secret.

Being, as you see, mere random roamers, it was
not very wonderful that, having got so far, we should
take Winchester on our way home. If Canterbury
stands first among English cities for the inspiring
memories that it awakens, I think we must give the
second place to Winchester. Here, again, we find
ourselves driven back into a past that has to do with
ages long before the Christian era. The Romans
came and made the place their own; they called it

Venta Belgarum. And after them the Saxons came
and made it the "capital" of Wessex, and *they*
called it Wintanceastre; and here King Kênwealh
caused "the old church" to be built in A.D. 643.
The Danes came in, about 200 years after that
building of the *old* church, and they took the place
by storm, and then for a while it was Danish
ground. And then—and then—and then : what
need to go on ? There are traces of all these successive waves that have swept over Winchester if
we have but eyes to see, and ears to listen, and
hearts to understand. " Brains, you mean ! " No,
my erudite and too algebraical critic ! I do *not*
mean brains. I mean what I say. My England !
my England ! who can know thee or understand thy
glory or thy greatness if he lack the patriot's love
for thee, and the patriot's burning loyalty?

In the old times, from which you may perceive
that I find it hard to get away, a great Roman road
ran from ancient Chichester to Southampton, and
hence, making a new departure, it started off in a
straight line to Winchester, and thence went on to
St. Albans (?). But at Winchester several Roman
roads converged, and one of them, crossing the
other at an angle, went through the country of the
Atrebates, and, twenty-two Roman miles from Winchester, it reached their chief city, which then was

known as Calleva Atrebatum, and now is known as the village of *Silchester.* The whole parish, I believe, belongs to the Duke of Wellington, and about the middle of it stands a farm of a hundred acres surrounded by a stupendous Roman wall ten feet in thickness and in some parts still twenty-five feet high. Outside this wall, on the north and west, there ran a tremendous ditch serving as a defence to a mighty outwork, and the great walls were pierced by four awful gates, each with its guardhouse, and through one of these the great road to London led. The place had been once a great British fortress or *oppidum* ; the Romans recognised its strategical importance, and they made it into a *city,* as, for convenience, we call such places now. For fourteen hundred years this mysterious Calleva remained forsaken—sometimes the haunt of wild beasts, sometimes a quarry out of which churchbuilders got their stone, and then at last, when corn was dear and farming was profitable, it was brought under the plough ! A hundred acres ! Two-thirds the area of Pompeii, not to mention the cemeteries and the amphitheatre outside the walls, and the *suburbs,* whatever they were and whatever may hereafter be found to have stood upon them. Five-and-twenty years ago the late Mr. Joyce, then rector of Strathfieldsaye, became consumed by the desire to lay bare some portion of the foundations of the city, and at his own expense he set to work in earnest. No one man can to any purpose uncover the foundations of a city that extends over a hundred acres of ground. Mr. Joyce, however, made a great beginning ; and first and foremost he opened out the whole area of `the great *basilica* of Silchester, and left it as you may see it there to-day.

What is a *basilica* ? Accept this as an answer. The *basilica* was the town hall of a city. That is enough for all practical purposes; and if my algebraical critic tells you that a *basilica* was something more, never mind what he says. The Town Hall of Portsmouth is a *basilica;* so is St. George's Hall at Liverpool. At Rome there were a dozen and more of them, just as in London there are a dozen and more town halls ; and the time came when the Emperor Constantine turned several of these *basilicæ* into Christian churches, and for anything I know to the contrary, he or his successors may have done the like with some of the *basilicæ* in England ; and he might very easily have done worse. The *basilica* of Silchester followed the almost invariable plan in its construction ; that is to say, it was a quadrangular building with a semicircular apse at each end. The length of the main building was usually about double its breadth, and it consisted of a nave with two aisles. The *basilica* at Silchester was 285 feet long; almost exactly the same length *as the nave of York Cathedral!*

This is that Silchester which the Society of Antiquaries has taken in hand to lay bare for us, if only we will find the funds. One royal-hearted gentleman has, for the last ten years or so, been devoting himself to throw light upon *village* life in Britain during the Roman domination, and most strange and instructive are the results arrived at. But there is not to be found, all the world over, another so heroic an antiquary as General Pitt-Rivers. You might as well look for a second Newton. Such men stand alone : they *must* stand alone. What is wanted now is that we should pursue our researches into the life of the British *towns* in Roman times ; and in this long-buried city we have all the materials lying ready for intelligent investigation. What may we expect to find at Silchester? Money? Yes! even money. In the great Chronicle under the year 418, there stands the following very curious entry : " In this year the Romans gathered together all the gold hoards that were in Britain; and some they hid in the earth that none might hereafter find them, and some they carried with them into Gaul." The late Mr. Joyce was no worshipper of Mammon, nor in his digging did he go very far ; but he tells us that the number of the coins he found in the course of his researches was "perfectly surprising." They dated as far back as Caligula (A.D. 37), and they went on in an unbroken series for nearly four centuries, down to the time of Arcadius, when the Romans abandoned the island. That is a tempting bait for the sons of cupidity ; but I am not so very, very sure that treasure-hunting would be found a paying quest ; and if we seek for our reward in coin or coins, I fear we shall not be able to show a satisfactory balance-sheet. No ; we must expect to find something better than that.

We shall find that those British folk, though they built houses and theatres and baths, and a great deal else, did not quite adopt the fashions of their masters ; that their houses were not as they were in the warmer climate of the south ; that they had their own methods of making themselves comfortable; that they had to provide for the long winters ; that they did not live so much in the open air ; that perhaps they did not affect the public baths so much as people did at Rome; and it may be, too, that they had temples and religious rites of their own, which were dying out and being replaced by the better way. Mr. Joyce found a seal and a ring which indicate that the Christian faith was not unknown at Calleva ; and what if it should turn out that a

Christian church was standing there when the
Teuton Longheads dashed in with a yell through
the gate that proved too weak to resist their terrible
assault, and the doomed city from end to end reeked
with carnage ? [1] But the work has only begun, and
it must needs go on slowly, or had better be left
alone. Happily it is in the very best hands. Mr.
Hope is, of course, the commander-in-chief; but
with him is associated Mr. G. E. Fox, a past-master
in Roman-British lore, chivalrous, sagacious, indefatigable, a perfect draughtsman, and one, too, who
can wield the scholar's pen.

It is impossible to conjecture, as yet, what a revolution may be wrought during the next few years in
many of our views of the civilisation of Britain
during the third and fourth centuries. As we stepped
from stone to stone, walked along the pavements
that had been buried for ages, saw the heaps of
pottery, fragments of glass, broken tools and implements and weapons, which had been tossed aside as
not worth preserving in the little museum—all the
mere refuse of a few months' or weeks' careful labour
—and as we stopped at this point and at that, while
our accomplished guides led us on and on, the hours
passed away; and when the time came for us to

[1] Since the above was written, the remains of a Christian
church actually have been uncovered at Silchester.

leave this city of the dead, eye and brain were fairly exhausted by the long tension at which they had been kept, though it was very hard to say good-bye !

There still remained two or three hours of daylight. We took the train to Reading, and came upon new surprises. I had got it into my foolish head that of that great Abbey there had been utter obliteration. Some good angel took me to the door of the vicar of St. Lawrence, and in a moment the spell of an enchanter's wand was upon me once more. But if you think that I am going to let my pen run on about Reading, you judge me harshly. Under that magician's influence, after humbly learning from him for many an hour and many a day—after some patient tutelage—perhaps I could a tale unfold—but not yet, not now.

II.

CASTLE ACRE.

Dr. O. Wendell Holmes has somewhere said that
" England is one vast museum." That is, that there
is hardly a town or village in the land that does not
contain some historic monument worth looking at,
some interesting record of a remote past, some unique
specimen of ancient art, or some spot where great
deeds have been done, or some great man whose
name is a household word has lived and toiled and
played the hero's part, or been laid to rest at last
with some monument to indicate the place of his
sepulchre. This is eminently true of our old towns,
whose corporate existence dates back centuries, and
in which, though much obliteration has gone on, and
sometimes much wanton destruction, yet there
usually survives some picturesque building—or mere
fragment of masonry or gate or mound or rampart—

round which old traditions hover, and the sight of which revives memories of great deeds. The necessity of carefully examining the history of our towns, if we hope to understand the history of England, its people and its institutions, has been forcibly impressed upon us of late, and it is surprising and disappointing to be told that the valuable series projected five or six years ago by Professor Freeman and Mr. Hunt, and now in course of publication, has not received that measure of acceptance and that extensive sale which it so well deserves.[1] The object of the series was to set forth the history of our more important English towns in a convenient form for the instruction of intelligent readers, and at a price accessible to all. The volumes are generally well written and the facts carefully—in some cases admirably — put together. To the occasional visitor, knowing little or nothing of the neighbourhood but anxious to acquire some trustworthy information, these little books are an immense improvement upon the trumpery handbooks which we waste shillings upon in our travels ; while to the resident—often as ignorant of a city's past as if it existed only in the moon—they will furnish satisfactory interpretations of many of those problems which press upon the per-

[1] " Historic Towns." Edited by E. A. Freeman and Rev. William Hunt. (Longmans.)

plexed stroller in the streets, and for which he would be glad to find a solution.

It is very rarely that any laborious study of the smaller area of a country parish can repay the long microscopic research which it involves, or that the chronicles of a country village can prove of much interest to any but the local few, with an inborn taste for antiquarianism. The events or the persons, which have here and there made a village famous can hardly be other than few. The rustic leads his quiet life without expecting to be startled by the presence of a hero, a genius, or even an abnormal villain, as often as once in a century. There is no attraction about him, except when he has a vote to cast into the ballot box; and when the rival candidates or their agents canvass him they are always bristling with promises to be redeemed in the future: of the past they know no more than he does, and they care as little. *We* have no history, in the sense of our having any sequence of events worth recording. If we try to construct our chronicles, we have often to pass on by great strides from one stepping stone to another standing out above the surface of the stream of time that goes faintly babbling through our borders; our tiny grains of sand get carried down into the great sea of oblivion—there they sink if they do not perish. It is otherwise with

the towns. There, there has been a greater *bulk* of
life, if I may so express it; there men have had a
constant succession of conflicts; there, there have
grown up slowly institutions, associations, corpora-
tions, implying the war of parties, the loud or the
low roar of discussion, the strife of tongues and the
stubborn, conscious endeavour to attain to some high
ideal. Thus it comes about that the annals of our
historic towns have nothing like the same wide breaks
in them which curious people in our country villages
complain of when they attempt to construct the story
of their humble birthplace. The great cities have
few blanks in their history; they can usually appeal
to some original documentary records deposited in
their archives ; they have always played some part in
the great movements and struggles of the people ;
they can boast of a long continuity of busy and
eventful life, with only here and there a break in their
annals. It is because this continuity in our village
life is so very rarely to be made out that our village
chronicles are generally found to be not only petty
and trifling but dry, fragmentary, and consequently,
as a rule, rather hard reading.

It is, however, not always so.

*   *   *   *   *

In the western division of the county of Norfolk
there is an irregular stretch of upland about twenty

5

miles in length from north to south, and never more
than ten miles broad, whose northern limit is the
low range of sandhills that extend from Ringstead to
the Burnhams, and its southern boundary is the
valley of the Nar; through its whole length, and
traversing it diagonally, there runs a mysterious and
very ancient trackway known as the Peddar's Way.
Straight as a ruler it may be traced from Hunstanton
till it crosses the Nar at Castle Acre, and thence
travels on, with hardly a swerve, into regions of desolation and dulness with which for the present we have
no concern.

Who laid down this ancient road? Antiquaries
are at issue upon the point. Some say the Romans
made it. Some say they found it where it is and used
it for their own purposes. If it be a Roman road
how is it that all along those first twenty miles
so very few coins or vestiges of anything that may
be called Roman has ever been found? And how is
it that it strikes the coast a good five miles from the
once tremendous fortress at Brancaster, whose walls,
we are told, were eleven feet thick, and where a
force of Dalmatian horse kept watch and ward in
the third century of our era, prepared to dash down
upon the pirate rogues who came to plunder and
slay?

There was a legend or tradition which the

chronicler Stowe treated as if it were veritable
history, and which told that when Edmund, the
martyred king of East Anglia, came from across the
sea to take his kingdom, in the year 855 A.D., he
landed somewhat near Hunstanton and "built a
royal town there " and kept his court there for a
whole year, for he was prosperous then. We may
accept the story for what it is worth; but, true or
not, there is a value in the details of any fabrication,
and this story points back to a time when there was
a port or landing-place in this neighbourhood—a
port which the shifting of the coast line has oblite-
rated long, long ago, but—which was the harbour
that the Peddar's Way led to from the interior ages
back, how far back it is impossible to say with confidence and idle to conjecture. In a matter where we
can only theorise one man's opinion is as good as
another's, and for my part I incline to maintain that
the Peddar's Way was an ancient road long before
the Christian era, and that this mysterious trackway
ran its course from the coast to the Nar without
crossing a single brook or tiny rivulet in all those
twenty miles. It passed over an open country of
heath and sandy hillock and rolling downs on which
the flocks and herds of a pastoral people wandered
to and fro, a people answering the description which
Cæsar gives of the " men of the interior " in Britain

during the century before Christ, "who for the most," he says, "grow no corn, but live on milk and flesh, and clothe themselves with skins" [of the animals they tended]. But the valley of the Nar makes a somewhat deep depression across this stretch of upland, and the spot at which the Peddar's Way crossed the river must always have been a "coign of vantage" of enormous strategical importance, giving as it did the command not only of the road, which traversed almost the whole length of East Anglia, but the command also of the stream, which was navigable for small flat-bottomed barges nearly as far as Castle Acre itself, little more than a century ago.

The utter defeat of Boadicea and the Iceni in A.D. 62 was almost the most important incident in the history of the Roman conquest of Britain. The country of the Iceni was bounded on the west by the vast fenland of Cambridgeshire, on the south by the Stour, on the north and east by the sea. It was a kingdom apart, and its king Prasutagus ruled over his people as an ally or tributary of the Romans much as our native princes in India administer their several principalities under the protection of the British Crown. When in the year A.D. 61 Prasutagus died and bequeathed the reversion of his dominions to the emperor Nero, subject to the life interest of his wife

Boadicea, the beginning of the end had come and the speedy annexation of the little realm was inevitable. The immediate effect of the annexation appears to have been the establishment of the great fortified camp at Caistor about three miles to the south of what is now the city of Norwich, and some four miles to the north of what appears to have been the great stronghold or "capital" of the Iceni on the high ground overlooking the little river Tas.

If on the heights overlooking the Nar there was another Icenian fortress close to the ford where the Peddar's Way crossed the stream, it would have been almost an absolute necessity to dismantle it—if we may use so grand a term—or to replace it by another fortified camp which would of course be constructed in conformity with the Roman methods of warfare. And this appears to have been exactly what happened. It was at Castle Acre that the Roman engineers threw up the entrenched camp whose mighty ramparts still tell their tale and testify to the audacious foresight of a conquering people whose military genius, if nothing else, fitted them to be the masters of the world. If the estimate is to be relied on which assures us that the camp at Caistor was capable of receiving within its area a force of 6,500 men, the camp at Castle Acre must have been able to take in at least 3,000 or 4,000. The great rampart

of this camp which runs north and south for almost
300 yards, whose height from the bottom of the great
ditch, after all the abrasion and wear of the elements
during 1,500 years, is still some forty feet high, and
must have made the fortress impregnable on that
side ; while on the south another rampart ran, less
formidable, because less necessary, inasmuch as
here the Nar, broadening out into an impassable
morass, served as the best natural defence for a force
that on this side had very little to fear from attack.
There stands the great Roman camp to this day, the
life all gone out of it, but even now bearing on its
dead face something that looks like a menacing
scowl.

  *   *   *   *   *

East Anglia was subject to Roman domination
just 350 years. At the end of that time the legions
marched out as they had come in, crossed the
Channel, and left the land and its people to take care
of themselves. East Anglia got home rule, and I
dare say there were a great many Britons who were
very proud and delighted at their newly acquired
liberty. But during those three centuries a prodigious
change had come over the Roman world and its
subject people. When Aulus Plautius carried his
invading hosts into Britain in A.D. 43, the world was
a pagan world. When the legions left the Britons

to take care of themselves, Christianity was the
established religion of the empire, and the Christian
Church, if not everywhere supreme, was rapidly
becoming dominant. It is noticeable that in many
places where Roman camps exist a church is to be
found in close proximity to the rampart ; sometimes,
as at Caistor near Norwich, we find it actually within
the inclosure of the vallum. Of course, the earlier
churches have long since disappeared, but the presumption is a reasonable one that the later churches
stand upon the site of a far more ancient Christian
temple. At Castle Acre the noble fourteenth-century
church is situated within a stone's throw of the great
western rampart of the Roman station and separated
from it only by the huge ditch out of which the
materials of that rampart were dug. I hold that
where that stately parish church now stands once
stood a humbler sanctuary dedicated to the worship
of the Most High, in which the Christian faith was
taught and preached, and prayer and praise was
offered up according to the prevailing ritual of that
age. When already as early as A.D. 315 the Bishops
of London, York, and Lincoln [?], attended the
Council of Arles, and during the next hundred years
the conquering Cross was everywhere extending its
sway, and the pagans were in their turn put upon
the defensive and pleading for no more than tolera-

tion, which was denied them, it seems to me that then East Anglia must have been a Christian land or nothing. Then came her baptism of blood.

From the lands to the northward of the Rhine and the Yssel—lands into which the sound of the Gospel of Christ had never travelled—a stream of pagan warriors, fierce and pitiless, come pouring in upon the Norfolk coast, forcing their way up every little inlet and carrying all before them, blotting out the civilisation and the religion which the Romans had fostered, and under which the Britons had prospered, and step by step getting a firm footing in the old kingdom of the Iceni, and calling the land after their own name. The realm of Prasutagus became the kingdom of the East Angles, and there for another 400 years they held their own. But they, too, were threatened by another stream of invaders, who in due time made good their landing and dispersed the others in their turn. But in the meanwhile these Angles or Saxons—call them which you will—got to learn that it was needful to make good their conquest by raising up other fortresses to serve as defences against the new invaders.

Abandoning the great Roman camp of Caistor they reared that stupendous earthwork on which the castle of Norwich now stands, and they planted it on the banks of the Wensum to check the advance

of the marauders who might strive to sail up that
important waterway into the heart of the country.
Leaving the mighty walled station of Brancaster to
its fate, they constructed another huge fortress at
Castle Rising. But they found that the position that
the Romans had occupied at Castle Acre could not
be improved upon, and so they utilised the mighty
ramparts which they found there, and out of them
they built up their great *burh*, which as long as
they could succeed in holding it gave them, as it
had formerly given the Roman conquerors, the command of the Nar.

But the tactics of these Teutonic conquerors were
very different from those of Rome. The camp of
the Roman legion was always quadrilateral, and for
the most part lay hard by a river's bank, with easy
access to the water for the horses and the cattle that
might chance to be within the lines of defence. It
was a camp of occupation, the home and the *dépôt* of a
force which was meant to be permanently settled in
a province, and intended to serve as at once a garrison town and a base of operations if it were necessary at any time to make a forward movement upon
an enemy on the march. The Saxon camp was
something very different. It was little more than a
place of refuge in the event of attack ; it was rather
a citadel than a fortress ; a stronghold in which a

stand might be made when the foe was too powerful to cope with in the field ; it was never meant to be permanently garrisoned; it was "a place to flee unto " rather than a *base* from which to issue forth on great military operations. The Saxons would never have dreamt of shutting themselves within the four great ramparts of the Roman *castrum ;* they had a system of fortification of their own. It consisted in piling up a huge circular mound surrounded by a deep ditch, and flanking this ditch with an outer line of "horse-shoe " earthworks, each supporting the other, and each affording a place of retreat if the attacking force had been strong enough to dislodge the de-fenders from their position. The central mound was called the *burh ;* the plateau on the summit was the last refuge for the besieged ; it was surrounded by a strong stockade, and might be held by a small force of brave men against an army.

When the Saxons found it necessary to throw up such a stronghold as this at Castle Acre they planted it on the north-east ·corner of the Roman *castrum,* and they utilised the eastern rampart from the materials of which they piled up their *burh* and the flanking earthworks which surrounded it. There to this day the two systems of fortification may be seen in wonderful preservation in immediate juxta-position. At Burgh, near Yarmouth, you may see a

Roman camp, its gigantic *walls* still standing ; at Caistor on the Tas you may see another camp, with its huge rampart still almost perfect on all the four sides. At Castle Rising you may see an almost perfect specimen of a Saxon *burh* with its horseshoe earthworks. But at Castle Acre you have the two systems of ancient fortification side by side, the one actually having grown out of the other, and the very materials of the more ancient line of defence having served for the construction of the more modern but more barbaric earthworks.

Barbarians these Angles undoubtedly were at their first coming, and in East Anglia they were, from all that appears, behind their kinsfolk outside their own borders in culture and civilisation. The great monasteries in the Fenland seem to have had more affinity with the West than the East. They were all outside the East Anglian diocese when the conversion of the Angles was effected, and submitted themselves to the spiritual guidance of bishops of their own. Of architecture they knew nothing. Even to the last almost their only weapon and their most effective tool was the axe; with that they cleared the forest, shaped the beams, and latterly hacked the very blocks of stone which they learnt so slowly and, as it seems, reluctantly to utilise for building purposes. Their art was confined to the

rude adornment of their sepulchral urns, to the
scratching of simple patterns upon rings and cups,
and the combs of the women. Once settled upon the
land in small communities they wandered but little :
the band or clan or family which had won a tiny
territory were chiefly concerned in keeping it to
themselves, and they call it their *tun*, or their *home*.
Walled towns they abhorred. Like gipsies, they
shrank from the thought of being imprisoned in the
streets. Even late in the seventh century, and when
they had become Christianised—after a fashion
—their moral perceptions and sentiments were
hideously chaotic. In their quarrels they dropped
the bludgeon and took to the knife, and they valued
life so little that they compounded for murder
according to a differential tariff. They burnt their
dead and collected the calcined bones into urns of
incomparably inferior make to the pottery of the
Romans. They buried these cinerary urns in cemeteries outside the *vill* where their habitations were
clustered. It is the only indication that we have
of their having any feeling of reverence. Even
when, much later, every settlement had its church
and its priest, it was necessary to forbid them by
ecclesiastical authority from using the timbers of
the church for fuel to save themselves the trouble of
going further afield when there was a scarcity of logs

for the hearth. It was not till 571 that the East Anglians chose, or submitted to, a king to reign over them ; before that time we may presume that something like anarchy prevailed, and every man did that which was right in his own eyes.

Such were the people who appear to have had a settlement of considerable importance at Castle Acre; and the great earthworks which they raised when a common danger forced them to unite and co-operate in the face of the foe are not by any means the only remains which the district supplies, and which speak to us with an eloquence of their own.

During the course of the year 1892 Mr. Henry Willett, of Brighton, with characteristic generosity, supplied the whole funds for exploring an early Anglian cemetery at Castle Acre which can hardly have been used after the sixth century. About half an acre of land was explored ; the place of sepulture has for some few generations been under the plough and the urns are never much more than a foot below the surface of the soil ; the modern tillage and our heavier agricultural machinery, furrowing much deeper than aforetime, has crushed and destroyed the sepulchral urns which at one time must have been deposited in this burial place by the hundred ; still, " though much is taken much abides," and the results of the exploration are not without their significance. Upon this branch

of the subject, however, I do not think it necessary
to dwell.

*   *   *   *   *

When the little East Anglian kingdom had
lasted some 300 years, and had slowly been learning some of the arts of peace, and enjoying some
of its blessings—not without the influence of the
Church, which became more and more potent for
good—the Norsemen came down upon the land,
and there was long war and pillage and carnage.
The invasion began in 838 ; that seems to have been
no more than a plundering raid by a Viking fleet
that came for booty. Twenty-eight years later Ivan
the Boneless, with a mighty host, landed on the
East Anglian coast, and soon showed that he meant
to stay. Where did he land ? There is no answer
forthcoming. But if it were on the northern shore,
then peradventure he and his marched down the
Peddar's Way and traversed the upland where the
flocks and herds were roaming, and where it may be
that he saw the droves of horses which next year he
seized for his march towards the north. If he sailed
up the Nar his first great fight would be at Castle
Acre ; that stronghold would be too formidable a
gathering place for the tribes to allow the invader
leaving it in his rear. Did he storm that terrible
burh ? Did he harry the country round with fire

and sword ? Did he give the villages to the flames ?
Of the ruthless character of the invasion we have
dreadful testimony. Of the line of his march we
have but vague notices, and conjecture is but waste
of time. But I suspect—I only suspect—that there
are traces of a Danish entrenched camp five miles
from Castle Acre which may have been thrown up
by the Boneless One ; and this is certain, that in
the long period of warfare during which the East
Anglian land was frightfully devastated by the new
hordes of heathen invaders, all the old Saxon fortresses shared the same fate. The Norsemen came
and stayed as conquerors, and for the next 200 years
East Anglia was a Danish province.

The Danes came in among us as pagans, and they
did their best to blot out the Christianity which they
found in East Anglia, but the Cross triumphed after
all. *Cedant arma togæ* is the great law of progress.
When Guthrum in 880 received baptism, and the
great Alfred ·was his sponsor at the font, a beginning was made in the conversion of the fierce
marauders ; East Anglia, left to settle its own
affairs, slowly recovered itself from the havoc that
had been wrought ; and Christianity became the
religion of the new ˌpeople.

Then came another conquest, and William of
Normandy burst in resistless and carried all before

him, he won the crown of England, and divided all the land as seemed good to him.

In Norfolk—for we must speak of Norfolk now by her modern name—the Conqueror bestowed 139 manors upon one of his sturdiest followers, William de Warenne, and of these Castle Acre was by far the most considerable and important. It was the *Capital manor* of his great Norfolk possessions, and though there is little evidence that he made it any-thing else but an occasional place of residence, yet it is inconceivable that the great fortress on the Nar should have been left ungarrisoned, or that it should have been allowed to go out of repair. But during the lifetime of the first Earl of Surrey—by which title William de Warenne became known—it seems more than probable that the defences of the *burh* remained pretty much as they had been—huge timber fences—stockades and palisades in-closing the wooden dwellings of the soldiery and their officers ; the seneschal of the fortress probably occupying an important position upon the *plateau* of the great mound. Of stone walls and masonry there was none. It was reserved for the second earl, who succeeded his father in 1089, to make Castle Acre a place of far greater magnificence than it had ever been before.

*   *   *   *   *

As the eleventh century was drawing to a close a tremendous cyclone of religious excitement—its centre nowhere, its circumference everywhere—was moving with an awful force over Europe. All ranks and all classes were affected by it; the upper ranks of society indeed more powerfully, or at least more conspicuously than the rest. Reprobates to whom conscience had been a word without a meaning through all their lives of vice and crime, found themselves shuddering with unaccountable spasms of remorse for sins they had felt no compunction in committing, and had till now well-nigh forgotten. Rugged warriors, coarse and relentless, to whom bloodshed and pillage had been a merry game and the clash of battle a kind of rapture, clutched at their heartstrings by a mysterious agony, shrieked aloud with uncontrollable horror at the prospect of judgment to come. Kings and queens, and nobles, men and maidens, careless, luxurious, gay, frivolous, sensual or debauched, awoke as out of sleep to the consciousness that their lives had been no better than a ghastly dream, and found themselves over-whelmed by an unbearable sense of emptiness, and an ecstasy of yearning and aspiration after spiritual exaltation and nearness to God. The emotional storm did not exhaust itself in the languor of mysticism, it translated itself into action, and

6

sacrifice, and good works. The history of that amazing and awful Religious Revival in the eleventh century has never yet been written. When it comes to be studied and thoughtfully dealt with, it will, I feel confident, be found to have originated in the famous Burgundian abbey of Clugny. There the fire kindled, and thence for well-nigh two centuries the warmth and the flame of the movement continued to be supplied.

Just ten years after the great William had landed at Pevensey, and not till then, his work of bringing the realm under his sway was completed, and his kingdom was finally consolidated by the suppression of the formidable rebellion of Ralph of Norfolk. That attempt at revolt collapsed at the beginning of 1076. When the Castle of Norwich surrendered it was committed to the custody of William of Warenne. It seems that during that same year, the earl and his wife Gundrada set out on a pilgrimage to Rome. Years afterwards it became necessary that the earl should set down the story of that Continental tour, and this is what he tells us about it :—

" . . . I William de Warenne and Gundrada my wife wishing to make a pilgrimage to St. Peter in Rome, went on our way stopping at many monastries which are to be found in France and Burgundy, and there we offered up our prayers. And when we had reached Burgundy we learnt that we could not safely go further because of the war which was going on then, between the Pope and the Emperor. Thereupon we took up our abode at the monastery of Clugny, a great and holy abbey built in honour of St. Peter. . . . And because we found there such great sanctity and devotion and Christian charity, and moreover so much honour shown us by the good Prior and all the convent—who received us into their society and fraternity—we began to regard that Order and that House with love and devout regard above all other Religious Houses that we had seen. But Sir Hugh their holy Abbot was not then at home. And because a long time before—and now more than ever—my wife and I had it in our purpose and wish, by the counsel of Lanfranc the Lord Archbishop, to raise up some Religious House for our sins and for the salvation of our souls, it seemed to us then, that we should not be willing to found it of any other Order so gladly as of the Cluniac Order. And therefore we sent and requested of Sir Hugh the Abbot and of the whole sacred congregation, that they would grant to us two or three or four monks of their flock on whom we would bestow the Church hard by our Castle of Lewes, which in ancient times had existed in honour of St. Pancras, and which we, from being a wooden church, had converted into one of stone.[1] And at starting we were prepared to surrender as much land and cattle and goods as might suffice for the support of twelve monks. But the holy Abbot was at first very averse to listen to our petition because of our foreign land being so long a distance off, and especially because of the passage by sea. But after that we had procured a licence to introduce Cluniac Monks into the land of England from our lord King William; and that the Abbot on his part had been certified of the king's will; then at last he granted and sent to us four of his Monks, to wit Sir Lanzo and three associates, on whom at the outset we bestowed all the things which we had promised, and we confirmed the same by a writing which we sent to the Abbot and convent of Clugny, because they were unwilling to send their monks till this had been done. And thus it was granted to me and to my wife to bring the Cluniac Monks into our English land."

This was the first introduction of the Cluniac Order into England, but this was not all. When the great earl drew up the record of his first foundation, ten years had past since he and his wife had,

[1] Compare the story of the foundation of Horsham St. Faith's. Blomefield, vol. x. p. 439.

resolved on the course they were prepared to follow. In those ten years the Conqueror had died, and the Queen Matilda and the lady Gundrada too, and William the Earl was drawing near his end. It is clear that the original intention of founding a monastery of prior and twelve monks at Lewes had developed into a much more ambitious scheme: The husband and wife seem to have kept residence sometimes at Lewes and sometimes at Castle Acre; for it was at the latter place that Gundrada died in childbed in 1085. Wherefore it seemed good to them that Castle Acre should not be treated worse than Lewes, and as there was a monastery provided for the one, so should the other be blessed with the presence of the Cluniacs in like manner.

During the first earl's lifetime, however, this intention was not carried out though a beginning was made. It appears that within the defences of the castle, which, as we have seen, were surmounted by the formidable stockades, a church or chapel, probably of wood, had existed before the Conquest and dedicated to St. Mary. To keep up the daily service in this church two or three monks, perhaps draughted from Lewes, were housed within the precincts, keeping up their cloister life in temporary shelters (as we know was done elsewhere while a monastery was building) and keeping to their

"Rule" as strictly as circumstances would permit. But when the earl died in 1088, his son the second William de Warenne lost no time in carrying out his parent's wishes, and as early as 1089, according to one authority,[1] he confirmed his father's charter of foundation, and he appears to have intended to make the capital manor of his Norfolk estates no unworthy rival of the great Sussex castle and the great Sussex monastery. As for the castle, the timber stockades were replaced by huge walls of flints, which may be easily traced along its whole circuit and which must have involved in its construction a prodigious expenditure of labour. The central mound or citadel of the Saxon fortress was crowned with an enormous *shell keep* as the technical term is: That is, the plateau on the summit of the Saxon *burh* was surrounded by a mighty wall of rubble, the outer side faced with masonry and strengthened at intervals by great buttresses. While radiating from the great *shell* itself five other lofty *walls* were carried right across the deep Saxon ditch to prevent the possibility of a besieging force concentrating itself in a combined attack upon any single point of the defences. Moreover, the *base court*, as it is called—that is the area into which the Saxon tribesmen would drive their wives and

[1] *Flores Historiarum, sub anno.*

children for defence when the Danes were pillaging
and burning and slaying—this base court was no
longer left to be defended after the old fashion by
a timber stockade. That would not suit the improved tactics of Norman warfare. The Norman
came not to plunder and carry his booty across the
sea, not to ravage and move on. He came to win
the land and hold it, and he meant to keep down the
subject people with an iron hand. So the whole area
of the base court was girdled with its frowning wall,
that too following the line of the Saxon rampart and
running along its summit; and the inclosure which
had once been the base court of the Saxon fortress
became the *inner ward* of the castle of the Warennes.
But it seems that during the thousand years or so
that had passed since the Romans threw up their
tremendous camp guarding the ford across the Nar,
a considerable change had come about in the stretch
of lowland to the south. In Roman times, as we
have seen, this was a wide and impassable morass,
so impassable that the Romans made their southern
rampart much less strong than on any other side;
the defence of the position here was comparatively
easy. If the old road, as seems probable, crossed
this morass by a causeway, that causeway would
in the lapse of ages help very powerfully to bring
about a gradual silting up of the little river; and

as time went on the land hereabout would slowly
rise and the marsh ground would no longer be as
treacherous as before.   Accordingly when the Saxon
base court was turned into the Norman *Inner Ward*,
it was found necessary to defend the approaches
from the south far more carefully than the Roman
had thought it necessary to defend his camp on this
side.   So the wall of the *Inner Ward* is found to be
at its highest on the south, as though by this time
the southern line was most open to attack though in
Roman days that line had been least assailable.

   *   *   *   *   *

And all this is to be seen " with half an eye " by
any one who likes to look about him at Castle Acre
and trace the course of those changes which have
left their ineffaceable memorials in the Norfolk
village, which was never anything more than a
village, never even rising to the dignity of becoming a market town as we understand that term
now.

Of any grand residence of the Warennes within
the line of circumvallation there is not a vestige
remaining.   I doubt whether the second earl ever
carried out the buildings he contemplated at the
castle.   He had quite enough upon his hands elsewhere.   He died in 1138, and his son the third earl,
from anything that appears, was never at Castle

Acre at all. The chroniclers say he escaped somehow from the battle of Lincoln in 1140—and that he
died in the Holy Land ten years after his father.
With him the Warennes in the male line came to an
end, and during the next hundred years at least the
Castle appears to have been occupied by the bailiffs
of the non-resident earls, and there is quite enough
in the complaints recorded in the Hundred Rolls to
show that these bailiffs were no better than they
should be, and were a bullying grasping extortionate
set, grinding the faces of the poor under pretext of
looking after the interests of their lord ; and when
the day of reckoning came shielding themselves by
putting him before themselves as their defence.

So it appears that the shell keep and its stern
walls as they startle us to day when we turn the
corner into the Norfolk village and come upon them
without a warning—" multiform, manifold, and
menacing "—were all built up in the lifetime of a
single Norman earl ; that they could not have been
begun much before the twelfth century had set in ;
that nothing was added to them after 1138 except
perhaps the somewhat imposing Edwardian gateway
which I suspect was erected by one of the bailiff
class to keep things snug within the *liberties* of the
castle, those " liberties " having step by step grown
into a little town which kept on stealthily creeping

up in the area included between the Roman ramparts and the great western ditch of the Saxon earthworks.

Meanwhile, all along the *Roman Vallum* on the north a steady and resolute invasion was going on by a new horde of barbarians; and their name was —The Squatters. I doubt whether any village or town in England can be found in which such audacious and continuous appropriation of little plots of land has been going on for ages, as may be seen at Castle Acre. The temptation to settle here was irresistible. There was a wide extent of ground which was valueless. Not even sheep, much less cattle, could be safely left to feed upon the earthworks and the mighty ditches, and the supply of building materials which the walls and ramparts afforded was practically inexhaustible. So the Squatters picked out the giant flints, and tore down the stone which had been brought by the sea and up the river from the Lincolnshire quarries, and they found their lime ready to hand, and they erected good substantial dwellings on the sites they chose and which they soon converted into their own freeholds. They had no need to square the stone—all they had to do was to square the bailiff. To this very day the people dig into the Roman Vallum for chalk and flints, and seem to think the great earthworks are no man's land. The great Saxon Burh is waste, and the huge Norman walls could only be protected at a heavy annual cost, and though the whole place possesses for the antiquarian a unique and absorbing interest, who is to keep off from it the hand of the spoiler, say for another thousand years?

We can only make an appeal to sentiment; but sentiment is an expensive luxury, and the Philistines and the Squatters laugh the sentimentalists to scorn. We are a practical people, a very practical people. We cannot tolerate fads. At any rate we say we cannot. We are almost angry and quite contemptuous when we hear that on the other side of the Channel the French government goes the length of protecting even the Cyclopean monolith avenues of the Morbihan, and at some considerable charge to the revenue actually puts pre-historic monuments under the supervision of the police. That's not our way. We go in for useful knowledge, horribly useful! We are for letting the dead bury their dead, and if they have not buried them deep enough, we set to work to dig them up again—be they cats or men; and we provide pianofortes for elementary schools, and encourage strumming and dactyllic volubility. What more can we be expected to do?

*   *   *   *   *

While the second Earl Warenne was taking away the wooden walls of the old castle and replacing

them with masonry and stone, was he busy at the
other end of the parish ?

Abutting upon the western ditch of the Roman
camp stood the church of St. Peter with a triangular
strip of land belonging to it. One side of the tri-
angle extended all along the western rampart; another
side continued the line of the northern rampart for
about 100 yards ; and the third side, which joined
the first at its southernmost extremity, abutted on
an old road which led down to the ancient ford
across the Nar. The Warennes left the parish
church where they found it and appear to have done
nothing to it. The inhabitants might be trusted to
take care of their own place of worship, and in those
days men were much more in the habit of paying for
their religion than is commonly believed. What
sort of place St. Peter's church at Castle Acre was
in the 12th century we have no means of knowing,
but we have only to look at it as it stands now
shorn of much of its old splendour though grandly
" restored " some five-and-twenty years ago, to form
some idea of what a noble church it became in the
14th century, even though it is pretty certain that it
owed very little of its magnificence to the later Earls
Warenne and much less to the Cluniac monks who
had their own church to keep up on the other side
of the road.

And this brings us to that which most visitors look upon as the real glory and boast of Castle Acre, to wit the Cluniac Priory.

How soon after his father's death in 1189 the second earl set about the project of carrying his parent's intentions into effect we have no means of knowing. He had a great deal on his hands; and the presumption is that he did not begin upon the Norfolk capital manor till the castle and the monastery at Lewes had been brought to something like completion. And as the great church at St. Pancras at Lewes was not consecrated till quite late in the reign of William Rufus, it seems probable, and the conjecture is confirmed by the internal evidence which the architectural features afford, that the works at Castle Acre were not begun till the reign of Henry I., and indeed not till more than half that reign was over. Into the early history of the monastery, however, I have no intention of entering here further than to hazard a conjecture that the Priory, not begun till the death of the first earl in 1089, was not completed till after the death of the second earl in 1138. In other words it took more than fifty years before the original intention of the first earl was carried out, and the church opened with the usual pomp and ceremony. During these fifty years the popularity of the Cluniacs did not increase; they were eclipsed in austerity by the Cistercians and quite surpassed in mere popularity by the Augustine Canons. Yet for all that it must not be forgotten that the Cluniacs were the first great reformers of the Benedictine order and that the founding of the Monastery of St. Pancras at Lewes was an event in English history; while the building of the *cell* or dependent house at Castle Acre, though its completion was deferred till another generation, was but a continuance of the first design. It gave importance to a movement in favour of making the religious houses on our side of the channel more strict in their discipline, and it helped in giving a decided impetus to the desire after a higher tone in the social life of the country at large.

Taking the first meridian west of Greenwich as a convenient dividing line, I doubt whether to the east of that line and south of the Humber, there is a monastic ruin in England that can compare with Castle Acre for the extent and condition of its still existing remains and for the facility with which its ground plan can be made out, even in minute details. If such an extensive ruin had existed anywhere except in a remote village, it must have been carted away bodily centuries ago. As it is, it has simply *fallen* into decay. It has been a quarry from

which all the beautifully *carved* work has been
industriously removed, but there was a far more
convenient quarry in the Castle and its walls for the
squatters and anyone else who wanted stone or lime,
than the more distant monastery afforded. Other
protective influences have contributed as a check
upon unlimited spoliation. The grand Tudor gateway appears to have been used as a dwelling a long
time after the suppression—and there are considerable fragments of the residences of some of the office
bearers in the monastery which have never ceased to
be inhabited to the present time. Large portions of
the pavement of the church have been uncovered for
the first time during the last few years ; the walls
of the cloister garth are still standing ; the refectory
remains as it was when the roof fell in. Anyone
who likes may climb the dormitory stairs which
the monks went up and down for more than four
centuries. The boundary wall may be traced with
ease from the great gateway to the ancient mill that
abutted upon the ford over the Nar. Four at least
of the altars at which mass was said for centuries in
the church are still *in situ* ; only their slabs of marble
having been torn away. In the chapel of the cel-
larer's lodgings the frescoes at the east end are still
to be seen—faint, of course, but distinctly traceable.
I believe that the prior's house is buried in its own

ruins; the arrangements of the infirmary and its members might be mapped out with certainty. As for the matchless west front of the church, with its two towers supporting it—one of which has survived —if it had not been for the swaggering improvers of the 14th century, who must needs insert a braggadocio "perpendicular" window in the place of the Norman lights, and in doing so hacked away a portion of the lovely arcading which still puts them to shame — the west front, I say, might have remained till now the most sumptuous specimen of Norman work in East Anglia.

In fact, the Norman work has outlasted all the additions that the later men erected. *They* pulled down the apse and built up an ambitious Lady Chapel, of which no more than the foundations remain; from two other chapels, one on the north and another on the south, the altars have never been removed, though their roofs and windows have perished. The piers of the central tower are still standing; but about their bases are the immense masses of masonry that came crashing down some day or night a couple of centuries or so ago. There they lie for little boys and girls to climb and dance upon while they scream out little nursery rhymes about the monks of old! Quietly browsing through the old aisles or cropping the sweet grass that grows

in the old cloister, the sheep wander and grow fat.
As you stroll—quite unconscious of where you are—
across the Convent Cemetery, where for centuries the
Cluniac fathers gently laid their brethren to rest,
each one shrouded in his monastic habit—the cattle
chewing the cud of bovine reflection stare at you with
their mild eyes—no speculation in those orbs—

Little heeding the past—bent on pasture alone.

It is not because Castle Acre can boast of a Roman
Camp, nor because it contains a Saxon Cemetery,
nor because its great earthworks are a wonder and
astonishment to the passer-by, nor because the Norman Castle has a tale of its own to tell, nor because
its parish church is a noble specimen of 14th century
architecture—nor even because the Cluniac Priory is
so splendid and interesting a monument of bygone
greatness, that this out-of-the-way Norfolk village is
so well worth a visit; but because *all* these things
are to be seen in so small an area, and all may be
inspected in a few hours. In their aggregate they
make up such a continuous series of historic—and
almost pre-historic—records as perhaps could hardly
be paralleled in any English village of the same size.
Happily the whole parish, with the exception of the
small holdings which have come down from the
hordes of squatters, belongs to a single noble owner,

who is not likely to let things get worse than they are. On the ruined Priory a good beginning has already been made by clearing away an immense mass of the *débris* which had accumulated, arresting the progress of decay, and protecting what is worth preserving. The Priory Church has been opened out from end to end under the able supervision of Mr. Hope, who has also cleared the walks of the cloister. The refectory still remains to be dealt with. The undercroft supporting the dormitory with the latrines, &c., have been uncovered, Mr. Willett again having contributed handsomely to the cost of that part of the work. Much more than this, however, still remains to be done, and in the meantime a caretaker has been appointed to keep the ground—to admit visitors at a trifling charge, and to warn off ragamuffins with a talent for pilfering. Lord Leicester is not likely to stop at that point, but it is too much to expect that the noble owner should provide a playground for the world at large unless they who are interested in the preservation of our ancient monuments are prepared to support any efforts that may be made to arrest the progress of decay. Hitherto the remoteness of the locality has protected it from being overrun by any very large number of mischievous visitors; but our facilities of locomotion are steadily increasing, and the danger becomes greater, from year to year, of Castle Acre being overrun by a new horde of invaders—not now of Romans or Angles or Normans or even Squatters —but an invasion this time of Trippers, who will leave no traces of their existence behind them except their crumpled paper, their broken bottles, and their offensive names scribbled upon every wall or cut upon every accessible tree. Other conquerors have each and all come here to build up—such invaders as these come only to destroy.

III.

HILL-DIGGING AND MAGIC.

AMONG all my acquaintances above the lower middle class I know no man of forty—except he be a country parson—who has not written a book, or who has not an account at a bank. We all write books, and we all *keep* a banking book. Yet there was a time when human beings did neither the one nor the other. Also there was a time when books were common, much written, much read, and when bankers were not common. Nevertheless in those days money changed hands—money in lumps with a stamp upon it, money by weight that was the price of lands and cattle and men's lives, and things much more precious than even these. The world had grown quite an old world when Pasion—the Rothschild of Athens—turned over the leaves of his ledger

to find out how Lycon of Heraclea stood in his
books. It was a much older one when Julius Cæsar
persuaded the bankers at Rome to make those heavy
advances to him as he was preparing for the pillage
of Gaul. But a thousand years after Cæsar's time
Europe had clean forgotten all about the finance of
the earlier ages, and banking, as we understand the
word, was a thing unknown. Yet men traded, and
bargained, and got gain, and some grew rich, and
some grew poor, and some were thriftless and some
were grasping—as it was in the beginning, is now, ·
and ever shall be.

In process of time the art of money-making
advanced again. Great capitalists rose up, fortunes
were made, estates changed hands. The great men
doubtless had their own methods of managing their
money matters. The Jews, the Carausini (who
bought out the Jews), and other such financiers,
made their accounts and negotiated loans with kings
and potentates, and throve surprisingly as a rule,
though by no means invariably.

That was all very well for the big men embarked
in important speculations ; but what was the small
man to do—the man who went about from village to
village and from fair to fair with a pack on his back—
the man of the market whom people called indif-
ferently John le Marchant, or Johannes Mercator, or

Jack the Pedlar, and whose gains counted by groats, not by shillings ?

What did he do? To tell the plain truth he found his money—his hard cash—somewhat of an incumbrance to him as he travelled about from place to place. It is hard, very hard, for us to realise in our time the difficulty of finding investments for capital in the middle ages. The merchant princes of Venice or Genoa and many another thriving mart built their palaces and got rid of a great deal of their ready money by indulging in their taste for splendour. But the " low man adding one to one," to whom fifty pounds was a fortune, if he could not hear of some neighbour in difficulties who wanted to sell house and land on a small scale, must have been, and often was, sorely put to it to know where to dispose his gains. Sometimes he made an advance to the landlord out at elbows, sometimes a neighbouring monastery was badly in want of money for carrying on those everlasting building operations which ambitious abbots or priors were never tired of undertaking. Sometimes there was a speculation in shipbuilding to tempt him when half a dozen small adventurers made up a joint-stock partnership, each contributing his quota ; but as often as not, when a small capitalist had a good round sum in his money-bag there was no opportunity of putting it out at use,[1] and the poor man had literally to carry it about on his person and take his chance. Timid men and women shrank from such a risk, and then the alternatives which presented themselves were few. If there was a religious house which bore a high character in the neighbourhood the spare cash was left in the custody of one or other of the *Obedientiaries*, the depositor receiving an acknowledgment which took the form of an *obligation—i.e.* a promise to pay by a certain date. In the meanwhile the lender in most cases received no interest—for was not the taking of usury a deadly sin, or something very like it ?—the security of his deposit was reckoned a sufficient equivalent for any advantage which the borrower derived from the use of the capital, and the money so lent lay not "at call " but invariably " on deposit."

In the case of a small trader who required a certain amount of floating capital for the purposes of his business, these monastery banks were of very little use. As the time approached for the holding of one of the great annual fairs, where the merchant laid in his stock for the year and paid ready money for it, it was needful that he should call in his small debts and gather his dues. That must have been a

---

[1] "Having money out at use "—i.e. *at interest*—is still a common expression in Norfolk.

very nervous time for Jack the Pedlar. The nights
were long and very dark ; folks said that a band of
landless rogues were skulking in the copses down in
the hollow yonder ; that two pilgrims coming home
from Walsingham had been stripped of their all ;
that there was a hue and cry for some ruffian who
had killed his mistress and was supposed to be
hiding, hungry and desperate, the Lord knew
where ; that in Black Robin's Alehouse on the moor
there had been much talk of Jack the Pedlar's
wealth, and grim Jem and cock-eyed Peter had
darkly hinted with some savagery that the pedlar
was a grasping knave whom it would be a good
deed to lighten of his burden.

Oh Jack! Jack! How you must have quaked!
Was it wonderful that Jack and Jill and many a
score of the thrifty ones who had laid by their tiny
hoards against a rainy day should have been driven
to think of a *cache* as the only possible way out of
the difficulty, and that hiding money in the earth
should have been a very common practice up and
down the land in the old days when security for life
and property was a very different thing from what
we now understand by the words ?

But,——what am I thinking about ? Did not
Achan, the son of Zerah, feel himself to be in
the same difficulty when he purloined that wedge

of gold and the fifty shekels of silver and all that perfectly irresistible accumulation which dazzled his eyes among the spoils of Ai ? Did he not hide it in his tent, dig a hole there and bury it, the accursed thing ? Verily a capacious receptacle, wherein that goodly Babylonish garment had a place among other objects of *vertu.* How blind avarice is ! The son of Zerah must have been distraught in his wits when he persuaded himself that he could remain for long one of that noble army of the favoured few who are *not* found out. Ages before Achan there had been buriers, the thing has always gone on. Why our dogs—our very dogs— practise the virtue or the vice, and Tip and Toby and Nick and Gyp—confound them !—can never be cured of hiding their stolen mutton-bones in the flower-beds and returning to them in the dead of night to scratch up the nauseous relics. It is a survival of some instinct or other, say the wise men. So we cannot cure our dogs of it, and we cannot eradicate it from the hearts of our fellow men. All literature is full of it—yes, and all law.

In the Digest, in the Institutes, the law of treasure trove is elaborately handled ; the law varied from time to time.[1] Constantine (A.D. 315) claimed half of all treasure trove for the crown ; Gratian in 380

[1] See, too, " Roger de Hoveden," vol. ii. p. 224.

surrendered all claim upon any share of the spoil, but assigned a fourth to the owner of the land; Valentinian ten years after this decreed that the finder of treasure should keep all that he found.

It is evident from all this legislation that in the Roman world the practice of burying valuables must have been very common. Can we wonder at it? Between the death of Septimius Severus in A.D. 211 and the accession of Constantine in 305, no less than twenty-seven names appear upon the Fasti, of pretenders to, or wearers of, the purple. Twenty-seven Emperors of Rome in less than a century! Mere names do you say?

> Distinguished names!—but 'twas somehow,
> As if they played at being names
> Still more distinguished, like the games
> Of children.

Ay, that was just the worst of it. There was no saying any day who was or who might be king over us. Of course men lost all sense of security. Men with the best intentions could not be trusted. These must have been the days of old stockings and of literally hiding talents in the earth.

But our concern just now is not with other lands. We have only to look at home; and here, " within the four seas," I am inclined to think that we in East Anglia have been at all times more addicted to the hoarding and hiding mania than elsewhere. There are innumerable stories of men and women digging up money and getting suddenly rich by a great find. Sometimes you are assured that old Hakes, who amassed such vast wealth that he was able to buy a farm of fifty acres without a mortgage, began by finding an old teapot full of golden guineas up the chimney ; or that Joe Pymer dug up a pot of money in his cabbage-bed ; or that Mr. Dixe, " him as is the builder now," what time he was a mere well-sinker came upon " a sight o' old gold cups and things " when he was making a well at a fabulous depth. Sometimes, too, the prevalent belief receives a startling confirmation in an undoubted discovery, as when some few years ago, in clearing out a moat at Bradenham, a silver jug was actually picked up ; and then it was remembered that some fifty years before there had been a robbery of plate at Letton Hall, and the report was that the thieves were hard pressed and had to drop their booty.

I was myself once present at a very remarkable function. Evidence had been adduced, so positive and precise as to defy contradiction, that a certain magnate at Ladon had been buried in the family vault and the family jewels had been buried with him. An application was actually made to the con-stituted authorities for a licence to disinter the corpse and open the coffin. The thing was done. Then the real explanation of the story that had got abroad revealed itself. When the arrangements for the funeral were approaching completion it was found that, by some mistake, the leaden coffin had been made too large for the oaken shell that was placed within it, and it became necessary to make use of something to serve in the place of wedges to prevent the inner receptacle from *shifting* when the bearers had to carry it to the vault. The undertaker's men were equal to the occasion ; they picked up a couple of old books which they found ready at hand ; the one was a battered old French dictionary, the other was, I believe, " The Whole Duty of Man." The fellows made no secret of the matter, and two volumes were wedged in accordingly. It would have been all one to them if they had been a couple of Caxtons or Wynkyn de Wordes. But the story got wind. Two *books* soon became changed into two *boxes*, and the two *boxes* became caskets of inestimable value, till it ended by people loudly proclaiming that the family jewels had been buried with the dead, and a cry arose and grew strong that "something must be done." It was to me a very memorable day, for I had the French dictionary in my hands, and, inasmuch as I had a very smart new coat on and " looked the character,"

I was much flattered by being mistaken for the bishop of the diocese, and being addressed as " my lord " !

But the widespread belief in the existence of large sums of money being concealed in the ground, and which wait only for the sagacious explorer to discover them, has really a basis of truth to support it. Such hoards of valuables have indeed been turning up continuously from the very earliest times, and they turn up still much more frequently than might be supposed. In 1855 a workman came upon a collection of nearly 500 silver pennies, of the reigns of Henry II. and Henry III., at Hockwold, in Norfolk. They had been hidden by some poor creature six hundred years ago, probably under his own doorpost. The house may have been burnt or tumbled down—who knows ?—ages had passed, and the ploughman had drawn his furrow over the place from year to year, and the corn had sprung up, been reaped and garnered, and then one day the nineteenth-century man with a patent improved share had driven it in a few inches deeper than any plough had ever gone before, and lo ! there rolled out before his delighted but hardly astonished eyes the sum total of that other poor miser's lifelong savings, scraped together in the times when every penny stood for at least a whole day's wages, laid by so

painfully, watched so very anxiously, gloated over so
ravenously, but all saved in vain for another to
gather! Had the poor wretch some dream of buying
his freedom or getting his only boy made a priest, or
making himself master of that other strip of earth
that marched with his own tiny patch? How easy
it is to find a pathos in some mysterious relic of
the past!

In 1852, again, upwards of 300 *British* coins were
found in a field at Weston. We may be sure it had
not been an open field when they were hidden there:
they are said to have been coins of the Iceni—struck,
it may be, in some rude mint of the great Queen
Boadicea, hidden away for a purpose when money
was very scarce and a little would go a very long
way, meant to be dug up all in good time by the
hider, who thereupon went into the battle with the
Roman legionaries, fought and fell, and took his
secret with him.

It was in the year 1887 that the largest find
of all was made. *Ten to fourteen thousand* Roman
coins, mostly of the reign of Postumus, were discovered at Baconsthorpe, where it seems a Roman
station once was. There they had lain for fifteen
centuries, and cunning scholars will have it that
some bold band of Britons made a raid one day upon
the weak Roman garrison, slew them to a man,

pillaged the station, burnt and rioted, but missed the treasure, which the legionaries, in view of the peril grown imminent, had buried so deep and meant to return for when the foe should have been repulsed or annihilated. Those legionaries never came back. How far did they get? And then those others who were waiting for their pay—waxing mutinous—and the commissary-general with a deficit of 14,000 pieces of silver lying in a hole in a gigantic earthen pot, and destined to lie there for ages—what did they do? And yet people will write fiction and think it is a mark of genius to be able to *invent* a story. Would not *telling* one do as well?

Gentlemen of the shires will perhaps tell me that they too had much treasure buried in holes among themselves. I deny it not, but I protest that incomparably more finds have been made among us in the east than among you in the west and the midlands. Moreover, there is a reason for this: a man thinks twice before he begins to pick a hole in the limestone or the granite. Such a hole would very soon betray itself if he did. Nor does he like to bury his hoard in a marsh or a river bank—your sloppy swamp is not adapted for concealment. But the dry and light soil on which most of our Norfolk villages were planted, and the old banks raised in primæval times for defence or for the enclosure of

cattle, and the old walls of *cobble*, sometimes three
or four feet thick, of which many of our humbler
dwellings and almost all our barns and byres were
made before the times came back when people set
to work to burn bricks again and build houses with
them—all these were exactly the spots which afforded
easy hiding-places for the small man's savings.
Even to this day such places are utilised by our
local misers.

Nevertheless, I do not want to hurt the feelings of
the gentlemen of the shires. I know that it was
somewhere between Wycombe and Onhandande-
decruche (*there* is a name to be proud of!) that
William Attelythe in the year 1290 was said to have
found a hoard of twenty pounds, the which he was
said *maliciose concelasse*, and that by favour of the
king he was pardoned his offence, whether he had
committed one or not.

Also I know that a hundred years after this Robert
atte Mulle and Alice his wife were put upon their
trial on the charge of having appropriated seven
hundred pounds *d'aunciem temps mussez souz la terre*
at Guildford in Surrey, and that the unhappy couple
were prosecuted and worried for years by Sir Thomas
Camoys; though it seems clear that the charge was
utterly false, and after seven years of shameful
exactions it was practically withdrawn and master

Robert restored to what was left of his houses and lands and goods and chattels, which during all this time had been left in the hands of the spoilers.

So, too, in the year 1335 a decree went forth from the great King, who was at Carlisle at the time, directing that an inquiry should be made regarding a hoard of unknown value which certain rogues had succeeded in unearthing in the garden of Henry Earl of Lancaster, in the parish of St. Clement Danes, outside Temple Bar. They found the treasure in the said garden under a pear-tree, and they dug it up and carried it off; and for all that appears they escaped with their booty, and none knew what became of it or them.

* * * * *

How did these rogues find that money in the Earl of Lancaster's garden under the pear-tree? How did it get there? The Earl (he was not yet Duke) was one of the greatest potentates in England. If his house was not his castle, whose should be? We cannot help thinking that the hoard must have lain there from a very distant time—it may be that it had been there for ages. How did the rogues find it? Why didn't the gardener dig it up? It was not his, and he knew nothing about it. It certainly was not found by mere chance, for there was a recognised term in use for describing such finds. In the formal documents they are spoken of as *subito inventum*; as in the case of that sum of gold and silver which William Whethereld of Brokford in Suffolk fished up from a well *infra mansionem ipsius Willielmi* in the year 1425, and about which due inquiry was made—the jury declare expressly that it was *subito inventum*; or that other hoard of money, which on the Monday after All Saints' Day, three years after this, John Sowter, alias John Richerd, of Bury St. Edmunds, cordwainer, came upon at Thurleston, in the same county, under a certain stone.   That, too, was a mere chance find, and that, too, is set down as *subito inventum*.   So, too, some finds were mere thefts, as when the Rev. Edmund Welles, parson of Lound, who had hidden away in a secret place in the church of Lound his little pile of seven pounds and saw it safe there on the 1st of April, 1465, and when he came to look at it again on St. Laurence's Day, the 10th of August, found it was gone, and by-and-by 40s. thereof was proved to be in the hands of Robert Prymour, a noted receiver of stolen goods. It was clear enough that some one had watched the reverend gentleman, peradventure through the leper's window, one dark night as he went to trim the lamp over the altar, and could not keep himself from having one more look at his savings, just to see if they were there in their hiding-place.

But when it come to such a hoard of treasure as Beatrix Cornwallis and Thelba de Creketon—two lone women, observe—dug up at Thetford, in the year 1340, and which was worth at least one hundred pounds, which they could not in the joy of their proud hearts hold their tongues about, which they forthwith began to spend in riotous fashion, so that mere guzzling seems to have been the death of Beatrix—which, too, when Reginald of Kylverston and his brother Henry and another rogue got wind of, they came upon the two women and despoiled them of; which, moreover, was the death of Reginald also and the ruin of all the rest, none could tell how; —when, I say, it came to this kind of thing, you must not hope to persuade any but the most feebly credulous that *that* was all a haphazard business, or that there were no occult powers enlisted in so awful and terrible a business as that. What! are we going to be persuaded that only the nineteenth century has anything to tell us about spirit-rapping and bogies ?

*   *   *   *   *

I will not intrude into the province of these profound philosophers, whose business it is, and their delight, to trace the origins and development of religion.

Haud equidem invideo : miror magis.

Only this I know, that there does seem to exist a stage in the progress of human beliefs, when the orthodox and universally accepted creed of the children of men may be summed up in the brief formula—

There are gods above, there are fiends below.

That seems to have been the creed of the earliest men who had any creed at all. What the gods could do, or would do, people were very vague about; for men learn very slowly to believe in the power of goodness and in the possibility of a Divine love, personal, mild, and beneficent. These things are matters not of experience but of a higher faith. Even the gentler and the more earnest find it hard to keep their hold of these. They are for ever tending to slip away from us; but there is no difficulty at all in believing in cruelty and hate and malignity. These things are very nigh to us, meeting us wherever we turn.

There may be heaven, there must be hell,

was not a dogma first formulated in our days. Heaven for the gods, there might be; but earth, and all that was below the earth, that was the evil demons' own domain. The demons were essentially earth spirits. The deeper you went below the outer crust of this world of ours, the nearer you got to the homes of the dark and grisly beings who spoil and poison and blight and blast—the angry ones who only curse and hate, and work us pain and woe. All that is of the earth earthy belongs to them. Wilt thou hide thy treasure in the earth ? Then it becomes the property of the foul fiend. Didst thou trust it to him to keep ? Then he will keep it.

" Never may I meddle with such treasure as one hath hidden away in the earth," says Plato in the eleventh book of the *Laws*, " nor ever pray to find it. No ! nor may I ever have dealings with the so-called wizards, who somehow or other (ἀμωσγέπως) counsel one to take up that which has been committed to the earth ; for I shall never gain as much as I shall lose ! " It was already, you perceive, an established practice. The wizards that peep and that mutter, the " cunning men " that dealt with familiar spirits, have been an institution time out of mind. " O ! if Hercules would but be so good," says the man in Persius,[1] " and I could hear the click of a pot full of cash under that harrow of mine ! "

Hermes was he who bestowed the lucky find; but Hercules—who was he but the *earth spirit* who claimed his dues ?

When the witch of Endor, to her own amazement,

[1] " Sat." ii. 10.

had summoned the shade of the dead prophet to commune with the doomed king, the wicked old woman cried out in her horror, "I saw gods ascending *out of the earth.*" Under the earth were the powers of darkness that could be dealt with somehow, and there were witches and wizards—who could doubt it?—possessed of awful secrets and versed in occult practices, who somehow or other (ἀμωσγέπως) exercised a hideous sway over the fiends below, and used them for their own ends. Has the race died out? Have the awful secrets been lost? Are there no more specimens of the real genuine article? Have all the railway tunnels and other audacious devices of our time let too much light and too much air into the bowels of the earth, so that the very demons have been expelled, or retired deep and deeper down towards the centre of our planet, where the everlasting fires burn, and whence sometimes they burst forth?

I am always finding that I know nothing of the present. I find it so hard to understand; it is so very near; it cramps a man with its close pressure. The past you can form a fair and impartial estimate of, and of the past you *can* know something—just a little but still something; the present *wriggles* so. This I know, that ages ago there were wizards, and potent wizards, too, who had dealings with imps

and fiends and goblins, and lived with those beings
upon familiar terms, and called them by their several
names, and compelled them to do service. Surely
this candid, truth-loving, sagacious, and most impartial nineteenth century is not going to resist and
set itself against the crushing force of cumulative
evidence.

    *   *   *   *   *

In the year of grace one thousand five hundred
and twenty-one—that is, in the twelfth year of King
Henry VIII.—a license was given to one Sir Robert
Curzon, commonly called Lord Curzon, to search for
hidden treasure within the counties of Norfolk and
Suffolk. The noble lord, like the unjust steward,
could not dig himself, but he could find others who
would act as his deputies and agents. Accordingly,
he made choice of three rogues, who were styled
his servants, William Smyth, William Tady, and
one Amylyon, whose Christian name, if ever he had
one, does not appear, and the worthy trio made
their headquarters at Norwich and began to look
about them. It was discouraging to hear sundry
rumours that they had been forestalled. Others had
been at work before them. There might be a doubt
whether or not they could discover hidden treasure ;
there could be no doubt that if they flourished their
commission in poor men's faces they might easily

succeed in levying blackmail from the suspected. They lost no time in pouncing down upon four unlucky victims. From three of these they managed to extort sundry small sums, amounting in the aggregate to two or three pounds, together with a *crystal stone* and *certain books*, which, being duly delivered up, an engagement was given that the culprits should be " troubled " no more. The offence committed by these poor fellows, and for which they compounded, was that they had been all *hill diggers ;* and though it does not appear that they had been by any means successful in their searches, yet *digging of hills* was, it appears, an amusement not to be indulged in by any but the privileged few.

Encouraged by this first success, the three went about trumping up accusations against any one of whom they could hear any vague story, and in the course of their inquiries they singled out one William Goodred of Great Melton, a village about seven miles from Norwich, whom they found ploughing in his field ; and, forthwith charging him with being a *hill digger,* they took him off to the village alehouse and "examined the said Goodred upon hill-digging." But Goodred was a stout knave and obstinate ; he had never been a hill digger—not he—and, moreover, the squire of the parish, Thomas Downes, happened by good luck to be in the alehouse when the rogues took their man there, and Goodred threw himself upon the protection of Mr. Downes, who offered to give bail to the extent of one hundred pounds. It was a very indiscreet offer, and Smyth and the others waxed all the more exacting when they heard of so great a sum. They dragged poor Goodred to Norwich, he protesting all the way that he would give them never a farthing. But when they came in sight of Norwich Castle the man's heart sank within him and he came to terms. He promised to pay twenty shillings " to have no furder trouble," and when it was all paid, Amylyon, acting for the others, gave him a regular receipt, or, as the deposition has it, " made to the said Goodred a bill of his own hand." The rascals had gone too far this time, for Mr. Downes, angered at the treatment which he himself had received, and indignant at the abominable extortion, managed to get an inquiry set on foot as to the character and proceedings of the fraternity, and then it came out that they had already begun their operations, not without the help of the black art.

It appears that they themselves knew nothing of the real methods of *hill-digging*, and the first requisite for ensuring success was to find somebody who knew what he was about. Accordingly they made advances to one George Dowsing, a schoolmaster dwelling at

St. Faith's, a village three or four miles from Norwich, who they heard say "should be seen in astro-
nomy"; and having opened up negotiations with
him he engaged to co-operate with them, but he
seems to have made his own terms. He would not
go alone—other skilled experts should go with him ;
and it was agreed that they should commence operations " at a ground lying besides Butter Hills within
the walls of the city " of Norwich. There, accordingly, between two and three o'clock in the
morning, a fortnight after Easter, the company
assembled—the three servants of Lord Curzon, *the
Parish Priest* of St. Gregory's Church, Norwich, *the
Rev. Robert Cromer* of Melton aforesaid, and *other
priests* who were strangers to the deponent. Before
starting, a solemn council assembled and the necessary ceremonial was rehearsed " at Saunders'
house in the market at Norwich," and then the
schoolmaster " raised a spirit or two in a glass,"
and the parson of St. Gregory's " held the glass
in his hand." Mr. Dowsing was not the only nor
the most expeditious hierophant present, for the
Rev. Robert Cromer " began and raised a spirit
first." When the fellow Amylyon was examined on
the subject he declared that when the Rev. Robert
Cromer " held up a stone, he could not perceive anything thereby, but . . . that George Dowsing did

areyse in a glass a little thing of *the length of an inch or thereabout,* but whether it was a spirit or a shadow he cannot tell, *but . . . George said it was a spirit.*"

The astonishing feature in this business is the prominent part which was taken in it by the parish priests. It is clear that among people of some culture there was a very widespread belief in the powers of magic, or whatever we may choose to call it, and that the black art was practised systematically and on a large scale.

In the first volume of the " Norfolk Archæology " there is a most curious and minute account of the doings of a certain worthy named William Stapleton, who had been a monk at the great abbey of St. Benet's Hulme in Norfolk, had misconducted himself, and, having been punished for his sins, had in consequence run away from the monastery and set up as a practiser of magic. The rascal was a stupid bungler, but in the course of his career he was brought into relations with all sorts of people, among others with Cardinal Wolsey and Sir Thomas More. His chief confederates, however, were half-a-dozen parish priests in Norfolk, who had awful dealings with familiar spirits, spirits that came at call and knew their names. The most notable of these fiends were *Oberion, Inchubus* and *Andrew Malchus*—a surly

and uncertain demon—and also a singular and
peculiar being which Stapleton describes as "a
Shower" and whom they call *Anthony Fulcar*,
"which said spirit I had after myself," he assures
us. All these spirits and their priestly confederates
were engaged in *hill-digging*. I regret that I cannot
report a single success, though it is certain that they
were not idle. They were intensely serious in their
proceedings, and seem to have made very little
secret of them. No one seems to have thought any
the worse of them for their converse with the fiends,
and only one instance is mentioned of their being at
all interfered with in their *hill-digging*. This instance
is, however, a remarkable one. In the course of
their rambles they got information that there was a
very promising digging place at Syderstone, a parish
not far from Houghton, where at the manor house
lived the widow of Sir Terry Robsart, a person of
some consideration. She was the grandmother of
Amy Robsart, and it is more than probable that in
this manor house Amy herself was born. The old
lady no sooner heard of the hill diggers than she had
them all brought before her, examined them strictly,
and told them plainly she would have no digging in
her domain ; " she forbade us meddling on her said
ground, and so we departed thence and meddled no
further." There was at any rate one woman of

sense who could deal with the cunning men and their " Shower."

But what did all these people mean by talking about *hill-digging* so often ?

I must defer answering this question for a little longer, until I have dealt with one more story of hill-digging which is much more complete than any of the preceding, and has, moreover, never yet, as far as I know, appeared before the eye of those who read only what is displayed upon a printed page.

*   *   *   *   *

On Saturday, being the Feast of St. Clement, in the fifth year of King Edward IV.—that is, on the 23rd of November, 1465—an inquiry was held at Long Stratton, in the county of Norfolk, before Edward Clere, Esq., Escheater of the king's majesty in the county aforesaid, and a jury of thirteen persons of some consideration in the neighbourhood, with a view to examine into the case of John Cans, late of Bunwell, and others implicated by common report in the finding of certain treasure in the county of Norfolk, and to report accordingly. The jury being duly sworn, and having examined witnesses and received their depositions, did so report, and this is what they found.

John Cans, late of Bunwell, and Robert Hikkes, late of Forncett, worsted-weaver, *during divers years*

past, on divers occasions and in various places in the
same county, had been wont to avail themselves of
the arts of magic and darkness and invocations of
disembodied spirits of the damned, and had most
wickedly been in the habit of making sacrifices and
offerings to the same spirits. By means of which
arts and sacrifices they had incited many persons
unknown—being his majesty's subjects—to idolatry
and to the practice of *hill-digging* and other disturb-
ances and unlawful acts in the county aforesaid [*ad
fodiciones montium et ad alias riottas et illicita*].

Especially, too, they had made assemblies of such
persons at night-time again and again [*sæpius*] for
the finding of treasures concealed in the said hills.
Moreover that the same John Cans and Robert
Hikkes, having assembled to themselves many
persons unknown on the night of Sunday before the
Feast of St. Bartholomew in the fifth year of the
king aforesaid [18th of August, 1465], they did cause
to appear before the same disorderly persons, practising the same unlawful arts, a certain accursed disembodied spirit [*spiritum aerialem*] at Bunwell aforesaid, and did promise and covenant that they would
sacrifice, give, and make a burnt offering to the self-
same spirit, of the [dead] body of a Christian man, if
so be that the aforesaid spirit there and then would
show and make known to the said disorderly persons

in some place then unknown within the county aforesaid, so as that a treasure therein lying might come
to the hands of them.

Whereupon the said spirit, under promise of the
sacrifice to be made, did show to them *by the help of
a certain crystal* a vast treasure hidden in a certain
hill [*in quodam monte*] at Forncett, in the county aforesaid, called Nonmete Hill. Upon the which discovery the same John Cans and Robert Hikkes and
many more unknown to the jurors, in return for the
aforesaid treasure so found and to be applied to their
own use, did then seize upon a certain fowl called a
cock at Bunwell aforesaid, and there and then in the
presence of their fathers and mothers, baptise the
said cock in holy water, and gave to the said cock a
Christian name, and slew the same cock so named,
and did offer it as a whole burnt offering as a Christian carcass to the accursed spirit, according to covenant. Which being done, the said John Cans and
Robert Hikkes and the other unknown persons
assembled at Bunwell aforesaid did proceed to
Forncett along with the said accursed spirit and did
dig in the hill called Nonmete Hill and made an
entry into the said hill, insomuch that there and then
they found to the value of more than a hundred
shillings in coined money in the said hill. For all
which they shall make answer to our lord the king,

inasmuch as the said treasure they did appropriate to their own use and do still retain.

We have come upon our real magician at last— one who knows how to use a crystal, who knows how to summon a spirit from the vasty deep and make him appear, who can carry the foul fiend along with him, make him tell his secrets, disclose the treasure that had been hidden in the bowels of the earth, at any rate *in the hills*, and, to crown all, a magician who can outwit the foul fiend, which is grandest of all.

For it is plain and evident that the accursed spirit intended to have the body of a Christian *man* handed over to him with all due formalities as an equivalent for the filthy lucre which he was to surrender. Some one was to be sacrificed to the powers of darkness, whose soul should be the property of the evil one for ever and ever ; and John Cans did manage the matter so shrewdly that, instead of a human carcass, only a certain fowl commonly called a cock [*quoddam volatile vocatum unum Gallum*] did duty for the human victim demanded.

But where did they get the holy water ? The Reverend Thomas Larke was rector of Bunwell at this time, having been presented to the living some twenty years before by William Grey of Merton, ancestor of Lord Walsingham. Did the rector con-

nive at the proceedings? Did he provide the holy
water for the occasion? I really am afraid he did ;
for the craze of hunting for treasure had been *endemic*
in that neighbourhood for several years past ; and
fifteen years before this time another worthy, named
John Yongeman, with other *hill-diggers*, had dug up
a hidden treasure said to be worth one hundred pounds
at Carleton Rode, which is a parish contiguous to
Bunwell ; and if the parish priests were delirious
with hankerings after crystals and familiar spirits in
1520, they certainly were not less so seventy years
before that time.

There remains little more than to speak of the *hills*.

✻   ✻   *   *   *

In East Anglia it is to be noted that we are *not*
rich in sepulchral *barrows*. I do not mean that we
have not some instances of these prehistoric structures, but that we have nothing to be compared to
the numbers which remain in Wiltshire or the Yorkshire Wolds. We have them, but they are not very
common. They were, of course, the burial-places of
great chieftains who may or may not have provided
for their sepulchres before they died, just as we know
the Pharaohs built their own pyramids and Mr.
Browning's bishop made *his* preparations for his
tomb in St. Praxed's Church. Were those sepulchral mounds on Salisbury Plain our British sur-

9

vivals of the earlier Egyptian pyramids? Or were
they even earlier structures?—and did those great
men of Egypt learn the trick of heaping much earth
over their dead of our primæval British forebears,
learn and perfect the art as the ages rolled? I
would not be too sure if I were you, Mr. Dryasdust.
One of the greatest of English ethnologists was bold
enough years ago to express a doubt whether the
migration of the Aryan race had certainly moved from
east to west, and ventured to suggest that it *might*
be proved hereafter that it was otherwise. Be it.
as it may, though our sepulchral barrows do not
swarm in Norfolk as they do elsewhere, we have a
sprinkling of them. It is unquestionable that when
some great man was buried in his earthen tumulus,
his arms, his golden torque, his brooches and what
not, were, as a rule, buried with him. In some cases
these would constitute a really valuable find. For
ages these buried great men were protected from
disturbance by the superstitious awe that haunted
the resting-places of the dead. For generations they
were left alone. Tradition well-nigh perished with
regard to them. But there came a day when a vague
curiosity which makes diggers of us all and

the lust of gain in the spirit of Cain

began to work, and some one said, " Let us search
and see what lies there in yonder earthy pyramid ! "

Then they made a hole into the mysterious barrow that none had meddled with for a millennium, and lo! there was something to pay them for the toil. It is easy to see that no sooner had a single success crowned the search of an excavationist than a mania would speedily spread. That it did spread we have proof positive, for I do not remember a single instance of a sepulchral mound in Norfolk having been opened in the memory of man which did not afford unmistakable proof of having been entered and disturbed at some previous time. Our Norfolk barrows have *all* been explored and rifled. The hill diggers of the fifteenth century did their work most effectually: they left nothing for that rabid band of monomaniacs of our own time who with sacrilegious hands have been burrowing into dead men's graves elsewhere, and, in defiance of the curse fulminated upon such as disturb a great man's bones, are prouder of nothing so much as of having unearthed a hero's *vertebra*, his skull, his eye-teeth, or the boss of his once massive shield. No dread of the foul fiend with these gentlemen, and no taste for familiarities with *Oberion* and *Andrew Malchus!*

With regard to this particular hill at Forncett, when first the case of John Cans became known to me, an unexpected difficulty presented itself. The country hereabouts, if not flat as a board, is at any rate almost as flat as the palm of your hand, and the little stream called the Tase goes crawling in tortuous fashion through the only depression that there is in the general level of the landscape, and nothing like a *hill*, or even a mound or tumulus, could be discovered, though a careful survey of the parish and neighbourhood was made. Had any one heard of Nonmete Hill? No. "Never heerd tell of no such place!" We were baffled, till by good luck the oldest inhabitant, as usual, came to our rescue. It was James Balls — aged nearly ninety-three years, parish clerk at Forncett St. Peter, who on Sunday, November 28, 1886, took his place at his desk as usual and gave out the responses in a full sonorous voice, as he had done every Sunday for more than forty years—who found for us the clue. "Nonmete Hill?" No, he had never heard the name. Mound? No. "A hill that folks had dug into one day and found something there?" suggested some wise one. "Oh! lawk! ah! You must mean *Old Groggrams!*" We had got it at last. The fifteenth-century name had long since passed away, and had been superseded by the name of the familiar spirit conjured up by John Cans four hundred years ago.

But where was "Old Groggrams"? From the recesses of James Balls' memory there rose up

straightway clear and distinct the scenes and incidents of his childhood and boyhood, and then he
told us in picturesque language, not without a certain
lively dramatic power, how when he was a boy there
stood on the edge of what were then the unenclosed,
open fields, in a somewhat conspicuous position, and
where four ways met, a slight artificial mound of
earth where the lads were wont to assemble and
practise horseplay. They used to slide down the
sides of *Old Groggrams* when the time was favourable,
and our informant had taken part in such *glissades*
now and then, though he was only "a little un." Then
came the enclosure of the parish; this was in 1809.
(I wonder if in the Act of Parliament there is any
mention of *Old Groggrams* ?) James Balls was then
a lad of sixteen, and he remembers " the piece of
work there was." Old Groggrams appears to have
been a source of disagreement, and it was finally
determined that the mound of earth should be levelled
and carted away for the benefit of the parish. Balls'
father had some patches of land "near by," and he
actually employed his horse and cart to carry off
sundry loads of the mound and spread it on his own
little field.

Earth to earth! This was the end of Old Groggrams.

But was this mound one of the many sepulchral
tumuli of which we have already heard ? And did

John Cans really find a treasure there, value five pounds and more in coined money? I think not. For the buried money, which appears to have been made up of silver pennies for the most part [*centum solidos et ultra in denariis numeratis*], I can hardly doubt but that it was deposited there by Mr. Cans himself, or his confederate, in preparation for the great unearthing that came in due course; but that anything else was ever hidden away in Nonmete Hill, even a hero's skeleton, I should find it very hard to believe.

What, then, was the artificial eminence, which undoubtedly did exist from very ancient times, and was only removed in the memory of a man still living? I believe it was the place of assembly for the old open-air hundred court of the Hundred of Depwade, for which the parishes of Forncett St. Peter and Forncett St. Mary constitute a geographical area most convenient because most central, and of these parishes this very spot where the old mound stood when our friend James Balls was a boy, is almost exactly the centre or *omphalos*. On the subject of these open-air courts I will not presume to speak. One man in England has made that subject his own,[1] and at the feet of such a teacher I sit

[1] See " Primitive Folk-Moots or Open-Air Assemblies in Britain," by George Lawrence Gomme, F.S.A.   London : Sampson Low. 1880.   Comp. Chron. Abb. Reculviarius (Macray), Preface xxxix., pp. 214, 266.

humbly as an inquirer and learner. But I am strongly inclined to believe that a few years of research will discover for us the site and the remains of many another ancient meeting-place of those assemblies. I believe that if Mr. Gomme, or some expert whose eye he may have trained to see what others are blind to, would pay a visit to the little parish of Runton, in the neighbourhood of Cromer, he would pronounce that curious circular protuberance on the hillside, which is called in the ordnance map " The Moat," to be another instance ; nor should I be surprised if even the tumulus contiguous to the churchyard of Hunstanton should turn out to be not a burial-place at all, but the site of another ancient open-air assembly. In such "hills" all the diggers that ever dealt with familiar spirits since the world began would never find more than they themselves thought fit to conceal. Furthermore, if other experts—experts in linguistics—should further suggest that the very name None-*mete*-hill may indicate, even by the help of etymology, comparative philology, *umlaut*, vowel scales, dynamic change and all the rest of it, that there was once a time when Old Groggrams was actually called the *Moot Hill*, I can have no possible objection, but, as we say here in the east, " That I must lave ! "

*   *   *   *   *

But what has all this clatter about open-air courts and the like got to do with magic and magicians? To that only too severe question I can but answer that I never did, never do, and never will promise in handling a subject of this kind to attempt a solution of all the difficulties that may suggest themselves to my readers, or to fetter myself by any such limitations as would keep me strictly to any one point. If, however, my readers are not satisfied, I must refer them again to the experts of the Psychological Society and other inquirers into the regions of Transcendentalism. I commend to them a study of "Mr. Sludge, the Medium," and of another large literature which may be purchased without much difficulty—a literature which will make it clear and plain and evident that John Cans and Thomas Stapleton and their fellows have not passed away without leaving competent successors behind them, and that Oberion and Inchubus and Anthony Fulcar, being spirits, are not dead, but are as ready as ever they were to come at call, if only you can find the *crystal,* or it may be even the *planchette.*

Only one caution would I venture to offer to all who are inclined to practise the black art in our days: Let them remember that a malignant spirit is not likely to be outwitted twice on the same lines, and that if, having been duly summoned, and duly put in an appearance, he should once again make his bargain for a Christian corpse, the adept in necromancy must beware how he tries to circumvent him a second time, even by the help of the baptismal font and holy water, with so poor a substitute as "a certain fowl called a cock." Terrible, I ween, might be the raging wrath of Old Groggrams. Who shall imagine what he might do in an outburst of malignant vengeance and pent-up rage? He might turn again and rend you!

IV.

A FOURTEENTH-CENTURY PARSON.

I⊤ is about thirty years ago since readers of history
—I do not mean historians—began to be consciously
tired of the details of campaigns and battles. We
had become a peace-loving generation, a generation
that was averse to having its feelings harrowed, a
generation that had begun to doubt whether martial
glory was the only glory, a generation that had set
itself to ask whether the uneventful humdrum life of
the present was not after all worth living, and then
went on to ask, rather hazily, whether there was
anything like it in the past. So a new school of
historians rose up, whose teachers began to investi-
gate the origin, growth, and development of our
institutions; and one of them, John Richard Green,

struck out a line of his own when he began and
brought to completion that work of real genius and
original research, the " Short History of the English
People."

When a man strikes out a new idea he may have
reason to complain that others appropriate it and
claim it as their own, but he certainly will not be
able to keep it to himself. The good seed with a
living germ in it is sure to spring up he knoweth not
how. And so it has come to pass that *the people*
have become curious to know how *the people* lived
in ages past, and feel only a languid interest in the
exploits of kings and great captains, or armies and
navies, and champions and conquerors. There is a
voice which is calling out from the hearts of the
very ordinary folk inhabiting these islands, and
which seems to be saying to those who know, " Tell
us something about ourselves in the past by telling
us how such as we lived, and thought, and struggled
in the old days." It is not easy to supply the
demand for this sort of information which has arisen
of late among us. In the first place, we have to
begin by combating the immense mass of gratuitous
assumptions and contemptuous prejudices which
have held the field so long ; we have to prove that a
great deal that we learnt of our accredited teachers
was wrong, and to attempt to gain confidence in our

own conclusions by showing that such as were before us were by no means infallible, and sometimes committed themselves to quite untenable theories. Of course, when men venture upon this line they are sure to appear presumptuous, and something more. But that is not all. The saying, " Blessed is the land that has no history " is a very pregnant saying, and part of its meaning is that when people lead a quiet and prosperous life, without much ambition and without great calamities or violent changes, the records of their lives and proceedings are apt to appear dull and uninteresting to those that come after, and so they are often without compunction consigned to the dust-bin, the rag-bag, or the flames. Only here and there does an eccentric nondescript, with a bee in his bonnet, find himself possessed by a mania for scrutinising the most *useless* documents that come in his way, and employ himself in deciphering parish papers, bailiffs' accounts, and other such lumber, and the older they are the happier he is to meet with them and transcribe them. It is a very curious and wholly irrepressible and incurable monomania ; but, I grieve to say—for by my confession I shall be sure to incur the ridicule and scornful pity of my fellow-creatures—I grieve to say that I am one who suffers from this form of madness.

When I am too weary to sleep, or to read, or to talk, or to think, or to listen, I have, for many years past, found a soothing and healthful recreation in simply copying something which has never been printed and is never likely to be, something which not everybody can read, and very few would care to read, if they could make it out. I " draw the line somewhere." I draw the line for the most part at the fifteenth century. Everything that comes to my hands before that time I fasten upon and set to work at ; but when a document is less than five hundred years old it is a little too modern for my taste. But when I get a roll, or even a conveyance, of the four-teenth century, or better—a great deal better—of the thirteenth, or sometimes even of the twelfth, I am a happy man, and I copy patiently on, and the result is—virtue rewarded.

Lest the reader should do me the injustice of supposing that this kind of employment is the busi-ness of my life, I must needs inform him that I spend only my leisure moments in this foolish diver-sion. It is the amusement of my odd minutes and odd half-hours; but I am sometimes amazed at myself when I see how my collection of miscel-laneous transcripts has grown. Nevertheless, it is a subject of constant regret, and of no little per-plexity, to observe how very rarely I come upon any documents which throw light upon the daily life and social status of the country clergy during this early time. My lamented friend, Mr. Cadaverous, used to say that we knew quite as much about them as was good for us; but this was one of his contra-dictious sayings, and of a piece with another saying of his that the English clergy and the English monasteries were deteriorated and corrupted by the rise of the universities, and by the fashion of young men seeking that sort of learning abroad which they could have found just as well, or better, at home, and that the clergy ceased to be interesting by reason of their being overgoverned, and cowed, and snubbed by the bishops and other overbearing functionaries, when the Academics began to lift up their heads on high and to walk with a proud look. This odd position of his he would take up with some vehemence at times, but I noticed that, like many other dogmatists, he was wont to support it less by evidence adduced than by unhesitating asser-tion. Peace be with him! I intend to publish the cream of his note-books some day. When they appear, the world will know that there has been a prophet among them.

Among the many old manuscripts which I have copied *verbatim* and *literatim*, one of the most curious and precious is what we should now call a

balance sheet, or account of receipts and expenditure of a certain bailiff, or clerk, or managing man
who was in the employment of the Rev. John de
Gurnay, Rector of Harpley, in the county of Norfolk, for the year ending Michaelmas, 1306. Harpley
is about seven or eight miles from Sandringham,
two from Houghton, and twelve from Lynn. Here
the Gurnays had a house of some pretension as
early as the reign of Henry the Second, and I dare
say even earlier, and they were the lords of a
small manor, which was called after them Gurnay's
Manor.

My friend the Rev. John was almost certainly the
son of a certain Sir John de Gurnay, and almost as
certainly a younger son, or he would not have taken
holy orders and accepted the family living as he did,
apparently, before the reign of Edward the First
was much more than half over. Now, it came to
pass that his elder brother died leaving no issue,
and, for anything that appears to the contrary,
unmarried, and the Rev. John succeeded to the
family estates, which were not inconsiderable, and
for the most part lying about in three or four
parishes in the neighbourhood. Bailiffs' accounts of
the fourteenth and fifteenth centuries are to be met
with by the thousand all over England ; they are
not very exciting reading—they are, in fact, caviare

to the general. I have handled many hundreds of them, I have copied or analysed many scores; but accounts of the thirteenth century are at least comparatively rare ; and of anything like a balance sheet rendered to *a country clergyman* by his factor during the reign of Edward the First, I have never before met with or heard of an example, except this one that lies before me.

*   *   *   *   *

It will be seen that this unique document furnishes us with a great deal of very curious and minute information regarding the rector's way of life, habits, social status, and other matters, as could only be gleaned from such a source as this. If we have now and then to read between the lines and draw our inferences from slight indications, this is only what we are always compelled to do in studying the past. For the past must be *studied*, or it can never be known.

I hesitated at first where I should begin—but after consideration it seems to me best to say a word about the house in which this worthy clergyman lived, and to show my readers what sort of a house it was. In that part of Norfolk where Harpley is situated stone is scarce and dear; the making of bricks was an art which had almost perished among us, and even if it had existed hereabouts, brick earth, such as our ancestors would have thought it worth their while to bake into bricks, was not to be found. Moreover, the rights of the *homagers* of every manor to "turbary" and collecting of furze, and lopping and topping of trees growing in certain parts of the manor—that is, the right of providing themselves with fuel in one form or another—was very jealously watched, and whereas in Harpley there were two or three manors whose territories overlapped or ran into one another, the attempt to appropriate any large portion of the common stock of fuel for the purpose of burning brick would have been resented with great indignation, and something like a rebellion ; certainly a succession of ugly riots would have been the inevitable result of such an invasion of the common rights of the inhabitants. On the other hand, there was a great deal more timber grown and standing all over the island, and especially over Norfolk, than is now to be found, and much more importance was attached to the woods of a manor than some good people are inclined to suppose. Timber was by far the most important building material used in East Anglia. But it was not the only one. The dwellings of the working classes were made almost exclusively of what we call " clay lump " in our part of the world ; but the houses of the gentry and well-to-do were either constructed wholly of timber, or more fre-

10

quently they were built, partly of timber and partly of *clay lump*, as the old stud-work houses were built, of which some very interesting specimens may still be found in Cheshire and Shropshire, and, in fact, everywhere where timber was comparatively plentiful and stone was costly or scarce.

So it was in the case of Mr. Gurnay's house. He had some substantial repairs to carry out this year upon his Harpley property, and chiefly upon a house which I suspect had recently been burnt down, for the house is spoken of as "*formerly* the house of David Faber," and it looks as if this house had been rebuilt from the ground. I think, too, that the great barn or "grange" adjoining the manor house had been seriously injured by the fire, and the rectory house itself had not escaped unscathed. Therefore it became necessary to provide timber and rafters and scantlings and beams, and several hundred weight of nails and bolts and clamps and other iron "fixings," for the new work. But the expense did not end there. In the account there are entries for *digging clay* and for the cartage thereof, and inasmuch as water was scarce—and it seems to have been very scarce—some expense was incurred in carting *water* for mixing with the clay, *i.e.* for making the clay lump of which the walls of the houses were in part built, while the barn seems to have been made exclusively of this material, and after it was finished the outside was daubed all over with pitch some time in the autumn.

Unfortunately, I have no means of estimating even approximately the real cost of all this rebuilding and repairs, because the worthy bailiff tells us that the rector had himself paid for the timber (which he had bought at Lynn), and also it is clear that he had done the same in the case of the iron work, and that all that the bailiff had to do with the matter was to pay certain small amounts which were still due upon the articles delivered, and which were paid only when it should be found on examination that the quantities agreed with the invoice. The same is true of the cost of the labour. The rector had paid the heavier part of the outlay, leaving the bailiff to discharge a few smaller payments out of the " petty cash " left in his hands. As for the rectory house, it was covered with reed ; one of the rooms appears to have been *panelled with pitch pine*, and it had a somewhat costly door studded with iron nails.

I incline to think that the rector did *not* live in the rectory house, but left it for the use of his curates or " chaplains." He himself, I infer, lived at the manor house, and lived there in some state, as a man of his means was entitled to do. If a

gentleman in those days had two manor houses—to
go no further—it was at once his interest and his
duty to spend a portion of the year at each of them.
It was his interest because, by his presence among
his people he "kept things together," as we say, in
more ways than one; it was his duty because he
was responsible for the little community over which
he was, to some extent, a petty king, and to some
extent morally a *paterfamilias.* A non-resident lord
could indeed save himself a good deal of trouble by
staying away and taking his rents and his dues, such
as they were; but the non-resident was not only in
the hands of his agent and bailiff, but he left the
poor people too very much at the man's mercy to
grind their faces and to extort from them all he
could get by fair means or by foul.

Mr. Gurnay had another good house at South
Wooton. Wooton, as everybody knows, is the first
station on the railroad from Lynn to Hunstanton.
Sir John de Gurnay had been lord of the manor of
Wooton, and thereby hangs a tale, which I am not
going to tell, because I am not in funds upon that
matter; but I have my suspicion that his son
somehow recovered the ancestral manor of which
his father had been deprived, and that here, too,
at the manor house the Rector of Harpley spent
almost half his time every year.

In the year 1305–6, he spent twenty-one weeks at Wooton, and thirty-one at Harpley.

Before I proceed to treat of the way in which the Rev. John lived, I must needs say a word about the church. Harpley church as it now stands is quite the handsomest ecclesiastical edifice in this part of the country. The chancel is about half a century older than the nave, and its east window is said to be identical with one in the vestry of Merton College Chapel, Oxford, which is known to be of the date 1310. The inference is that this chancel was built about the same time, probably a few years later. I am not going to weary my readers with architectural details; it will be sufficient to refer them to a paper upon the church contributed by Mrs. Herbert Jones to the eighth volume of the " Norfolk and Norwich Archæologia."[1]

This, however, can admit of no doubt, viz., that the present church is a very different building from that which existed in the year with which our

---

[1] If people when they stay at Hunstanton, with nothing to do, find their time hang somewhat heavily on their hands, I venture to advise them to spend a day in going to see Harpley, where the church will very well repay them for their trouble ; and if they can bring pressure to bear upon the rector and churchwardens to remove that organ from the south aisle, where it is flagrantly out of place, to the north aisle where it ought to be, they will do a good work.

bailiff's account is concerned. To begin with, the old church was covered with thatch and reed, and the bailiff enters on his debit side a payment for reed for the roof. But this is not all. It appears that the church, too, was built of *clay lump* or stud work. For, as in the case of the house, which we have seen was repaired and rebuilt this year, a certain expense was incurred in carting water for mixing with the clay, so also was it necessary to pay for cartage of water to the church for the same purpose ; and there are two other charges, one for some iron work, possibly for the door, and another for two *gates,* which can only have been to protect the approaches to the churchyard. The rector can hardly have been yet in a position to build the beautiful chancel in which his body was laid some twenty-five years later, for he had only recently come into possession of the family estates, and his first duty was to erect a handsome tomb to his father, which accordingly he did erect at Lynn, as we find from an entry for the expenses of a certain John de Chewyngton, who appears to have been commissioned to look after the aforesaid tomb, and was sent to Lynn *ad imaginem patris domini.* Some years later the rector undoubtedly did build the chancel of Harpley Church much as we have it now, and it is a noble monument of the good man's large-hearted liberality, and of his cultured taste, and of his zeal "for the houses of God in the land."

It appears that the rector farmed some 800 acres of land, including the pasture, the sheep walk and meadows. The account shows that he sowed a total of 183½ acres, of which 43½ acres were in wheat, 55 in barley, 21 in oats, and the rest in peas (22 acres), beans (1½ acres), and the coarse grain known as *siligo* (20½ acres). The peas, we find, were chiefly used for porridge, as some quarters of oats were, and the barley was chiefly used for beer. The beans, it seems, were given to the poor, except a single bushel which went to the stable. There had been two great barley stacks standing when the year began : one had yielded over 92 quarters, and the other a little over 19 quarters ; the allowance for barley seed was three bushels an acre, and if we may assume that the same numbers of acres were laid down in barley in 1305 as were sown in 1306, we must conclude that the yield on the barley crop was more than six times the seed, and the yield per acre something over two quarters. But such calculations are very likely to mislead us ; we really have not sufficient data to go upon, and I should not have ventured to touch upon this problem, if I were not strongly persuaded that the late Mr. Thorold Rogers very much underrated the yield of the arable land of the country in the middle ages. I do not for a moment suppose that the soil was adequately tilled, or that the maximum crop upon any farm was to be compared with that which was raised among us in the "roaring times," or is raised by good farmers now; but it is not conceivable that the cultivation of any land could have been carried on for a succession of years if the harvest yielded no more than three or four times the quantity of seed sown; the margin of profit would not have sufficed to maintain the labourers.

The Rector of Harpley, or his father before him, was a man who was in advance of his time; for whereas there were at the beginning of the fourteenth century many manors on which the personal services —or enforced labour—of the tenants were still exacted (the tenants being compelled to give so many days' labour in the year to the cultivation of the lord's domain, and to assist with their cattle in ploughing, harrowing, and carting over the acres the lord kept in his hand), it appears by this account that these *services* had been compounded for by a money payment before this date. The tenants of the manor had been relieved of their most burdensome imposts.

Taking the *manor* as a little domain which comprehended a geographical area of limited extent,

with so many acres under cultivation and so many
more of waste, woodland, and heath, the greater
portion in the hands of the tenants and scattered
over the open fields, but the compact central farm,
as it may be called, in the hands of the lord, and
cultivated for his behoof—the most noticeable
feature of the village community is its self-
supporting character. The corn grown on the land
was ground at the manorial mill ; the wool was
spun into thread, and the thread woven where it
grew. The cattle were slaughtered where they were
bred, when they had been used for a year or two to
drag the plough or the cart. Then their hides were
dried and prepared to be made into harness, and a
large portion of their flesh was salted down for
winter consumption.

Adjoining the manor house was a garden in which
vegetables were grown, and some garden seeds were
distributed to the poor, gratis. There are few
subjects over which so much obscurity still hangs
as the subject of mediæval horticulture ; and in the
account with which we are dealing, the only vege-
table named is the leek, which our forefathers
appear to have loved extremely and to have cultivated universally. The gardeners' rolls of the priory
at Norwich form, perhaps, the most important series
of such rolls during the *fifteenth* century which could

anywhere be found in England, and they deserve
to be printed for the benefit of students; but we
must wait for better times before we can hope for
their publication. The bailiff at Harpley includes
all his vegetables under the single designation of
Olera. Besides the garden there was an orchard,
and the crop this year was a large one; for, after
using all that were needed in the house, many
bushels of apples were sold by the bailiff. The late
Mr. Thorold Rogers, though he had frequently met
with mention of hemp as cultivated in England, said
that he had " never seen any entry of payment for
such kind of labour " as the manufacture of ropes
(" Hist. of Prices," i. 28). It is plain that at Harpley, as in many other places, there was a *hempland,*
and this year the bailiff brings into his account two
payments for the manufacture of hemp into traces,
head-stalls, and ropes.

There are indications that the Rector of Harpley
was rather a " high farmer." His implements, such
as they were, had a good deal spent upon them, and
whereas at this time wheeled carts were in Norfolk
by no means universally used, Mr. Gurnay's carts
appear to have been all not only furnished with
wheels, but the wheels had iron tyres, or the next
best substitute for tyres, to wit, thick iron plates,
called *strakes,* attached to the fellies by long spikes

which were riveted on the inner surface of the woodwork. The sheepfold, too, was apparently constructed with exceptional care, and afforded much more protection and warmth for the lambs than was customary in Norfolk, even fifty years ago; among any but the leading sheep breeders of the county.

At the beginning of this century it was not uncommon for the Norfolk farmers and resident gentry to let out their herds of cows at so much a head for the "season." The owner had to feed the cattle and house them, and if a cow chanced to die, he had to supply her place with another of equal value. When a cow became dry the owner took her back and the calf was his; the hirer took all the milk and made his profit by it if he could. This practice still survives extensively in Dorsetshire, and the payment for the hire of the cows is very high—so high that it is said to amount to as much as two-thirds the market value of the animal for the mere annual hire. The Rector of Harpley in 1306 let out his herd by the year in this way, reserving three cows for the requirements of his own large household, and his dairymaid's name was Emma. The three cows reserved were apparently not more than enough to supply the milk for the porridge: the servants were very liberally supplied with oatmeal;

also, they had rations of cheese, which, however, was not made in the dairy, but was bought perhaps from the hirer of the other cows. Goats are very rarely met with in our Norfolk records; but Mr. Gurnay had a flock of goats at Wooton, which he let out in the same way as he did his herd of cows. I rather suspect he did not like a bevy of women about him and his household; and milking and butter-making he therefore would have nothing to do with. Let others milk the cows and the goats, and make their profit of the dairy business if they could—that should be their affair.

I have said that when a cow or bullock was slaughtered the hide was turned into leather, if leather was needed, for the harness room or other purposes. Sixty years ago—I am told by old men who can look back so far—in every considerable village in Norfolk there was a *tan vat*, where the farmers took their hides to be cured. It appears to have been a very long and a very nauseous process; but, of course, the *laudatores temporis acti* assure me that there is no such leather now as they used to have when they were boys.

"*That* was more juicy like! There was more suppleness and *heart* to the old leather. Why, Lor' bless you, I never remember my father with more than one pair o' leather breeches all his life. You *couldn't* wear that leather out. My father 'd think nothing of riding fifty miles in they breeches, and going to church in 'em o' Sunday ! "

In the account we are dealing with, I find a payment entered for making tallow into *dip* candles. Here again I have met with some curious explanation of this entry in the reminiscences of our reverend seniors. Sixty years ago, on a substantial farm, the *dip* candles were almost always bought of the tallow chandlers, by whom they were made on a large scale ; but the *mould* candles were always made in the house, and generally by the mistress of the establishment. The mould was nothing more than a tin tube which was set upright on a dish, half full of moist sand, to keep the tallow from escaping. There was a great deal of knack and dexterity required in working the cotton-wick (the housewife used to buy this in balls of the travelling pedlars) into the middle of the tallow, which was poured hot into the tube ; and my informant told me, with some pride, that his mother was noted as the best candle maker in the neighbourhood, her wicks were always " straight and stretched as they ought to be."

There are two or three omissions in the account which are a little puzzling. There is no mention of butter, eggs, or honey directly or indirectly. As to the butter, it is just possible, but very improbable, that none was used in the household, but it is hardly conceivable that there should have been no beehives, and no careful storing of the produce, and quite inconceivable that no account was kept of the eggs. In the thirteenth century—and it. must be remembered that we are now only six years out of that century—I doubt whether it would be possible to produce a rent roll of any Norfolk estate which does not enter the rent paid by the tenants in eggs, as well as the other portion paid in oats, in addition to the mere money payment. In this balance sheet the bailiff sets down—(1) the payment in composition of personal services; (2) the number of bushels of oats; (3) the money rent; and all this very minutely, but not a word about the eggs, which, in a manor of this pretension, would amount to many hundreds and probably thousands. Another significant omission is all mention of any tithes, except the tithe of lambs or offerings paid to Mr. Gurnay as rector of the parish; although his payments of tithes due from himself at Wooton and elsewhere are duly entered. I can only explain the difficulty by conjecturing that another functionary had to keep account of such small matters as the eggs, honey, hemp, flax, and perhaps garden produce, and that this account, with the

tallies, was rendered to the steward of the household probably at the same time as the farm bailiff
presented his account, viz. at the Michaelmas audit.
The state kept up by the Rector of Harpley during
his thirty-one weeks' residence at the manor house,
fairly staggers us when we come to analyse it. He
resided there during the winter months only. During
this time two horses were kept in the home stable
for domestic as distinct from farming purposes, and
they had the liberal allowance of about half a peck
of oats a day. The rector had besides his " palfrey,"
and during the whole period of thirty-one weeks the
account shows that there was an average of seven
other riding horses belonging to the guests, and at
least two more belonging to one Simon Tripping,
who, I think, must have been the great man's
huntsman.

The allowance of oats for porridge in the kitchen
was about a bushel a week. There were about 110
quarters of barley and malt made into beer, which,
reckoning an average of two bushels to the barrel
for the strong beer and at least as much more for
the small, gives us certainly not less than 1,000
barrels for the year's consumption.

But the consumption of food was enormous : 31
swine, *i.e.* a hog a week, 11 sheep, 4 piglings, 113
head of poultry, and no less than 86 geese, were

consumed by the household, and no less than 52
quarters of wheat—not to speak of the inferior sorts
of " bread stuffs," which I suspect were largely
distributed as maintenance allowance for the dependents on the estate. Making all due allowance
for the great feast to which we shall come by and
by, I can hardly estimate the number of persons
eating the Rector's bread—and by that I mean
eating the *white bread* he ate himself—during his
winter residence at Harpley at less than fifty or
sixty persons. It is a startling view of the way of
life which a rich man led in those days—but it must
be remembered that he stayed at home and that he
had no luxuries—absolutely none. There is indeed
one payment made to Stephen the *Jeweller* at Lynne,
but it was a payment not in money but in corn ;
the good man received four bushels of wheat *ad
oblacionem*, which I suspect means a present, and
I further suspect that it was in return for work
bestowed on Sir John Gurnay's tomb.

After all, " it's the *hoffle weemen* as takes it out
of yur," as an old misogynist of my acquaintance,
long since dead, used to delight in asseverating.
Men can do without luxuries, and only begin to crave
for them when the enticements of ladies' society
makes them effeminate and dandiacal. There would
be no peacocks with the dazzling plumage if there

were no peahens. And the Rev. John Gurnay had
no milliners' bills to keep him awake at night ; no
drawing-room which had to be "done up" periodically; no ball dresses to provide for wife or daughter;
no school bills to pay for the boys ; no nurserymaids
or governesses ; no wife to worry him with her ex-
extravagance. No ! Nothing of this sort. That's
one side of the picture—and every picture has two
sides, the front and the back—and you may take
your choice which you prefer if you can't have
both.

The Rector of Harpley could not marry if he
wished, and when he was admitted to Holy Orders
—and, let us hope, received them with a view to
doing his duty according to his light as a country
parson in the Norfolk village—he gave up all dreams
of wife and children. The joy of wedded love and
the serene happiness of what we understand by
domestic life were not for him. So it is not to be
wondered at that in his bailiff's account we have the
name of only one woman—Emma, the dairy woman,
who milked the cows, presided over that brewery
which had so much to answer for in those thirty-
one weeks of the rector's residence, looked after the
poultry, and had her hands full ; but it is almost
certain that she was married and had perhaps a
family, for the account shows that she had her

rations of corn supplied her, which she of course took home and dealt with as she pleased. In the manor kitchen there would be just as many women cooks as there are in a college kitchen ; that is, there were none at all.

How did the rector spend his time from one week's end to another ? Well, he may have spent it in various ways. In the first place, I suspect that he spent a great deal more of his time in his church than some country parsons do now. We have seen that he rebuilt a portion (and that the most sacred and important portion, as it was then esteemed) of his church within a few years of the time that we are dealing with—and in any case it was much more the habit of clergymen then to worship God in the church itself than it is now.

As the services of his church required his attendance, and the elaborate ritual in that church, varying with every saint's day or festival, gave him always something to prepare for, something to interest him in the actual conduct of divine worship, so the claims of his parishioners were in those days much more defined and much more imperative than we quite realise now. The people may have been very ignorant, and they may have been very superstitious ; but they were very scrupulous, even the worst of them, in their religious observances.

The Sacraments they had a *right* to, and the parish
priest who was not ready at the call of the penitent
to listen to the cry of remorse and to give the awful
absolution to such as were agonised with a horror
of sin, would have had to answer for his cruel
negligence and suffer severely for the wrong. At
any moment of the day or night the call might
come that the angel of death was knocking at some
lowly door; and the priest must needs go forth to
touch with the holy oil the frail body that had
almost done its work, carrying with him the Host,
and standing by the bed of the dying while the
passing bell was tolling. In the stormy moonless
night, before he had laid his head upon his pillow,
he had to be sure that the lamp over the altar,
which it was sacrilege to neglect, was burning
brightly and duly fed—and there was work to be
done for the dead as well as for the living—the
masses to be said for the souls of the departed, and
the commemorations which had been imposed upon
the ministers of the sanctuary, and which they
neglected at their peril. It was not an age of
mother's meetings and tract distributing and district visiting, as we do these things now; but we
mistake it very much indeed if we assume that the
absolutely necessary daily duties of a village priest
in the first half of the fourteenth century were as

few in number as those of our modern country parson.

Moreover, the way in which he was looked after by his superiors would make us feel very uncomfortable now. Twice a year he had to present himself at the Synods held in Norwich Cathedral, and to give an account of himself; and although it may be true that, if he sent up his fees by deputy not much was said about his absence, yet in theory he was bound to be in his place, and might be called upon to answer for his non-attendance. Every year, too, the Archdeacon, who was a very formidable personage with very real power at his back, held his courts and made inquiries, and irregularities and neglect were looked into, and sometimes grave charges were brought against the parson which might involve serious consequences if they were not disproved. The *machinery* of ecclesiastical discipline in these times was incomparably more powerful than we have any acquaintance with in this nineteenth century, and if it was not always employed effectively, and if it tended to fall out of use and to be well nigh forgotten, it could be put in motion at any moment when occasion served; let but the fires be lighted and the wheels would "grind exceeding small."

I do not mean to imply that in the thirteenth

century any Norfolk parish was left to only a single ministering priest. So far from this, I suspect that no one man could have done all that was expected of the parson of any considerable village then. As a fact, I believe it would have been difficult, perhaps impossible, to find a Norfolk village in which there were not two or more ministering clergy, the un-beneficed " chaplains " as they were called, who constituted a very numerous class. These "chaplains " were the will-makers and conveyancers, the accountants, "men of business," and the school-masters of the villages: in fact, the educated class and the educators of the country folk, while they were always ready to take the heavy work off the shoulders of their more fortunate brethren, whose income was certain and their position secure. Yet, after making all reasonable abatements, it is certain that the resident Rector of Harpley had a good deal more on his hands, and was responsible for a great deal more pastoral work than the present rector of the parish, and if he did not do it all himself he had to provide that it should be done.

But the Rev. John Gurnay was not only Rector of Harpley, and so responsible for the religious life of the parish as an ecclesiastical territory, he was besides this a man of considerable landed property. As such he had other duties and responsibilities than those which fell upon him as a beneficed clergyman. Periodically—probably at intervals of two months—he had to adjudicate upon the disputes and serious quarrels of the people who were his subjects in the little domain—to safeguard his own and their interests against any invasion of their rights, to inflict punishment upon the unruly, to arbitrate between man and man, to be the general referee in matters great and small in a hundred different ways. A busy man and an energetic one, he was also a man before his age. He was before his age in his architectural taste and knowledge, for the specimens of church building of the Decorated period are rare in Norfolk. The rage for church building in the county began at least half a century later.

*   *   *   *   *

We have seen that he was a hospitable gentleman who entertained his friends in a bountiful way. Everybody hunted in those days—even bishops and abbots and monks and country parsons hunted. The foxes and the badgers and the weasels and such like *vermin* had to be kept down, and, moreover, their skins were worth money. The hares and the rabbits had skins too, and their flesh was good for food, and the big bustard was a dainty dish to set before a king, and the dogs could run them down if you kept them up to the mark. But they had to be

hunted with care and skill. Even nowadays it is
not everybody who is fit for an M. F. H., and the
care of the kennels calls for brains. In this very
year, 1306, some of those Harpley hounds had mis-
behaved themselves. Mr. Bulur sternly records the
fact that they had killed two of the geese—the
curs!—mangled them so that they were not fit to
send into the kitchen. Oh ! Don and Juno, and Tig
and Ponto, and Samson and Stormaway! How you
did catch it for those geese ! Don't think the
worse, I pray you, of Mr. Gurnay if he were a
hunting parson. Men have been that before now,
and yet have had the fear of the Lord before their
eyes, and have been no unfaithful or unfeeling
pastors of their little flocks, nor neglected the poor
and needy, the sick, the sad, or the dying.

But, as I have said, and I must needs say it
again, the Rector of Harpley had other duties and
interests besides those which his parish and his
people imposed upon him. He was clearly a very
busy man.

It may safely be affirmed as a general rule, that
the less a man has to do the less you can depend
upon him for doing that. If you want to get a job
done in a hurry, beware of looking to the man of
leisure to do it for you. It is the man who has all
his time employed and who has not a minute in the

day to spare, who is the man who can always find a minute to help a lame dog over a stile. The Rev. John Gurnay was one of these restless energetic men— with a head upon his shoulders and a full allowance of brains inside that head—and I am now going to tell you what the worthy gentleman did and what he brought about in this year 1306—that is, well nigh six hundred years ago.

If you look at an old map of Norfolk—not one of your modern ugly things all seamed and scarred with the tracks of those odious railways which are the great obliterators of so much that is picturesque and romantic and peaceful and humanising on the face of the earth ; but if you look at an old map, say of a hundred years ago—or, if you can get it, earlier —you will see that there really was only one way of entering the county from the west, and that way was by Lynn. Lynn was the key to Norfolk from the west and north, if you wanted to get into it by land. I am not going into the physical geography of the matter, and I am not going to prove my point—

> . . . the proof is complete
> If only I've stated it thrice.

During the long reign of Edward the First, which was now drawing to a close, the trade and com-

merce of the county had been going on increasing
hugely, and from Norfolk there was a large export
trade of wool and fells and hides. That means that
Norfolk had become a land of flocks and herds more
than it had ever been before, and the time was
coming when men would begin to grumble loudly
that so much land which had grown corn in their
fathers' days was now turned into sheep-walk. But
at present the cry was for more sheep and larger
herds. Where were they to be got? Wherever
there is a demand, there the supply will follow; and,
as the Norfolk men could not breed the sheep and
cattle fast enough, they looked about them for a
source of supply. It came. From the dreary high-
lands of the Pennine range, from the Yorkshire
moors and wolds, from the Cheviots—for Scotland
by this time was—for Scotland—peaceable and tame
—the sheep and stunted cattle were driven slowly
along; and Lynn became naturally in the fourteenth
century what it is at this moment, by far the largest
cattle market in the east of England. Our Norfolk
dealers persist that it is " the largest out of London."
The more the trade grew the more apparent it must
have become that Lynn itself was ill adapted for any
great assemblage of the shepherds and their flocks.
In the rich meadows and marshes the cattle might
do very well; a few days of such pasture for the

sheep would be ruinous—they would die by the hundred. It occurred to the Rector of Harpley that he might make a great *coup* for himself, and in doing that might be an immense benefactor to his neighbours, and indeed to the whole county in which he was born. So he made his advances in due form to his lord the king, and he made out his point so well, and managed his diplomacy so adroitly, that in this year 1306 he received the royal licence for holding a fair annually on his own estate at Harpley and inasmuch as Harpley Church was dedicated to St. Lawrence, the fair was to be held on St. Lawrence's Day—that is, the 10th of August. There was good reason for fixing this date, for it is just the time of the year when the sheep-breeders " make up their flocks," in preparation for the next lambing season, and it is just the time when the drovers who have more hoggets than they can keep during the winter are glad to turn them into money.

St. Lawrence's Day fell on a Wednesday in this year 1306, and since the feeling against Sunday trading had been steadily growing for well nigh a hundred years, from the time when Eustace de Flay had gone about from place to place preaching against the desecration of the Lord's Day, I assume that the king's writ had ordered that the Harpley Fair should be held in future on the first Wednesday after St. Lawrence's Day. And on that day the fair continued to be held for more than five hundred years, and there are scores, and perhaps hundreds, of living men who remember it, and have even attended it.

There was a stretch of open heath in Harpley which extended from a spot called Harpley Dam to a place called Kipton Ash, where still grows a clump of ash trees—trees that are the successors or descendants of some venerable and conspicuous old tree which stood as a landmark in the days of old ; and here the drovers and flockmasters used to assemble, and here the fair was held. At the beginning of this century the fair was far and away the largest sheep fair in the county. Old men, and men hardly yet old, remember the strange look of the Scotch shepherds, with their bare legs and their plaids, stalking about and bargaining; remember the booths and stalls and the impossibility of finding any shelter for their horses, ridden or driven a score or two of miles in the heat; remember the crowds, and the noise, and the fights and the drunkenness, and, above all, the dreadful difficulty of getting water, which in the morning was to be bought for a penny a pail, and at night was not to be had for love or money. There is some conflict in the reports that have reached me, but this is certain, that the fair was called Kipton Ash Fair, and to this day men talk of the very mixed quality of the animals that were brought there; and to this day when a Norfolk dealer wishes to commend a horse, he calls it a " Hyde-parker "; but if he wishes to express his contempt of the broken-down old beast, he bursts forth into what in Norfolk serves for poetry, and says—

> That there hoss be a Kip'n Esh,
> High in the bone and low in the flesh !

Kipton Ash Fair had a sudden and tragical end. About fifty years ago, when the flocks were assembled in the old place, a frightful form of what my informants assure me was small-pox broke out among the sheep, and they died by hundreds. There was dismay amounting to despair among the drovers, there was panic unspeakable among the dealers and the farmers. Of course there were high words, and of course everybody explained the calamity after a theory of his own. But there was one theory which prevailed extensively among the chief sufferers. That year there had been an enormous number of starlings observed in this district, and, as most people know, starlings like nothing better than to settle on the back of a sheep and hunt for *ticks* and other parasites that are to be found in the fleece. Where there are sheep there are sure to be starlings. This year the shepherds were appalled by the number of the starlings, and they swore that the starlings inoculated the sheep, and that the Norfolk farmers had caused the plague by not keeping down the starlings. But any way the poor dead sheep had to be buried where they dropped, and the area which a few days before had been one living mass of flocks and herds and human beings became, at the end of a week or so, a vast breadth of land which had been turned up to hide the carcases, and it was as if a great blight and curse had swept over the sweltering heath, and the sickening stench of the half-covered mass of putrefaction was horrible. Then the farmers round about said they would have no more fairs at Kipton Ash, and they posted great bills and notices on the barns and gates along the roads for miles round about, and the annual gathering came to an end; until after a year or two the need of a fair had made itself felt as a very pressing one; and then—the terror of the plague being still upon them—the farmers agreed to remove it to another spot, and since then it has been held a mile or two off, at Hempton Green.

But I did not sit down to write the history of Harpley great fair. If I had, I should have taken more pains to find out accurate information about its death and burial, as we may call it. My business is with the Rev. John Gurnay who started the fair. What does this shrivelled bit of vellum, with Adam Bulur's account upon it, say about the fair? It says a great deal, though, of course, it says much less than some of us would wish to find there. What is told us is set down in a very simple and *stolid* way, and the bailiff has no notes of admiration in his manuscript. One has to read the whole thing through and pick out the several items which are to be found under very different heads. Having done that, this is what comes out as clear as daylight.

Mr. Gurnay was mightily pleased that he had gained his object, and there was just the least little shadow of anxiety as to whether the king's license would arrive in time. It did come in time, how-ever ; and when the official who carried it produced it to the rector, he was so pleased that he there and then tipped that official's boy who had come with him. It was not a very heavy tip, but then such tips were not the rule in those days, and the boy, you may be quite sure, had as much victuals and drink as he could carry ; and I am not sure that this *tip* was anything more than the earnest of some-thing more substantial, but it was all that Mr. Bulur had to account for on the audit day. You would like to know what the amount of that tip was, I dare say,

but I am not going to tell you. When the rector
had got his licence, and due notice of the fair was
published far and wide, the least the good man could
do was to prepare for a great feast, and it should be
a real feast too. The neighbours came from all the
country round ; the Mayor of Lynn I doubt not was
there ; and Stephen Astley, the great man of Melton
Constable ; and Sir Richard de Rokele, who had
only lately acquired the manor of Sandringham ;
and peradventure Sir Hamo le Strange from Hunstanton ; and Sir Thomas de Ingoldesthorpe from
Rainham, what time the Townshends were but very
small folk there, though their time would come a
century and a half later ; and Sir Henry de Walpole,
too, from Houghton. His brother Ralph had ceased
to be Bishop of Norwich some seven years before,
and was now Bishop of Ely, and he himself had got
his foot upon the ladder—not the lowest rung of that
ladder either—and many another whose posterity
English history would remember in the after time.
But why dwell upon the possible or probable guests
at the Harpley manor house ? I know it was a
grand feast, and I know that all the servants of the
guests could not be accommodated ; for Mr. Bulur
had to pay for the lodging and expenses of some of
them even on the Sunday before. But when the
Tuesday came—*i.e.* the Vigil of St. Lawrence, being

a Tuesday, remember, and therefore by no means a fast day—there was a little special dinner for a favoured few, at which they had fish, and actually wine! Fish was a very dear luxury in the middle ages, no food was dearer. By fish I do not mean herrings, though they too were dear, but I mean fresh fish, such as we serve up as an adjunct to our dinners now. On Tuesday the 9th of August, 1306, the rector provided herrings galore, but he provided some *plaice* also, and some other fish which the bailiff does not give us the name of; and I make no doubt that the good man had to send for it to Lynn, as many a worthy rector has done hundreds of times since those days and will do again. As to the wine, that too must have come from Lynn, for the rector had no wine cellar and only indulged in such prodigality as this on very, very, very rare occasions.

But when the next day came and the fair was opened, and the king's letter read, and the people shouted, and the buying and selling began, then indeed there was a real feast! Fish? I should think there was fish! There was fish enough to come to at least £15 of our money, but the guests appear to have gobbled it all up, so that the rector actually had to give an order for an extra allowance of herrings to be bought for the servants the day after the feast, and he sent a man to Lynn, as it seems, to buy the herrings and bring back the bill, and that man was Adam *the Harper.* What! should there not be "a taking down the fiddle and the bow?" Should there not be minstrelsy and song?

Though Mr. Gurnay had the good of his people and of the neighbourhood and of the whole county at heart in obtaining the king's licence for holding this fair, and though it proved for several centuries a real boon and a solid advantage and a very important matter for the agriculturists of Norfolk, it is not to be supposed that it did not bring profit to the lord of the manor and the landowners in the neighbourhood. Of course the hundreds of people who gathered together would want meat and drink, and these had to be supplied on the spot. Living men remember the booths and stalls at Harpley Fair. Accordingly there came in a very respectable amount from the rents of the stalls and the dues that were levied, and these are set down in Adam Bulur's account. Moreover, it appears that the rector was not above having a stall of his own, at which bread was sold and what else I cannot tell; and though I do not find any record of his buying any sheep or cattle, yet I do find that he bought a horse with some formalities, and the witness to the trans-

12

action[1] was Mr. Henry Spendlove, who was, I think, the rector's agent and steward and friend and right-hand man, and whose name is mentioned more than once by Adam Bulur, with a certain sort of respect. We have a word to say about Mr. Spendlove before we have done.

*   *   *

But all things come to an end.—*Debemur morti nos nostraque.*

The fair came to an end as we have seen, but it outlasted the founder more than five hundred years. He must have been in the prime of life in 1306, and he lived twenty-five years after that date. He had a younger brother, as it seems, who died young; and when he had finished building the chancel of Harpley Church, he bethought him that life was uncertain, and that he had duties to those who should come after. So he made over his manor of Harpley and other property hereabouts to two trustees, who, I am pretty sure, were members of the Astley family, of which the Marquis of Hastings

---

[1] On this subject some readers will be glad to be referred to the "First Report of the Royal Commission on Market Rights and Tolls," p. 15. That and the "Final Report" issued in 1891 exhaust the subject. It is obvious that this splendid *résumé* of an enormous body of evidence must have been the work of a single hand, and that a master's hand, however many signatures it may bear at the end.

is the present representative: one of them was
Rector of the adjoining rectory of Little Massing-
ham, and the other was Lord of the Manor of Burgh
Parva, a mile or two from Melton Constable; and
he settled the estates upon his nephew John and
his heirs, with remainder in tail to his two other
nephews, William and Edward, and this settlement
was made in the ninth year of King Edward II., *i.e.*
in the year of our Lord 1316, ten years after the
Harpley fair had been established, and he himself
was little more, I take it, than forty years old. It
is pretty certain that the nephews were still but
boys, for the eldest of them did not marry till eight
years later, and their uncle survived that event nine
years, and then his summons came and he passed
away some time in December, 1331, and was laid in
his own church, and they raised for him a costly
tomb, and they laid upon him a marble slab, and on
it they carved his unpretending epitaph:

HIC : IACET : CORPVS : IOHĪS : DE : GVRNAY :
QVONDAM : RECTORIS : PATRONI : HVIVS :
ECLESIE :
CVIVS : ANIME : PROPICIETVR : DEVS : AMEN.

There the good man lay undisturbed for 498 years.
But in the year 1829 they opened that tomb and
they "displaced" the roof thereof.

And underneath, about a foot and a half from the surface, a figure was revealed, clad in a silk priest's robe [query, a cope?], and holding in its hand a sacramental cup, from which the stillness of five hundred years had only stolen silently the flesh from the bones and the gilding from the cup; all else remained unimpaired.

What became of that plundered cope and that precious chalice? Did they find their way to Wardour Street?

There is one more little fact that comes to light, and to my mind it is a very eloquent and pathetic fact as I read it.

Henry Spendlove, who had been, as it seems, the lifelong trusted friend and steward of the rector, had, I think, a son, and his name was Thomas. When the rector died and the living fell vacant, Thomas Spendlove was a lad at Cambridge, but he had already. been admitted to minor Orders. In those days it was never safe to keep a benefice open an hour longer than was absolutely necessary, and it so happened that the Bishop of Norwich, William de Ayremine, was away in foreign parts at the time the living of Harpley fell vacant. The Bishop had, however, left his brother Adam as his commissary, in charge of his diocese. Adam de Ayremine was a great don at Cambridge, though what his position in the University was I have never been able to discover. Before him, on the 2nd of January, 1332,

young Thomas Spendlove presented himself armed
with the necessary legal instrument, and by him he
was instituted in due form, as Rector of Harpley, on
the presentation of " John de Gurnay the younger,
then lawful patron of the benefice."

And here my story ends. But I have my day
dreams as I walk through the lanes and fields of
Arcady ; and I have my visions in the night as I lay
my head upon my pillow, and at times there rise up
before me scenes and sights and sounds, words and
men and women so vividly present, that I find it hard
to believe them other than real. I find myself standing beside the deathbed of the old parish priest of
the Norfolk village, and there are others round him,
and one of them is John de Gurnay the younger,
who is holding his uncle's hand. And I hear the
dying man speak low but clearly ; and this is what
he says : " Nephew mine ! I am passing away and
going home. I have lived my life and I have not
lived in vain. They that come after will have no
bad report to make of me and of my doings, and
that which I have done may He within Himself
make pure ! You I have in no wise wronged, you
are my heir. But have a thought for the young
man whose father was my friend, and let him take
my place and follow me as shepherd of the little flock
whose pastor I have been for thirty years and more."

And then a young man's voice breaks in, and there is a promise given, and the dying village parson sinks back and there is silence ; till somehow there comes up the sound of many voices chanting loud and sweet, and their song is

O all ye priests of the Lord, bless ye the Lord : praise Him and magnify Him for ever.

And there are other voices that make answer again, and their song is like unto the first :—

O all ye holy and humble men of heart, bless ye the Lord : praise Him and magnify Him for ever.

Do not try to persuade me that all this was no more than such stuff as dreams are made of.

NOTE ON PAGE 164.

On the 3rd December, 1892, I was favoured with a letter from the Dowager Lady Buxton, of Colne House, Cromer, in which her ladyship assured me that "she remembers the interest of the opening of the tomb. A small piece of the silk garment (about two inches) was given to her in 1833, which she still has in her possession."

This lady is the daughter of the late Samuel Gurney, and niece of the late Daniel Gurney, Esq., of Runcton Hall.

V.

1799.

A RUSTIC RETROSPECT.

I HAVE long intended to write the annals of my country parish. "Good intentions," however, as Dr. South puts it, "are no warrant for good actions," and "one of these days" never comes. The difficulty lies in determining at what point to begin. I could not start at an epoch less than ten thousand years ago at the very latest, and to bring the history down to our own time would occupy me — according to a calculation which I recently elaborated—during a period of at least a century and a half. I shrink from this protracted labour. Most men. desire to be at rest a little after they have attained their ninetieth year. Accordingly, my

projected *opus magnum* seems to be vanishing from
my hopes of execution.   I am losing

—the dreams of doing, and the other dream of done.

What if I take a single year, and see how it will
look ?
I was asking myself this question the other day,
when a lady-friend of mine put into my hands a lock
of hair.   It was a thick, straight lock ; the hair was
very fine, not now silky ; indeed, it was very dry,
very straight, about nine inches long, and auburn in
colour.   It was wrapped up in a bit of brown paper
of ancient manufacture, probably quite a century
old.   The hair was much older.   On the paper there
was an inscription dated 1799.   I will tell you more
about it by and by.
As I meditated, a desire came strongly upon me to
know what was going on in this Arcadian paradise
when this lock of hair was found, and I could find
no rest till I had gone some way towards recon-
structing the little community and bringing it to life
again.   But it is idle and foolish to give the reins to
Imagination unless Fact acts as charioteer and holds
the ribbons.   So I went to my documents, and the
past came back at my call, gradually peopled with
living forms that rose about me, the dry bones stir-

ring, "bone to his bone," and the flesh mysteriously
growing round the skeletons, and men and women
standing up and staring at me, "a very great army."

In Skeorn's Inga in the year 1799 there were just
434 inhabitants. Yes, that was the exact number.
There was a census held in 1801, as every one
knows, and this is the return: "We find four
hundred and thirty-nine Persons, including children
of every age, of whom two hundred and twenty are
males, and two hundred and nineteen are females.
Most of our males, except children, are employed in
Agriculture; but we have one Blacksmith, one
Wheelwright, and one tailor. We have *fifty-five
inhabited houses, occupied by seventy-five families,* and
two houses uninhabited." To this there ought to
have been added, as there was added ten years later:
"There is one School Master, who employs one
Usher to teach the Parish Children Gratis, one
Publican, and one Bricklayer [who keeps a beer-
house]."

But during the two previous years there had been
fourteen births and nine deaths, leaving the actual
population 434 in the year 1799.

Before we go on, let us pause to notice the ghastly
fact that there were in the whole parish no more
than fifty-five houses all told, and that in those fifty-
five houses there were living *seventy-five families.*

Exclude from these fifty-five houses those that were occupied by the farmers and others who were above the labouring-class, of whom I could tell you more than you would care to listen to, and the conviction is forced upon me that in the year 1799 there was an average of at least two families living in every labourer's dwelling in the parish, and the consequent average of illegitimate births was at least three a year, as shown by the registers. I for one have been loud in denouncing the shameful condition of our cottages in Arcady, and in lifting up my voice against the abominable hovels in which our peasantry are allowed to bring up their families. But it is fair to say that the state of things disclosed by this dreadful return for the year 1799 has passed away. We have no such shocking record as this against us. The world does move on, for all our grumbling. Here things are not as they ought to be, but they are surely better than they were, and, with a population increased in a century by more than one-half, we have three times as many houses as we had; and as for two families occupying one house, the thing is hardly tolerated.

The return quoted above is by no means a satisfactory one, for it tells us nothing about the *aristocracy* of the parish, among whom I happen to know that there were in the year 1799 no fewer than three clergymen, of whom the schoolmaster was one, and his "usher" another. But let us descend to particulars.

In the first place, there was Christopher Andrews Girling, Esq., J.P., who took up his residence in the parish in this year—1799. That of itself was an event; for it had been a long time since any one of his degree had lived at Skeorn's Inga, and he stood alone. He lived in what is still sometimes called the "Gentleman's House"; and such as it was, so it has remained, substantially unaltered for a century. It had only recently been erected, and I think it must have been built for Mr. Girling, as it certainly was upon his small property, and was within a stone's-throw of a farmhouse which his posterity own at the present moment. "A mansion," do you ask? That depends upon what your notion of a mansion is. It was and is an eight-roomed house, with an appendix consisting of a larder and a dairy, and two small chambers over them. There was a dining-room and a drawing-room on the ground-floor. Behind the drawing-room there was the study and business-room of the worthy magistrate; behind the dining-room, the kitchen; and there was only a single staircase.

Please to note that our grandfathers of the gentry class in our country villages, as late as 100 years

ago, were not all spoiled by the march of luxury;
they stood upon their rank and recognised position;
they did not think that gentility is nothing without
a princely income. They had still the foolish super-
stition, now almost extinct among us, that "gentle
is as gentle does." We had *grades* in those days,
and distinctions in social grade were acknowledged
as realities; they stood for something that was
behind, but they implied something that would
display itself in the outward bearing too. When
a man has some deference shown him by his neighbours who are as rich or richer than himself, it may
increase his arrogance and conceit if he is at bottom
a vulgarian, but it will tend infallibly to increase his
self-respect if he is not only of gentle birth, but of
gentle nature too. Mr. Girling was a gentleman,
and it came quite easy to him to live in an eight-
roomed house with no back staircase and no back
kitchen. You, Mr. Gigadibs, would resent being
invited to eat your mutton in such a mean domicile;
and yet, it may be, it may be, that the door of our
gentleman's house would not have been thrown open
to such as you a century back; and if you had
had the audacity to slap the J.P. upon the back, and
address him as "Old Fellow!" you would have
suffered rather surprisingly and very promptly for
your presumption and impertinence.

There was another gentleman's house in Skeorn's Inga in the year 1799, to wit, the Rectory; but that was a more pretentious edifice. To begin with, it had once been surrounded by a wide and deep moat, over which a drawbridge led from the rectory to the church, which stood to the north of it. The moat had, however, been filled up long before this time, though it is easy to see the traces of it to this day; and the high-road, which in old times had gone curling and meandering round the little fields hereabout in the most fantastic fashion, had at some time or other been tyrannically carried straight across the northern side of the parson's moat, and the carriers' waggons had been saved a long *détour*, and the parson's house had been thereby separated from his church by the aforesaid high-road. A grievance, doubtless, to the reverend gentleman, who peradventure had grumbled not a little, and fretted and fumed, and said to his neighbours, " It's always the way! The parson is always made the scapegoat, and if some one's land has to be taken, it's always the parson who has to suffer ! " All which is perfectly true, as it was in the beginning, is now, and ever shall be ! And yet, why should I not take the other view ? Is not it just as probable that when the road wanted altering—and wanted it badly—it was the parson who suggested the improvement; and that it was he who took the initiative, and offered to give up his old moat, and gave it to the parish, and took all the trouble, and bore the chief burden of it, and was worried by the people for his proposal, and yet somehow managed to carry it through at last. For that, too, is "always the way," and if in our country parishes some one has to make a sacrifice for the public convenience, it really is always the parson who shows the example ; and I am happy to know it is almost always the case that he is the last man who is " backward in coming forward."

Be it as it may, in the year 1799 there stood the old rectory, with its garden and its meadow, as it had stood for centuries, in the very centre of the parish. Six or seven roads from all the points of the compass seemed to start from this spot, where the church and the rectory stood side by side ; and, now that the moat was gone, the parson's house and bit of glebe were surrounded on all sides by a road from which the others branched off. All the little world of Skeorn's Inga wanted the parson in those days, couldn't do without him, knocked at his door day and night, and found him at home ; for it so happens that during the last seven or eight hundred years a non-resident rector of this parish has hardly been heard of. Here they have lived, as a rule ; here they have died. If we have not been among the best of the clerical order, we have not been the worst—in fact, we have been a very fair average lot on the whole. I am not ashamed of my predecessors, though I am bound to confess that the best of them was not he who was the last occupant of the *old* rectory. Alas! of that old rectory there is not a stone left except the wall that protects the mouth of the old well, which is still a dangerous abyss for calves and colts and lambkins; and the old meadow no longer belongs to the benefice, and several of the old roads have been thrown into the adjoining fields —and things are not as they were.

In the year 1799 the rector of Skeorn's Inga was a personage still : he had another living, which he served by a curate. A man can't be in two places at once, you know, and if a man has two houses and two estates, he makes his choice for the most part, and he lives in one and he puts a housekeeper in the other ; unless, indeed, he can let it to a tenant who will pay him rent for the convenience. That was the way in which our grandfathers looked at the matter, whether the estates in question were ecclesi- astical or lay; and I am not so very certain that the day may not come when the noble army of the have-nots will begin to denounce pluralities among the laity in the same way that they denounced pluralities among the clergy a generation back. But I shall be dead before that comes to pass, and I do not think that by the time such gabble begins to be riotous

> My dust will hear it, and beat,
> When I've lain for a century dead !

*   *   *   *   *

Those stars mean that I have left out an immense mass of the most delightful and deeply interesting information which—because I do not think that many of my readers will estimate at its true worth —I omit with a sigh. I may, however, at this point tell you who the rector was, even though I tell you as yet nothing more than his name. He was the Rev. John Beevor, and he had been rector here ten years in 1799. His curate at Scarning was the schoolmaster mentioned in the Census return. Do not make the mistake of supposing that this school-master was one of your certificated elementary gentlemen, employed in screwing up small boys and girls to pass their standards in the three R's. The dignified personage who acted as schoolmaster here left that work to the usher, whom he paid a pittance "to teach Parish Children Gratis." He himself flew at higher game.

Mr. Priest was the Senior Wrangler of his year in 1780, and was elected master of Scarning School

in 1789. His predecessor was the Rev. Robert
Potter, the first translator of Æschylus and of
Euripides into English verse ; and if you super-
ciliously assume that they were but indifferent
performances, it is only because you don't know
what you are talking about. Scarning School was
a famous school under Mr. Potter; and under Mr.
Priest it was not likely to go down in public estimation. Mr. Priest had a good house, warranted
to hold twenty-four boarders, and he enlarged it
after a fashion, and took a great many more than
the twenty-four. They say that he was the real
author of "Valpy's Greek Grammar," and I believe
the fact is so. At any rate, he published a great
deal else ; and he was a leading agriculturist too,
and a man of various accomplishments ; and he held
two or three livings while he kept on his school;
nevertheless he continued to reside in the school-
house, and to act as curate of the parish, which had
for him a strange attraction, till his death. He was
a man of *tastes*, and therefore of expensive habits ;
but there was "a rift in the lute," which, as this is
not a Scandalous Chronicle, I am not going to tell
you about. One thing is certain, that he died in-
solvent, though his wife bore him no children, and
though he must, all his life, have enjoyed a much
larger income than his neighbour, Mr. Girling, who

lived within his means and made a liberal provision
for his family.

I cannot refrain at this point from putting on
record certain traditions that were still handed
about, only a few years ago, regarding the once
famous school at Skeorn's Inga; they have almost
faded from memory now, and some of them will die
out altogether when I pass out of remembrance.
The school was founded by a certain William Seckar,
a thriving yeoman, who lived all his life in the parish,
and died there at the beginning of the seventeenth
century. The good man left the bulk of his property, consisting of a house and an estate in land,
now extending to about one hundred acres, to his
wife Alice for life, and after her death " for the maintenance of one free school, to be kept for ever in the
said house, while the world endure, in Scarning."
Mistress Alice was a prize, and a prize not hard to
win neither. Her first husband died on the 1st of
November, 1604, and Alice married her second on
the 3rd of December following. This second husband was buried on the 6th of December, 1608, and
Alice married her third husband on the 7th of
January following. A month and a day was regarded by this buxom widow as a reasonable interval
to lapse between " the funeral-baked meats " and
" the marriage-tables." When, however, she was

left a widow for the third time in 1622, no fourth
aspirant for her hand came forward, and she died,
lonely and neglected, in 1638, and our school was
forthwith started. Then followed seven or eight
years of abominable jobbery and robbery and litiga-
tion as the natural consequence, and the school was
only brought into actual working order about forty
years after the founder's death, and ten or twelve
years after his relict had joined the majority. At
last, however, it did begin to work in earnest, and
the usual precedent was followed : The sons of the
labourers were by no means allowed to contaminate
the children of the yeomanry and the farmers. These
latter were taught by the master himself. And they
were taught well and carefully and successfully too.
The school for more than a century had a surprisingly good record at the University of Cambridge.
The labourers' children were taught by an " usher,"
whose time was given to teach the three R's, while
in the evenings his business was with the master's
boarders, who came from all parts of Norfolk and
Suffolk, and were the sons of the gentry great and
small. Two grandsons of Roger North of Rougham
were educated at Scarning, and I have a note somewhere which says that one of these boys twice—
actually twice !—set the school-house on fire, and
was *not* tried for arson ; because, I suppose, the fire

was put out in time, and because his father was an important person in the county. Later on the future Lord Thurlow was at the school; and the tone of the place was not likely to have been raised by the influence of that coarse and boisterous Lord Chancellor *in posse*. Peter Routh, the father of the venerable Master of Magdalen College, Oxford, was one of Thurlow's schoolfellows, and many another who need not be named. Lord Thurlow seems to have had some sort of sneaking regard for his old school; for when he became Lord Chancellor he promoted Mr. Potter to a prebendal stall in Norwich; though that was but a poor recognition of the literary labours of a scholar who was the first translator of the Greek dramatists into the English language.

But consider how things have changed. Note that we have found a county magistrate living, in a little out-of-the-way village, in an eight-roomed house with a lean-to. A school which had a high academic reputation, though it never could have had fifty boys in it, with a Senior Wrangler as its master—he, too, a beneficed clergyman, and yet acting as curate of the parish for the resident rector; and a third clergyman, usher of the school, itinerating through a rather large circuit of adjoining parishes, where there were no parsons to look after the poor sheep, and no parsonage houses for the vicars or rectors to live in, if

they had been so inclined. Another noticeable indication of the frugal manner of life which prevailed
among the lesser gentry in Norfolk, and elsewhere
too, a hundred years ago, is afforded by one tradition
that has often been repeated to me. Here it is.
" I've heard grandfather say that when Mr. Priest
was at his best there was scores o' young gents as
used to come to school as day-boys, 'cause there was
no room for 'em to board ; and they used to come on
dickies [donkeys], and some on 'em used to have
a dickie for two—ride and tie like. I've heard
grandfather say he's seen a good dozen of 'em turned
out on Podmoor—that wasn't inclosed in those days
—and the *mischeevious* boys as didn't like the young
gents, and used to fight 'em pretty hard when they
got a chance, would take and hunt them dickies a
mile or two off on to Daffy Green, so as the young
gents when they came out o' school had a rare dance
to get their dickies!" Poor little weary urchins!
" But why didn't they come in donkey-*carts* ? " My
benevolent and commiserating friend, what an inno-
cent you must be to think that there was a spring
donkey-cart in Norfolk a hundred years ago, or a
parish road in Norfolk over which a donkey could
drag a cart with a couple of lads in it for, say, a
couple of miles, when the ruts were three feet deep !
Mr. Priest had a comfortable house enough, but I

gather that his boarders did not live with him, but in a range of squalid, rickety buildings, of which some portion still remains. They must have been wretched places, for the best part of them are now turned into four miserable and disgraceful hovels, where four families still continue to "pig" it after a fashion, and where no human beings ought to be allowed to live. I suspect that young North's soul revolted at the accommodation provided for him and his school-fellows, and that in righteous indignation he applied the torch; or it may be that he only wanted to burn that luckless usher in his bed, and to roast him alive for acting his part as gaoler over "the young gents." But this outbreak of virtuous indignation (assuming it to be such—and you know we ought to make the best of our fellow-creatures' little pecca-dilloes) happened long before 1799, though of course at that time it was one of the well-worn traditions of the school.

Among the "young gents" who were Mr. Priest's boarders at Skeorn's Inga a few years later than' the time I am writing of, was a small boy named Edward Hall Alderson. His father was Recorder of Norwich, and the son was an infant prodigy. Unlike many another infant prodigy, he lived to justify, and more than justify, all the great expectations that were formed of him in his childhood; for at Cambridge he was the last man who ever won the Chancellor's Medal for classical scholarship after being declared Senior Wrangler, not to mention other distinctions, which make his academical career the most brilliant on record; and he ended by being raised to the Exchequer Court, as Baron Alderson, in 1834, retaining that high position till his death in 1857. I assume that it was Mr. Priest's reputation as an eminent mathematician which led the Recorder of Norwich to send his promising son to be *grounded* at our school. The boy remained here some two or three years, and then he was removed to Bury St. Edmunds. But Mr. Priest ought in justice to have some credit for the great lawyer's early training; and if the pupil was Senior Wrangler of his year, it should be remembered that the master was Senior Wrangler of *his*. I have known one of his schoolfellows who remembered little Alderson here; but my aged friend was a big boy when young Alderson was a little one, and between the big boys and the little boys in a school, except in cases where the younger is the elder's fag, there is a very broad distinction, whatever the difference may be.

I think you have had enough about our school, though not nearly as much as my inveterate garrulity would give you, if you were worthy of it. I must

get back to the rector of Skeorn's Inga in 1799.
The Rev. John Beevor was presented to this rectory
by Sir John Lombe, the patron, in 1789, and he held
the living for nineteen years. He had not been
many years in residence before the good folk in
Norwich all went wild about a young painter who
had become the fashion, and who was now rising in
estimation every day. He managed to win a very
beautiful and accomplished bride in the person of
Amelia Alderson—a cousin, I think, of the future
Baron of the Exchequer; and among other people
who gave Mr. Opie a commission was the rector of
Skeorn's Inga. When the present writer first took
root in this neighbourhood, this picture of the Rev.
John Beevor was still hanging up in the little dining-
room. It was very far from being a good specimen
of the artist's workmanship, and so when, ten or
eleven years ago, somebody laid claim to it as his
property, I let him have it without weeping, though
for old tradition's sake it might better have been left
where it was. I like to think that young Alderson
saw that picture painted here—going in and out
while his beautiful and gifted cousin watched the lad,
not without many curious speculations as to whether
he would turn out all she and other of his kindred
hoped and expected he would develop into. As
to Mr. Beevor, the best thing I know about him

is that he gave Opie one of his earliest commissions.

He was a big, burly, sloppy sort of a man. They tell how he had an enormous appetite, and could never get enough to eat at home. There was, and still is, a second-rate inn at the adjoining town of Dereham, where some of the coaches used to change horses and the carriers put up their vans. Here a good deal of eating and drinking went on. The people say that when the parson had devoured all he could find at the rectory—and in those days people used rarely to dine later than four—he would be driven down to the "George"; and, as one of my old people put it, "there Parson Beevor'd *George hisself*—leastwise, that was what I've heard 'em say!" He had married a lady of some fortune, and the rustics had a strong regard for her; but their affection seems to have been mixed with pity. "I've heard my mother say as she used to come and call in sometimes, and talk won'ful quick-like and kindly, for five minutes at a time; and then she'd sit still and say nothing for ever so long, only look wistful-like at the children, and take and pat 'em, and say nothing, only pat 'em and pat 'em. Sometimes the little 'uns 'd get scared, and she'd get up and go away, and say nothing, only look wistful-like." It was just as well the poor woman had no family, as things turned out.

The Rev. John was a masterful sort of a person. There were oak benches in the nave of the church in those days—they were all "restored" off the face of the earth some thirty years ago; but I cannot hear that there were any in the chancel. So the Rev. John took it into his head that he would put up two pews in the chancel; one for himself and the *wistful* lady and his family, whoever they might be, and one for his servants. But Sir John Lombe was a masterful man too, and, moreover, he too was Rector of Scarning. For this benefice consists of two medieties; one is of necessity held by the clergyman of the parish, the other may be held by anybody, male or female. When the Rev. John took it into his head to put up two pews in the chancel, Sir John Lombe, as lay-rector, intervened, and reminded his clerical better-half that he too owned the chancel, and was rector of the benefice, and inasmuch as Mr. Beevor had thought fit to erect two pews without consulting his colleague in the preferment, he, Sir John, claimed one of the pews as his—and he appropriated it accordingly. What happened I cannot tell. But that the masterful baronet ever actually did come and take his seat in the rectorial pew, and thereby assert his right, I never heard, though there are strong reasons for suspecting that he did come to Skeorn's Inga now and then. But thereby hangs a tale, and a romance too, which I am not going to tell, though I am prepared to sell it at a price to any distinguished and competent novelist who wants a plot and cannot invent one.

Now it came to pass that on the 28th of April, 1799, Elizabeth, wife of the Rev. John Beevor, died aged forty-five years, and she was buried on the 5th of May. The wistful lady laid her down and slept. At last her earthly yearnings and dreams and regrets were all over. In those days, it must be remembered that the place of dignity for the parson and his belongings to be buried in was the chancel, and in the chancel accordingly they prepared to find a place for all that was left of the wistful lady. But the chancel was very very full of the mortal remains of Skeorn Inga's rectors, not to speak of all the small gentry who had been laid there in large number for centuries. It would never have done to disturb the grave of any man whose representatives were still living in the parish. That would have resulted in such a revolt from authority as would have been frightful to contemplate. But about a hundred years before this time there had been a certain Mr. Blackhall living in Skeorn's Inga, who was one of the gentry of the place; the family had long ago been extinct, and the name almost forgotten in the parish. It would have been altogether forgotten but for certain rather handsome ledgerstones that were lying in the chancel. One of these covered the mortal remains of a little daughter who had survived her two sisters, and who, just as she had entered on her thirteenth year, had been taken away from the grieving parents. There were no Blackhalls now to enter a protest, and so, when the Rev. John Beevor wanted to find a place for the wistful lady, he bethought him of the little damsel's place of burial, and he resolved that there his late partner should be laid. So the great stone was raised and the old grave was opened, and there lay the little damsel, or all that was left of her. The coffin fell to pieces, and in it, lo! there was the skeleton of a little girl, all shrouded in long auburn hair, which had grown in great profusion apparently for years after she had been entombed; and as they looked there was a change, and the muddy vesture of decay crumbled, but the long hair remained; and first one and then another cut off a lock, and it is one of these locks that I have had in my hand.

I know there are many authorities who stoutly deny that the thing is possible. I know that an accomplished friend of mine, who is one of the aristocrats of the world of science, smiled the chilling smile of incredulity when I told him what I had heard, and what I had seen, and how I had held that lock of hair in my hand. But I know, too, that facts are stubborn things, though we all do resolutely accept such facts as square with our pet theories, and bravely reject such facts as go against our views of what the laws of the universe are. Also, I know of one eminent man of science, who was a burning and shining light in his day, who had one magnificent saying, which stood him in good stead many a time and oft, which I seriously commend to the notice of all sceptics and Philistines of every sort and degree. They are welcome to it. " Give me theories, sir ! I can understand them ; but confound facts ! I don't believe them ! "

⁂   ⁂   *   ⁂   ⁂

There is a sequel to this my account of the year 1799 in Skeorn's Inga. The Rev. John laid his wife in her grave, and he went home from that funeral a lonely widower on the 5th of May, and he found absolutely nothing to eat in his house. There is a ghastly tradition that he was seized with fierce spasms of hunger, and that he found the kitchen-fire out, and nothing but dry bread upon the premises. Decency would have suggested that he should fast ; the dreadful sense of emptiness drove him to the " George." When the sun arose on the next May morning his appetite had returned ; to his dismay, he found nothing to satisfy his cravings but the driest of dry bread. It was terrible! Then his cook demanded an interview, and, in reply to his complaints and inquiries, she announced that she was going to go. Why people should ever declare that they are going to go, instead of simply going, it is difficult to understand; but this is the way that some people have when they signify their resolve to proceed on a certain course of action. The Rev. John was at his wits' end. Starvation stared him in the face. He had never engaged a servant in his life; if this woman should desert him he was a lost man. To die of starvation in his own house was a fate too tragical to contemplate. There was only one way out of it. Would that cook be induced to stay? Wages should not part them. What would secure her services? She smiled contemptuously, but only too significantly. Slowly came the *ultimatum*. On one condition, and one only, would she continue to act as the provider for that unhappy widower, and that condition was—marriage! The bargain was struck, and on the 6th of July, two months and a day after the wistful lady was laid in her grave, "John Beevor of this Parish, Clerk, Widower," says the Register, "and Bridget Lee of this Parish, *likewise Widow*, were married in this Church by License . . . by me, Samuel Horsfall,

Minister," and the book was signed by John Beevor
and by Bridget Lee, × *her mark.* The woman could
not write her name !

Did the happy pair start upon their honeymoon ?
Did they stay where they were ? What did the
neighbours say ? How did such a disgraceful and
disgusting *mésalliance* turn out ? Only this much I
know, that the reverend gentleman from this day
simply dropped out. He appears never again to
have officiated in the church. The rectory was soon
let to a gentleman of independent means, of whom
nothing is known, and who possibly may have settled
in the parish for the sake of such advantages as the
school in those days afforded. The church was
served, and the pastoral visitation of the people,
such as it was, was carried on by Mr. Priest and
his usher; and Mr. Beevor took up his abode at
Norwich, in the principal street of the city, and
made himself conspicuous there by affixing to his
front door an enormous brass plate, on which was
inscribed in huge letters his name and title, " Rector
of Scarning."

There is one tradition, however, or there was one
a very few years ago, which reflects some credit upon
the rank-and-file of the peasantry here a hundred
years ago. However much the neighbouring clergy
and others of their degree might have been willing to

condone this indecent marriage, and however much the farmers might be ready to hold their tongues and say nothing when there was nothing to gain and something to lose by protesting, the labouring class were indignant, and did not hold their peace. In their rough way they retained some regard and affection for the wistful lady who had patted their little ones, talked with their wives, sat down in their poor hovels, and somewhat shyly and awkwardly had done them many a kind service. They resented the wrong done and the disrespect shown to their only gentle friend. The lady was gone, and in her place had come a common woman, to whom they gave such names as suited their humour — and they did not spare her. Then they hooted the Rev. John if he showed himself outside his own gate. They watched for him on his way to and from the little inn, where he still would go " to George hisself," and the place became too hot for the rector and his mate. In fact, the people hunted him out of the parish, and he went his way, and was heard of no more.

And thus it was that this year 1799 proved to be the *annus mirabilis* of Skeorn's Inga—now ninety-five years ago.

All whose fathers had any stories to tell about that time have gone from us. Now we live a mere humdrum life ; though, who knows but that, a century hence, some gossiping antiquarian chronicler may fish up here and there a scrap of old-world scandal, and hold it up to the light for our posterity to smile or wonder at when distance lends enchantment to the view. Who can tell what that line of beauty is which separates the sublime from the ridiculous, or how infinitely subtle are the distinctions which make almost the very same incidents mean and vulgar or tender and heroic as they emerge from the mists of the past ?

I sometimes wonder what the chronicler of the future will have to say of me and my concerns if, by some queer chance, he finds a fragment of my personality intruding itself upon his notice in ages to come —say in the year 3000 A.D. What a huge accumulation of *mythus* will have grown up by that time concerning the habits and status and belief and character of the country parsons of England ! By that time, will there be anything picturesque in the world ? Who shall say ?

VI.

A SCHEME FOR CLERGY PENSIONS.

WHEN a man has the audacity to propose any important reform in the management of property which has for ages been left in the hands of administrators who have dealt with it as their own, he must be prepared to be denounced as a dangerous fellow with a bee in his bonnet. His scheme is proclaimed by some to be a veiled plot for introducing wholesale robbery; by others he is denounced as an idle dreamer; by the majority, who have never thought at all about the matter, his proposals are confidently declared to be impracticable. I have lived long enough to see too many "impracticable" measures become legislative enactments to the enormous

advantage of the community, to be frightened by a
sounding word, even though it be an adjective of five
syllables ; and I have read enough history to convince
me that any scheme which has the merit of striking
at the root of great evils, and has in it the germ of
such reform as insures healthy growth for a great
social or religious organism, is quite safe to work its
way to acceptance sooner or later. Also, I have observed that the authors of such schemes very rarely
receive what men usually understand by reward.
Why should they ? They are not labouring for *that*.
The man who would fain be the bringer-in of new
things has to suffer for his temerity. The Philistines
protest that he is stealing their weapons, and invading a territory where they have planted their flag.
The Have-nots shriek at him as a traitor in league
with the Haves, and as only anxious to keep off the
hands of *the People* from their own. Timid spokes-
men of the orderly and well-to-do classes, whose
temptation is to mistake indolent inaction for a
policy of defence, earnestly advise prudent reticence,
and warn him with mournful insistence, *Quieta non
movere.*

That chilling maxim—the wet-blanket of enthusiasm—has its good or its bad side, according to the
point of view of him who uses it. If there be real
quiet—the quietness and assurance of living energy,

the quietness that results from stable equilibrium—
no wise man will wish to disturb it. But if there
be *no* security and *no* stability, then to let things
be is to let them fall without an effort to avert
catastrophe.

Every sincere and loyal churchman—be he layman or cleric—must needs be *ad hoc* a Conservative.
But there are three kinds of Conservatives. The
Retrospective Conservative, who is for ever whimper-
ing for the days that are gone, and is for ever trying
to put back the clock. He knows so little of history
that he believes he can restore the past by dressing
up the present in antique costume, and returning to
plate armour and bows and arrows. He and I are
one in this, that I too love the past, and have
lived in it, perhaps a little more than most men,
but my eyes are not in the back of my head as
his are. For me and those who are of my way
of thinking "Our path is onward—onward into
light."

Secondly, there is the Retardative Conservative,
whose mission is to keep down the pace of progress,
to put the drag on, even when we are travelling
up hill, to prophesy ruin as the certain consequence
of any meddling with things as they are. With him,
too, I sympathise often enough to make myself
uncomfortable. Meddling and muddling somehow

do seem to be near akin, and the late Mr. Lowell was quite right when he wrote—

Change just for change is like them big hotels
Where they shift plates and let you live on smells.

But this earth of ours will go on spinning about its axis and wheel in its orbit round the central sun though you hang on with all your weight to the pendulum that swings in Greenwich Observatory. You can no more stop the great clock that keeps on "marking centuries with the minute finger" than you can put it back.

Lastly, there are the Progressive Conservatives. These are they who cling with a grateful love to all in the past that is still instinct with life and force and energy, and still full of promise of abundant fruitfulness. They are more, much more, than merely Liberal Conservatives, for there is a certain ring of condescension in the sound of those very ambiguous words ; they are *Radical* Conservatives, in that they look to the root of things, and if it comes to root-pruning of a living institution, they will not shrink even from that at the last resort.

I shrink not from avowing myself one of these Radical or Progressive Conservatives. In my love for the Church of my baptism I yield to none, nor in my loyalty to her as an institution whose history ought to be the pride of every Englishman ; but in our Church polity I see there are some things that call for change —change for the better, that the future may not be less glorious than the past.   Change for the better, that is true reform, but it *must* go to the root of evils that calls for remedy, or it is a spurious reform— mere political quackery or something worse.

*   *   *   *   *

We talk of this Church of England of ours as the *Established* Church.   It seems to some of us that that is exactly what it is not.   As a divine society, the Church is a body with which I am for the present not concerned.   But in the lower sense, as a society holding property, and recognised as such in the body politic, it seems to me that the Church exists on sufferance only, tolerated *ad interim,* and if allowed to hold its own as an institution, yet with very hard measure dealt out to it ; an institution or society restricted in its action, crippled in its natural growth, fettered in its liberty.   Call this Church the *non*-Established Church, and you call it by a name which may truly describe it.

This anomalous *polyp* is a very big something, which in one form or another makes itself seen and heard wherever we move.   It is so bulky that it is felt to be a power whose formidable mass compels politicians of all shades of opinion to reckon with it.

It is so huge a mass that they know not how to deal with it.

There are those who would destroy it by pillaging it—who would despoil it of its resources, and so deprive it of its means of material activity. These men are for *dis*establishment—that is, they demand that the Church, as an institution recognised by the State, shall cease to exist ; that its property shall be confiscated ; and that the clergy, if any remain, and the churches, if any be left standing, shall be supported, as the hospitals are, by holding round collecting-boxes in the streets.

There are others, again, who plead that it is no more than fair and just that the Church should be put upon a footing of equality with every other great corporation. They demand that the Church shall be allowed to " live of her own," to frame for herself a reasonable constitution, to govern herself according to some intelligible principles, to exercise her functions, whatever they are, without fear of external dictation, and to manage her property without menace of periodical plundering. They who claim this are they who, in very truth, are asking that the Church shall be *established.*

Lastly, there are those who call upon us to let well alone. These are they who are content with the Church being *not* established. They are content with the position of the Church as an institution which is just tolerated; they tell us that she may last as long as she is harmless. Too much activity, any semblance of an aggressive movement upon the vices or the supineness of the " classes," or any sign that she is acquiring a preponderating influence over the " masses," would be the signal for withdrawing even the measure of toleration at present vouchsafed to her, not to speak of the haughty protection and support of the politicians.

That things should be allowed to go on as they are, and that the Church should be left for another generation without being subject to some organic changes, or, failing these, should continue even to be tolerated as a political institution, seems to some of us an assumption entirely untenable. *Quieta non movere* will not do. There are only two ways of escape from the present position of the Church : we must either boldly embark upon some statesmanlike experiments in the direction of reform, or we must make up our minds to submit to extinction.

Because I believe that this latter alternative would be found to be the heaviest calamity that could befall this country, and because I believe that the keeping up the existing old-world *régime* on its present footing is impossible, I have already ventured to mark out the lines on which I humbly conceived some constitutional reform in the Church should be carried out. I believe they are such reforms as are imperatively called for, without, of course, being so presumptuous as to hope that any proposal for conservative reconstruction would ever be accepted in its entirety. Reform of our political institutions in every department has been accepted by the nation during the last half-century. It was felt to be inevitable, and our national life has become incalculably more vigorous by the great changes that have been effected. Reform of our ecclesiastical polity must follow.

Assuming that some important changes in the tenure of Church property in England and in its administration are inevitable, common prudence suggests that we should all endeavour to take an intelligent view of the outlook, and prepare ourselves for what is coming. No question is pressing itself more upon the attention of churchmen at the present moment than this, how provision may be made for aged and disabled clergy, and something like a maintenance fund may be raised for their widows and families. The initial difficulty suggests a painful reflection. Every other profession is going up, the clerical profession alone is going down. It may be, as it is, saddening to confess the fact—to deny it is impossible.

A great economist of the last century is reported to have said that "the clergy of the Church of England bring more into their benefices than they take out of them." I believe there never has been a time when, in the ranks of the beneficed clergy of this country, there was not a considerable number of men who had "private means," from which their professional incomes were supplemented. In the times before the Reformation we are perpetually coming upon such instances. In the century that followed we find the pages of Walker in his "Sufferings of the Clergy" full of bitter complaints, not only that the dispossessed clergy under the Commonwealth were ejected from their livings, but that their "temporal estates" were sequestered also. When Goldsmith wrote his "Vicar of Wakefield," he made a great deal of the interest of his beautiful story turn upon the good man's loss of his private fortune; and down to our own time it may be said to have been the rule that the country clergy have had resources outside their clerical incomes. Unhappily, the number of clergymen who are in any sense men of fortune is diminishing year by year, and their place is being supplied more and more by men who look to live by their benefices, and by them alone. Meanwhile, we have begun to provide for the maintenance of such clergymen as are no longer able to

discharge their duties, and who are anxious to resign
their livings—not to speak of the compulsory retirement of others, which is advocated as a needful
measure of reform by not a few of our magnates.
According to our recent legislation, it has been laid
down that whatever pension is to be awarded to the
superannuated or retiring clergyman is to come out
of the income of the benefice which his successor is
presented to. In the same proportion that the retired
officer is thus provided for—in that proportion is the
new man's income diminished, and the parish suffers
by the withdrawal of the funds supplied for the
maintenance of the superannuated, who, as a rule,
removes from the scene of his earlier labours. The
method adopted is not unlike that which prevailed
under the purchase system in the Army. An officer
paid for his *step*, and sacrificed the income derivable
from the sum paid down, receiving in return an
increase of pay and a higher rank in his regiment.
If he were fortunate, he recouped himself sooner or
later ; if the reverse, he might lose all.

But in the case of the retiring rector, his pension
becomes a first charge upon the living he vacates;
or, in other words, the benefice becomes less in value
as long as the pensioner lives. During all his term
of service this pensioner may have contributed
nothing to any pension fund—he has not been called

upon to make any provision for old age ; as far as his benefice is concerned, he has lived from hand to mouth, the pension he enjoys has cost him no sacrifice of income during the term of his incumbency; it is paid by his successor, and by him alone.

Surely this is hardly fair to the working man, who takes over all the duties and responsibilities of his new charge.   As a financial arrangement it is open to very grave objections ; on higher grounds it is even less defensible.   Whether a better scheme might not have been proposed and a better arrangement been formulated it is hardly worth while just now to discuss, and the less so because no attempt to deal with the problem before us should stop at considering the claims which any one class of the clergy may put forward.   It is a problem in the solution of which all the clergy, beneficed or unbeneficed, are interested.   When this matter is discussed people seem to forget that the numbers of the unbeneficed are steadily increasing upon the others, and that curates, too, grow old, and, as time goes on, become less fit for the discharge of their exhausting labours.

Why should we begin to make provision for old age only when old age has begun ?   Why should they who are in their full vigour be excused from sacrificing any of the comforts and luxuries of life in preparation for a time when they will need them more than now ?

If the clergy of the Church of England were indeed an organised body, subject to real, and not merely nominal, discipline ; if they were really doing their duty in some sort of subordination to their commanding officers ; and if the same sort of solidarity existed between the clergy of every diocese and their bishop as does exist between the officers of every regiment in the Queen's army and their colonel—it would be a matter of no difficulty to insist upon a certain quota of every man's pay being *stopped*, and invested as an insurance fund, accumulating at compound interest, and payable only on the retirement or the death of the contributor. Nor would there be any difficulty in so taxing the clergy for the benefit of themselves and their families if the clergy were, as some pretend they are, a department of the public service. It is because they are neither the one nor the other that any proposal for introducing compulsory life assurance among the clergy of all grades is denounced by some as impracticable, and by others as a scheme flagrantly Erastian in its character. As long as the clergy continue to hold their livings on their present tenure—*i.e.*, as

long as a man's benefice is his freehold for life,
with, practically, no trustee responsible for im-
peachment of waste, and no tenant in tail who
can interpose to prevent mismanagement—so long
will *any* scheme be impracticable which contemplates the taxation of an incumbent, even for his
own benefit, or which interferes with his liberty
of spending the income of his benefice exactly
according to his own pleasure, and without any
regard for the interests of those who may come
after him in his cure, or of those whom he may
have brought into the world.

It was stated in the Convocation of Canterbury
the other day that the numbers of the unbeneficed
clergy at this moment stand to the beneficed clergy
in the proportion of more than two to one, and,
therefore, that not more than one clergyman in
three can ever hope to receive any but a subordinate
charge. Meanwhile, it was added, these latter are
marrying in the most reckless fashion, and bringing large families into the world, who, as a rule,
are "dragged up," no one knows how. In other
words, a class of pauper clergy is rapidly increasing
upon us, and the hat is being held round every
week for the support of those who find themselves
left absolutely unprovided for. They cannot dig;
to beg they are not ashamed. It is a scandal and

a reproach to somebody. The question is—to whom does the reproach belong?

The enforcement of clerical celibacy is not to be thought of. Can nothing else be enforced? Granted that they who preach the Gospel have a right to live of the Gospel; yet it surely is too much to claim that they who preach the Gospel have any right to expect that their widows and families should be supported and advanced in life out of the alms of the laity indefinitely. It is a discipline of finance that we want, and we want it grievously. As for those who are already ordained, and have been so for years, they must, I suppose, be left to take their chance. As for those who are admitted into the clerical body in the future, they ought to be protected from themselves, in the interest of the community at large. Let us begin at the beginning.

It is not too much to assume that the average stipend which the deacon expects when he enters upon his first cure is £100 a year. As a rule he is then twenty-three years of age. The sum is not large, but somehow the young men live upon it; they very rarely get into debt, which proves that they can and do live upon it. Let this stipend be charged at starting with an abatement of 10 per cent., for which the paymaster, not the payee, is liable. Let this abatement be placed to the credit of the payee, as a premium upon a policy of insurance standing in his name—a policy not transferable, and not negotiable in any way. That is, let it be impossible for the assured to mortgage his policy, or borrow money upon it, or deal with it in any way as property which he can dispose of except by will, and even so let his power of appointment over it be limited by reasonable restrictions. Let the premium be at once invested by some board, or commission, or other duly-authorised body, incorporated *ad hoc*, and let the interest as it accrues be added to the premium in the ordinary course. Let this be done year by year, the annual premium in all cases increasing by compound interest, and the capital growing continually, in which the clergyman or his representatives have a reversionary interest. Assume that our young curate never gets more than his original £100 a year, and is therefore never called upon to pay more than his annual £10—a very unusual case ; and assume, further, that the premiums accruing are invested at only 2½ per cent. Even so, the aggregate standing to the credit of this account after forty years will be something over £690, the clergyman being then only sixty-three years of age. Or let the process

go on for another ten years at only the original
rate of payment, and instead of £690 there will be
a very little short of £1,000 to the credit of the
account, though the aggregate of annual payments
has amounted to no more than £500, and the
clergyman is no more than seventy-three. At this
age many a man has still some vigour, and is far
from unfit for the discharge of his clerical duties.

But this example puts the case at its worst, and
applies to those who never get more than £100 a
year all their lives. Moreover, it assumes that the
premiums are invested annually, at no more than
the low rate soon to be the normal rate of interest
of Consols. It assumes, further, that the premiums
are always invested at par. But it is very seldom
that a man's clerical income remains at £100 a
year during his life. If he chooses to take one of
those " small livings " which yield him a mere
nominal income, the presumption is that he has
some private means from which he supplements
his professional stipend. In such cases—and they
will be very few—the annual abatement of 10 per
cent. upon his net clerical income will be less than
£10, the amount to his credit will go on increasing
more slowly than before, and the aggregate at the
end of thirty or forty years will be proportionately
less than in the previous instance. But in this

case the presumption is that there will be less need for making provision for a family than before, and less chance of the wife and children being left destitute.

But take a more frequent case. Our curate who starts with £100 a year at twenty-three, finds himself with £150 a year at twenty-six, gets a living of £300 a year at thirty, is promoted to one of £500 at forty, and at fifty is advanced to the discharge of archidiaconal functions, with an increase of income corresponding to the lofty title to which he has succeeded. Then, at every step up the ladder of preferment the 10 per cent. abatement increases at the same rate as before; every successive increment goes on at compound interest to swell the aggregate that stands in his name; till, in the case of that favoured few who are born to succeed in their profession, and who do succeed in carrying off the prizes, their credit balance in the end will count, not by hundreds, but by thousands —the increase of the fund going on automatically, the annual premium rising as the man's income rises, and at the same rate at which this later grows.

But other cases will present themselves for special consideration. Many men are admitted to Holy Orders without any stipend. Assistant masters in our endowed schools are very frequently ordained in some dioceses—and I wish with all my heart this were the practice in all dioceses, and that many more were so admitted to the ministry of the Church; such men do excellent work as kindly helpers to their clerical brethren, and are among the most valuable of those clerical volunteers who, to the parochial clergy, are their best friends—their friends in need. Such men, it may be said, have no *clerical* income that can be dealt with as stipends can, but they continue to be members of the clerical profession; they are eligible at any moment for preferment, and, for the most part, they look to obtain such preferment sooner or later; they are not at all anxious to renounce their Orders.

These men, being (as they undoubtedly are) by far the most cultured and learned of the clerical body, and having acquired, by their long training, habits of business and the faculty of making the most of their time, make very good working clergy when they take to pastoral work; while, on the other hand, during those years that they pass in, what I may call, the reserve, they are usually making a larger income than they ever make afterwards when they join the ranks of the town or country parsons.

It is almost certain that such men would willingly

contribute their annual payments to their own assurance accounts: no pressure would be required in their case. But if there were any reluctance, and if some should object, and if in their case compulsion were objected to, might it not well be insisted that any clergyman whose name did not appear upon the register of the assured should be considered as having retired from the profession, and should therefore be considered as no longer eligible for preferment by means of his having so retired ?

And this brings us to another aspect of the scheme proposed. The annual payment, which I have hitherto treated as an insurance premium only, would really be something more : it would be an annual levy upon the members of the clerical *profession.* It would be a *fee* which all the members of the *profession* would be called upon to pay. Just as every graduate of Cambridge or Oxford who has not withdrawn his name from his college books ; or every barrister, whether practising or not, who still continues to be a member of his inn ; or every solicitor whose name remains upon the rolls—is called upon to pay his annual fees for the privilege of belonging to a learned corporation or a profession of which he is a member, so should every clergyman be compelled to pay his annual fee ; though in his case such fee would be, not only a payment in the nature of a tax upon him as a member of the clerical profession, but it would be also the principal of a fund which would be accumulating for his own benefit, and standing to his credit against the time of his death or voluntary retirement.

That word "retirement" introduces another question : What is to prevent any clergyman retiring from the profession at any moment and claiming his savings ?

(1) In the first place, it will have been seen that the annual abatement, or fee, or subscription—call it what you will—is not to be regarded or treated as an insurance premium and nothing more. It is also the annual fee which a man pays as an equivalent for his continuing to be a member of the clerical *profession.* Of course, he may retire from his profession if he chooses ; but would it be equitable that, on his retirement, he should claim, not only all the principal sum which he has been called upon to contribute, but the compound interest as well ?

Without venturing at this stage to go into details, it seems to me that in some cases it would be wise and equitable, in others it would not. Every case would have to be dealt with on its merits. At the worst, there would be the case of the clerical scamp whose career as a clergyman is practically closed, who could never again hope to make any professional income. At the other end of the scale there would be the hopelessly disabled man, who could no longer continue to pay his fees, and whose future in this world was a blank. In the one case there should be reserved the right to withhold at least the accumulated interest; in the other, it might easily be provided — sometimes that the annual fee should be remitted, sometimes that the whole of the fund standing to his credit should be handed over to him without conditions, sometimes that a portion of the accumulated interest should be reserved for his family in the event of his death. Where a clergyman deserted his profession—either because he was practically compelled to resign, or because he was tired of it, or because he was in debt, or from any other unworthy motive—it might be provided that a certain discretion should be left in the hands of the body in whom the management of the fund was vested; and where, in their judgment, the retiring cleric could not make out a good case for himself, the accumulated interest at least might be withheld, such interest being paid over to a general fund, which might go to swell the resources of the corporation, and thus become a bonus fund for the benefit of the assured.

(2) Very different from the cases of clergy retiring from the profession on insufficient grounds, from caprice, or because of some moral pressure brought to bear upon them, would be the cases of those who were really past work and past hope of professional usefulness.

(i.) In the case of the disabled clergyman *still retaining a benefice*, I incline to think that, *as a rule*, he should not have control over the sum standing to his credit during his lifetime. On the other hand, he might be relieved from all compulsory subscriptions at the age, say, of sixty-five. If he chose to go on adding to his accumulations, he could, of course, do so.

(ii.) In the case of the clergyman retiring with a pension paid out of his former benefice (always supposing that this vicious practice should be allowed to continue), it would certainly be advisable that any sum for which he was liable for *dilapidations* might be paid out of the accumulations standing to his credit ; but, inasmuch as he would be still receiving some income from his profession, it would be advisable that the balance should be paid over only to his representatives at his death.

(iii.) In the case of the *unbeneficed* there might be, and there would be sure to be, instances where a poor man would find himself without employment for months at a time, and even for longer periods. Would it not be hard to compel him to pay even the minimum annual fee when he was earning nothing? Observe that here, again, it would be no harder than it is for a lawyer to pay his annual subscription while earning nothing by *his* profession. But there always is, and there always would be, so much sympathy among the laity for the unbeneficed clergy that there would be very rarely any difficulty in providing for the minimum annual professional charge. There would be sure to spring up societies and associations for arranging this; and, moreover, it would be found pretty certain that, as time went on, the financial position of the assurance fund itself would be such as to allow of the annual increment being placed to the credit of many needy clergy, whose cases might be considered and dealt with from time to time.

What would be the effect of a clergyman's retiring and claiming a return of his money? He would cease to be a member of the clerical *profession*, and be incapable of accepting preferment or officiating as a *licensed* curate.

But might he not again return to work if he returned to a better mind? Clearly a *locus pœnitentæ* should be allowed in all cases which admitted of being satisfactorily explained. On the other hand, it would be impossible to allow of a man's withdrawing from his profession (and so withdrawing from all restraints of discipline and responsibility) for as long as he pleased, and yet to give him the option of coming back to it at any moment, and being presented to a benefice, without passing through some period of probation, or being subject to a searching inquiry as to how he had been spending his time and as to his present fitness to resume professional duties.

It may be said that the minimum annual payment to be required of the clergy under this scheme is too large.

In the first place, it may be answered that such payments are not to be levied from the receivers of stipends in the case of the unbeneficed, but from their paymasters, whoever they may be. The curate would not be called upon to pay back anything that he had received. It would be his rector or vicar who would be chargeable.

In the case of the beneficed clergy, again, the annual payment would be a *first charge* upon the income of his living ; and in accepting preferment the incumbent would take this annual charge into account in making his calculations, just as he now takes into account the amount of land-tax for which he is liable, or the interest upon any mortgage effected through the Governors of Queen Anne's Bounty.

Thus far but little has been said on that part of the problem before us which is concerned with the pensioning of the aged clergy. We have assumed that they will leave families behind them, and for them our scheme aims at making some provision. But suppose the reverend gentleman has never married—what then ? Then, on his retirement after loyally serving his time in the ranks, and finding himself, say, with a thousand or two pounds standing to his credit, two courses would be open to him : he might either withdraw his capital, and so withdraw from the profession ; or he might compound for a life annuity, surrendering all claim upon the principal and interest due to him. If he declined to accept either of these alternatives, a middle course would be at his option whether married or not, whether a celibate or the father of a family : he might leave his capital where it was ; but instead of adding to it he might, on superannuation, be entitled to receive interest upon it during his life. This would be his pension. At his death his family would receive whatever sum stood to his credit at the moment of his retirement.

In putting forth a proposal like this, which aims at dealing with a great and acknowledged evil, an evil which is rapidly growing to the proportions of a scandal, I repeat that I am not so presumptuous as to expect that it will be received without objections more or less reasonable, wrathful, or contemptuous. This generation is very strong in criticism ; we all have to run the gauntlet of that— we get quite as much of that as is good for us. What we really do want, however, is not such criticism as goes no further than pointing out faults, but such as may help forward the cause of reform wherever reform is urgently needed. This scheme may be as crude as you please. The present writer may be a mere country parson, as ignorant and silly as—of course—they all are ; but he does not speak without having long and honestly thought over the measure he advocates. He has at length felt himself compelled to say his say in all earnestness, and with the deep conviction that in this matter the time for taking action has come.

VII.

SOMETHING ABOUT VILLAGE ALMSHOUSES.

I AM informed on good authority that my grandfather's grandfather ended his days in a picturesque retreat for decayed gentlemen, somewhere in the West Riding of Yorkshire. I sometimes think that my grandfather's grandson will be a lucky man if nothing worse happens to him in his old age than that he should close his career in a similar asylum for destitute gentility. When this thought presents itself to my mind, so base and abject is my nature that I contemplate the prospect with a strange equanimity. I believe I *could* resign myself to a chamber in the Charterhouse, or a tiny cabin at St. Cross, without repining, if only my companions were anual。

not profane, my allowance of soap were not limited, and my linen were tolerably clean.

All
Life needs for life is possible to will,—

says the great laureate, which being interpreted means, as I take it, that if a man be wise enough to accommodate his requirements to his circumstances he becomes master of the situation, whatever the situation may be. And yet there is a limit even to this. I frankly confess I shrink from "coming to the workhouse," as the phrase is. I was for some time a kind of volunteer chaplain to a union workhouse, and I have visited more than one. I do not think they improve upon acquaintance ; they are not savoury—of course they are not gay—but they are not savoury, I know only one that is beautiful to look at—or rather it was beautiful to look at thirty years ago—I mean the union house of Falmouth in Cornwall. But to look *at* a workhouse is one thing, and to look *into* it is another ; and to live in it and die in it, that I shrink from. That be far from me !

I used to be told that my respected progenitor, whom I have alluded to above, had shown an altogether mean and vulgar spirit in extreme old age, inasmuch as he resolutely refused to leave the retreat provided for him by the gracious bounty of some dead benefactor, rather than make a home with his grandson, who had risen to something like affluence by his own energy and steadfast continuance in well-doing. The elder gentleman persisted in saying that he preferred to be independent rather than live on the generosity of his children's children, whom by his earlier imprudence he had wronged. He died in that almshouse accordingly, more than a hundred years ago.

Many years after that event I remember hearing some one say that *my* grandfather had never been able to get over the distress which his grandfather had caused him by refusing to come out of the alms-house, and as I listened to them talking the subject over, I had great discussions with myself in my small mind, and debated the matter again and again. I came to the conclusion that the old man was right, and I got to reverence his nobleness, and often and often I have said to myself, " If I am ever a grandfather and have to live in an almshouse, I shall be proud to entertain my grandson with suitable hospitality, but I will not permit him to patronise me ! "

I mentioned the Charterhouse just now. Who can think of it without thinking of Colonel New-come? I went there the other day, and I am sorry I went. There was no one there remotely resembling

Colonel Newcome. The place is fusty, shabby, sulky, frowsy—sweetness and light nowhere. The very air the old gentlemen breathe is stale, their very potatoes must be sodden, they talk of things gone by, they are specimens of a bygone era, and all around them there are things of the past and of the past only ; and that not a living past, but a dead one, dead, stagnant, and profitless, with no lessons, and out of all touch with the present, let alone the future. I spoke to this one and to that, and the tone was that of the dreary refrain—

I know not ! What avails to know ?

I would rather not die there among the brethren of the Charterhouse, and as one of them. No! Somehow the old gentlemen are out of place there, and I cannot but believe that if Master Sutton were to rise up from his grave and make a visitation of the place as it is now, even at its best, the founder would say : " This is not as I would have had it. This is no place for such as these ! "

But a while ago I was at the Hospital of St. Cross. It was an autumn afternoon. The leaves were still upon the trees, but they were changing from green to ruddy gold. Each leaf as it trembled in the gentle breeze seemed to whisper, " Thank God for life, the life upon the kindly earth. And

thank God that the earthly life does not last for ever.
We have lived through our fresh greenery, and the
golden days have come, and are passing. Thank
God for life, thank God for death!" That was
the whisper that came to me from the leaves that
fluttered and laughed upon the boughs. Through
the rich meadows the little Itchen flowed quietly;
yonder rose the cathedral tower, and a sound of bells
came softly to my ears—not riotous with too much
mirth, not telling of sadness or suggesting parting.
I went to that beautiful church within the gates—
there was a certain atmosphere of joy about it.
The richness was not the splendour of proud display;
it seemed to tell of mere thankfulness, and one old
gentleman was sitting there far down in the aisle—
sitting, not kneeling—and looking upwards; looking,
not I think praising or praying, but taking in a calm
delight, as if there was a serene enjoyment in idly
gazing at that luxury of colour and form. He rose
as we entered, and passed out, as if we had disturbed
him. I hope he did not resent our intrusion, for
what right had we there, we who came only as
chance visitors, while he was at home?

I asked where B. was to be found. They showed
me where his chambers were. The rich red creepers
had climbed to the very roof. The little window
was bowered in leafage. The sun was going down,

but the casement was opened, and as it faced the west the diamond panes gleamed with an evening glory. B. was drawing at the window. He looked up, knew me, and smiled a gentle recognition. The last time I had seen him was at my own house, where he had come professionally, when he had charmed me by his wide knowledge, his refined taste, and his attractive conversational powers. We talked for long; he told me much about the history and the architecture of the hospital. He had only one regret, that was that he could not move about without inconvenience or pain. " But was he not straitened ? " He appreciated the delicacy with which the subject was approached, but he waived it off. " Thank God ! you see my pencil and my brush are not quite idle. They have always been a source of happiness to me, and though I have not prospered as well as some, I cannot reproach myself, nor will they who alone have any right to do so reproach me. I am happier here than I have been for many a long day, because I have learnt to acquiesce. I know the worst now. There was a time when I used to think it would be dreadful. I find it what you see. Isn't it a very peaceful and beautiful retreat for a man who aimed just a little too high, and failed ? "

Yes ! It is this, and much more than this. It is just what such a refuge for the unsuccessful in the

16

great battle of life should be—quiet, orderly, not without discipline. The roar of a great city very far removed. Nature all around smiling in her serious fashion—even the very semblance of her wrath kept away from those bowed heads, sheltered as they are from the storms that must needs rage elsewhere. As I passed out I asked myself : " Is it always autumn at St. Cross—golden autumn, with its glowing leafage, its lush meadows and their placid kine, and the gentle river too content to hurry on its way ? Is the sun always sinking in the west there, and always streaming forth a gleam of hope and promise for the day that dawns after the lengthening of the shadows ? "

Why are there not more such resting-places as St. Cross for such as have run their race and run it bravely, have done their work and toiled manfully, and yet have not where to lay their heads ? Such retreats were numerous enough once upon a time. They called them " hospitals " in the old days, but they were all swept away ruthlessly, savagely, horribly—all but some very few, and I know not how those few were spared. How is it that they have never been revived ? There was one I wot of in this county of Norfolk once. It lived on for some four hundred years at Coxford, and when the suppression of the religious houses came it was blotted out, and the thirteen poor men who cowered and huddled tremblingly round the cruel visitors were turned out in the cold. " Sir John Mendham, Pryst of yᵉ Hospitall," received ten shillings to comfort himself with, and seven servants of the Priory got thirteen shillings and fourpence each for their "wages and lyverys."; but those thirteen old creatures were left to beg their bread, the doors of their old home being shut against them for ever on that bitter 22nd of January, 1537. *Their* autumn had lasted all too long. They had to face the winter now.

Aye! Why are there not more such resting-places as St. Cross? Is our age an age of genuine pity? I have my doubts. It is pre-eminently an age of bustle and fuss and fidget, but I think we are lacking in tenderness. We are all for organising; we subscribe guineas, we get up societies for the extinction of poverty, and publish reams of statistics. Then we hold up our heads and pull down our waistcoats, and comfort ourselves with the reflection that we have done as much as a certain widow at the treasury. She gave her mite and so have we given ours. Blessed are the givers of mites! Amen.

I confess I do not love to see an almshouse in a crowded thoroughfare. There is one—or was till very lately—in Gray's Inn Road, a dreary, dismal-looking place, suggestive of rats. There is another in the city of Norwich, six feet below the level of the street. I went down to it the other day and shuddered. Faugh! it should clearly not be there. And yet in that same city of Norwich there is the magnificent " Old Man's Hospital," which I hold to be the glory of our East Anglian metropolis. Yes; for it is one of the best managed eleemosynary institutions in the kingdom, if we estimate its efficiency by the sum of happiness which is to be found within those walls, and the cost at which that happiness is provided. The poor old souls, I admit, live disgracefully long; I have seen them go in skeletons, and, in a year, they have grown as sleek as brewers' dray-horses. I have known a man go in there with every line in his face telling of chronic bitterness of spirit, and in a little while I have seen him sitting on a long bench in the sunshine spinning yarns and laughing like a clown. " What, Dolly, you here? " I said one day to a worthy old laundress whom I had known for long and often wished she were there. " Yes! bless the Lord, I'm here, and all I've got to do now, sir, is to live as long as I can. I don't want to die till I'm ahundred, and that'll give me thirty years of joy here, and everlasting glory—you know where, sir ! "

The Great Hospital of Norwich is one of the very few survivals of those many refuges for the aged

poor which existed in considerable numbers down to
the time when the detestable oligarchy which made
havoc of the land in the name of King Edward the
Sixth swept them all away. It owes its preservation
from the general pillage to an accident—the accident
of its "foundation" being attributed to the boy
King, though in truth its "new scheme," as we
should call it nowadays, had been drafted before the
death of Henry the Eighth. People talk as if the
spoliation of the monasteries were the monster act
of robbery of that bad time. We are perpetually
assured that *that* measure dealt a crushing blow to the
labouring population, as if they were the great losers
—the great sufferers. I am by no means sure that
it was so. It was the pillage of the hospitals that
was the first great wrong done to the poor; but it
was the infamous confiscation of the funds belonging
to the *guilds* that wrought immeasurably greater
mischief. It has been calculated that five hundred
hospitals—let us call them almshouses, for they
were that, and little else but that—were plundered.
Poor old men and old women lost their homes and
their maintenance, and were turned out into the
roads to beg their bread. That was bad enough ;
but there were more than *thirty thousand guilds* that
were stripped of their all by a sweep of the pen.
The guilds answered partly to our trades union

societies, partly to benefit clubs. Some of them had
existed for centuries; some had large accumulated
funds, the savings of generations of penurious thrift,
grown habitual to those poor toilers by the discipline
of long training in the duty of providing for the
future. There was not a village in the land that
was not ruthlessly despoiled of its little hoards.
The guilds were absolutely looted: they lost every
farthing they possessed, every rag and cup and
platter. The gangs of ruffians did their work so
thoroughly among the frightened villagers, that not
only were they beggared, but the whole machinery
of self-help which had been at work from time im-
memorial was absolutely extinguished. Our modern
trades unions and benefit clubs are things of yesterday.

For more than two centuries after that hideous
spoliation Englishmen of the working classes never
rose to the conception that they could help themselves. They belonged to the parish and the
parish belonged to them; the parish bred them as
the parish bred the owls and the polecats; the
parish used them till they were past work, then the
parish put them into the *poor-house*, where the idiots
drivelled, and the palsied mumbled, and the halt and
the blind howled and cursed and raved; and there
they huddled, gaunt and stolidly desperate till they

died, like rats in their holes; and then they were
tumbled into their graves, sometimes two or three
at a time, the sexton taking care not to go too deep,
for decent burial couldn't be done at the money.
Ah! my masters, you must live in *an open parish*
where there hasn't been a gentleman's house for
centuries, where the land is owned by eighty or
ninety proprietors, and where the parson was looked
at askance as an intruder " arter no good " had he
dared to show his face on any day except a Sunday,
if you want to know what was going on in some
favoured spots in merry England less than a hundred
years ago.

Happily it was not as bad as this everywhere.
God never leaves Himself without witnesses even in
the worst times. To be sure, the labouring classes
never had the heart to try and help themselves
again for many and many a long day. Poor
wretches! They had lost all heart, as the phrase is.
There was only a sore where a heart ought to have
been. The guilds had gone, and no man had uttered
a word. Even historians held their peace, and up
to this hour have said almost nothing. But as for
the almshouses, they were no sooner gone than they
began to rise up again. They who had lived for
years among their tenantry and dependents, were
saddened and shocked at the sight of poor old people,

who could no longer earn their daily bread, being reduced to something like beggary in their old age, with no means of subsistence but the pittance grudgingly awarded them out of the parish allowance ; and here and there kindly and pitiful people made provision in their wills, or were beforehand with death, and did their work while they were alive. These kind people soon began to build new almshouses as refuges for the poor battered old folk who had few friends now, had no longer the power of earning their own living, had seldom had the chance of laying up in store for the evil days " in which thou shalt say I have no pleasure in them," and had not where to lay their heads. The new almshouses were not as the old ones had been. For the most part they were very unpretentious and unambitious institutions ; a row of three or four tiny cottages by the wayside, such as we see them now. Half a dozen old creatures housed and little more ; the endowment provided just enough, and sometimes barely enough, to keep the dwellings in repair and to find the aged inmates in food, fuel, and bare necessaries. The hospitals " of the older foundation " had grown up under very different conditions, and had been, almost always, started on a much grander scale : they were in many cases affiliated to some religious house, or, when this was not the case, the poor people who were provided for were put under the guardianship of some warder and a chaplain or two, whose duty it was to look after the other inmates, and far the larger share of the endowment went to support the governors of the house, not the governed. In a large number of cases, as the income declined—and somehow it almost always did decline—the poor people suffered first, and their numbers were not kept up. Sometimes there was no income for the poor brethren or sisters, and again and again we read that the houses became ruinous, or that the revenues were absorbed into those of some larger foundation. It is an ugly history, and as we look into it it saddens us. At any rate, it always saddens me to find that our forefathers were no better than ourselves for all their professions of aiming at a higher ideal than we profess to follow. And yet, if it be indeed true that the human race is growing slowly upward, what right have we to expect that our forefathers should have been more noble and truer, more far-seeking and consistent than ourselves?

The new almshouses rose up but slowly, but they did rise up during the century that passed between the spoliation of King Henry the Eighth and the Great Rebellion. When men of pity and generosity desired to make some permanent provision for the destitute, the way was not easy for them. Million-aires like Allen and Sutton were few and far between, and their millions were in shillings, not in pounds sterling; it was not the time for doing things in the grand style. As long as any great eleemosynary institutions were in some sort of working order, they offered themselves naturally as the accredited recipi-ents of charitable benefactions even of the smallest ; but for one man who could build up a new asylum from its foundation and provide for its maintenance, and draw up a body of statutes for its regulation, and make all those provisions for the future which such a considerable undertaking implies, there were hundreds who would be willing enough to enrich such an institution after it was once in working order ; and the aggregate of such smaller benefac-tions contributed by men and women of no great resources made up the real wealth of the house, which without such accretions would be pretty sure to decay. Our modern orphan asylums and dispen-saries and homes and the like would fare very badly indeed if it were not for the perennial flow of that stream of benefactions which keep them all going. But when the " hospital " or the refuge had become a ruin, roofless and desolate, they who had the wish to leave or give a hundred or two of pounds or an acre or two of land for the maintenance of the decayed artisan or the housing of the widow, found themselves in a practical difficulty. Who were they to leave their legacies to? How could their intentions be carried out? Every donation, subscription, or bequest helps to keep up a going concern; but if there be no going concern—What then?

The first almshouse built in England as a home for the aged poor, after the suppression of the monasteries, is said to have been that founded in Queen Elizabeth's time at Greenwich by William Lambard, whom Camden calls "a goodly good gentleman." The polemics of the Roman persuasion sneered at the fact that almsgiving had ceased among us since the Anglican Church had broken off communion with Rome, and were not slow to remind us that Lambard "was the first Protestant that built an hospital." [1] We may let the sneer pass.

I do not know the exact date of the foundation of Lambard Hospital, at Greenwich, but if it were started before 1594 his example was very soon followed; for in that year Clement Paston, Esq., left a considerable estate to certain of his kindred,

---

[1] He had, however, been anticipated by *Thomas Lewin*, who by his will, dated the 20th of April, 1555, founded an almshouse in St. Nicholas Olave, Bread Street, which almshouse is, I believe, still kept up by the Ironmongers' Company. But then Lewin was not a *Protestant* by any means.

which was to be held by them conditionally upon their providing six poor men in the parish of Oxnead, in Norfolk, with house room and a somewhat liberal maintenance, according to a scale that was carefully laid down by the testator. If the almshouse was eventually plundered and the poor men were left to shift for themselves, that was no fault of Mr. Paston, and the less said about that piece of iniquity the better. Three years later, William Cecil, the great Lord Burghley, founded his almshouses for thirteen poor men at Stamford, and there they are now.

In this instance, as in many others, the sagacious statesman took good care that there should be no mistake about his intentions, for he built and endowed his hospital during his own lifetime. Two years later again, Richard Platt, a London brewer—he too during his lifetime—founded his almshouses at Aldenham, in Herts, for six old people, who were not to be eligible till they were sixty, "except they be impotent, and therefore thought fit to be relieved at a lesser age, and such as have been known in their youth to have lived by their labour." House room and allowances for fuel, food, and raiment were provided for them, and careful regulations were drawn up for maintaining discipline and guarding against abuses. In this case the estate left was well husbanded by the Brewers' Company, and the

establishment is still kept up ; though, as usual, it
is now treated as if it were a mere encumbrance
upon the school, which is also supported out of the
same endowment. And exactly as in mediæval
times the tendency always was for the *monastery* to
absorb the income of an hospital affiliated to it, to
treat the property held by it in trust as only part of
the common funds available for the support of the
domus, and to grumble that the bedesmen cost them
so much annually; just so it has come to pass in
even modern times, that the *school*, which was more
often but an adjunct to the hospital than the reverse,
loudly complained that its income was seriously
burdened by having so many old impotent folk—of
no use whatever to the community—to support in
idleness. Thus history repeats itself. There was a
time when asceticism, or that which passed for the
religious life, was regarded as the one thing needful.
Now we have got to worship education as the god of
our idolatry. I wonder what will be the favourite
interest next.

During the reign of James the First, the fashion
of founding these refuges for the destitute prevailed
rather widely. William Goddard left rather a large
estate to found the Jesus Hospital for old people
at Bray, in Berks. This was in the year 1609.
Henry, Earl of Northampton, in 1616 built and

endowed his almshouses at Castle Rising, in
Norfolk, and Sir Ralph Hare established others
on a smaller scale at Stow Bardolph, in 1622. The
number of these hospitals went on increasing year
by year down to the time of the Rebellion, after
which it is observable that the stream of benefac-
tions almost ceases to flow. The earliest and most
considerable instance of any such foundation after
the Restoration was that of Smith's Almshouses at
Maidenhead. In this case, again, the buildings were
completed and the income secured to the inmates
and their successors in 1661, while Mr. Smith was
still living.

*   *   *   *   *

It is to be noted that, with one or two exceptions,
all the almshouses of the new foundation were set
up *after* the passing of the famous statute of Queen
Elizabeth in the forty-third year of her reign (*i.e.*
A.D. 1601). There is a very general belief that no
provision was made by the common law of England
for the relief of the poor till this statute was passed.
I am told that this is one of our many popular
delusions. Be it as it may, there can be no doubt
that ever since the Elizabethan time "competent
sums of money" were to be raised by the parishes
for the maintenance of the destitute poor, that such
money was regularly distributed to them, and that

a list of such as were the recipients of the "alms" was kept by the officers appointed to give it out. It is equally certain that where an almshouse was set up in any locality, it was almost invariably limited to the inhabitants of a certain area, and that whatever relief it aimed at affording was supplementary to such as was provided out of the parish alms ; or, as we should say, the almshouses came in as an important assistance *to lighten the Poor Rate.*

The same holds good of the doles of bread and money which were left so frequently by testators with some bowels of compassion. These doles were to help out the overseers' allowances. Thus, when Thomas Stretchley, in 1678, left £5 4s. to the poor of the parish of Christ Church, he ordered that the income should be spent in buying " twelve twopenny loaves, to be set up in the church every Sunday, and to be distributed by the churchwardens and overseers to twelve poor helpless men and women, *who take alms of the said parish."* The principle in both cases was the same. It was enacted by law that no man or woman should be allowed to starve, but charity came in where legal obligation stopped. It was enough in the eye of the law that the ratepayers should keep people alive, but it seemed abominable and atrocious to Christian sentimentalists to reduce the pauper's allowance down to the last straw. Of course, where these doles increased and multiplied, and no restrictions were placed upon the distribution, vagrants would crowd into the parishes, on the one hand, and substantial people who were in easy circumstances would lay claim to a share of the spoil on the other. But this did not prove even that the doles were in their nature mischievous : it only went some way towards proving that the " unearned increment " of any institution, if it exceed a certain reasonable limit, may require to be administered according to regulations better adapted than the old ones were for carrying out the original object aimed at. Is the amount of income enjoyed by this or that parish, or other geographical area, larger than is at all sufficient for providing for the aged and destitute whose characters will bear looking into, and who have been *boná-fide* labourers, artisans, or even substantial tradesmen in their time, but in old age find themselves destitute ? *Then extend the area, and let the advantages of the endowment be extended as far as it will go.* But do *not* go grovelling before your idol of education, and proceed to appropriate every scrap of margin of income that you can pick up, and then say with much self-gratulation : " Lo ! we have made ample provision for the poor and needy in this small corner of the earth, and for the residue, we will appropriate it to the sacred cause of culture, by stimulating boys and girls to spend their days and nights in getting up books for examination."

Let us take an instance in point. Thomas Cuttell, by his will dated the 17th of March, 1556, left a house on St. Dunstan's Hill, which at that time was let for £7 a year, to the churchwardens of St. Dunstan's-in-the-East. They were to spend £3 4s. of the rent yearly to provide a dinner for the poor prisoners in Newgate, 2s. 6d. in remunerating the aforesaid churchwardens for their trouble, and 34s. 8d. for providing " two poor women *to look after any persons that should be visited with the plague or other sickness.*" The balance—£1 18s. 10d.—to be reserved for the cost of any repairs that might be needed from time to time. I do not know where St. Dunstan's Hill is, but I suppose it is somewhere near the Tower. I read, however, that this house was let in 1829 for £56 a year on a repairing lease, and I should not be surprised to learn that by this time it has been turned into a warehouse, and brings in to the churchwardens £500 a year. There are no prisoners in Newgate, nor need to feast them now if there were ; and I can see no sort of objection, and quite the contrary, to the whole of such an endowment as this being utilised for the support of a great Nurses' Institution, the geographical area to enjoy the

17

benefits of worthy Mr. Cuttell's endowment being extended as widely as you please. But I see every objection to your laying your hands upon half of that endowment because there are no Newgate prisoners, and applying it to the founding of scholarships in the City of London School.

It may be in consequence of my impenetrable stupidity, or it may be from some other cause, but I never have been able to see any rational ground for accepting that position of certain theorists which has been repeated so persistently that the world at large have got to acquiesce in it from mere weariness —I mean the position that an endowment ought never to be allowed to save the pockets of the ratepayers.

You can't help an endowment benefiting the ratepayers, no matter what the endowment is. You might just as well try to prevent a border in your garden from receiving the rain of heaven upon it when the showers fall, because the peas want all the moisture and the potatoes can do without it. Even though you hold up an umbrella over the potato patch, some of the moisture will be sure to trickle through to the podgy tubers. If you go the length of saying, "Better then have no endowments at all," there is an end of the argument, for that means that you would rather the poor and needy were left in

their misery, than that any one except the poor and
needy were the better for any boon bestowed. But
where is the sense of all this cry about not allowing
the ratepayers to benefit directly or indirectly by a
charitable endowment? Why should not a man be
permitted to leave his money to lighten the burdens
pressing upon his surviving neighbours, and likely
to press more and more heavily upon his and their
children? In the wills of our forefathers, made not
so very long ago, you may find hundreds of bequests
for all sorts of public objects, such as the mending
of roads, and the reparation of churches, for which
the parishioners were liable, and by these bequests
the ratepayers were gainers to the extent of their
several assessments. When the Rev. Abraham
Colfe in 1656 left his estates to found a school and
almshouses at Lewisham, in Kent, he also left a sum
of money yearly " in working drains out of the highways into the ditches and water-courses, and in
amending the footpaths of the parish." Sir Martin
Bowes Knight, an Alderman of London in 1565,
during his life-time provided for a payment of
£6 13s. 4d. to be made annually for the repairing
of the conduits and the conduit-pipes of the city of
London. About the same time Elizabeth Gavener
left her manor of Shabcombe in Devon to be sold,
the money to be " distributed and given away *in*

alms, as well as towards the reparation and amending of highways." Ought such funds as these to be confiscated whenever the charge of providing for the roads is thrown upon the rates? You might with equal fairness confiscate all the money left for the repair of churches, because church rates are abolished.

But there is another assumption just as baseless as the other, namely, that no *paupers* ought to receive anything from ancient endowments, inasmuch as they are already provided for by the ratepayers. It would be nearer the truth to say that such endowments as take the form of doles and almshouses were *only* meant for paupers. As we have seen, these bequests were intended to supplement the minimum provision which the law compelled the ratepayers to supply. The statute of Queen Elizabeth enacted that in every parish house room should be supplied for the houseless, and the bare means of subsistence be allowed to the destitute. At this point charity stepped in and offered better house room for a favoured few, and additional sustenance to those who were dependent upon the parish alms. What the giver of almshouses and doles did *not* contemplate was that the " sturdy beggar " and the vagrant should participate in their bounty. The " sturdy beggar " was whipped out of the parish if he dared to show his face in it. Let him go back to where he

belonged. There was no thought of encouraging the
" casual." In many instances, nay, in most, it was
a condition that no one should be admitted ·to the
almshouse who had not been known as a *bonâ-fide*
labourer or artisan in the parish for a longer or
shorter term of years; and, as we have seen, none
might·lay claim to any share of the doles unless his
name were in the parish books as one of the recognised recipients of parish relief. If that condition
had been adhered to we should never have heard of
troops of vagrants crowding into a parish a week or
two before the annual " gifts " were distributed, and
scrambling each for his share ; nor of the rents of
fever-dens in a favourite locality reaching an almost
fabulous figure in consideration of the amount of
doles which the inhabitants of the parish had a right
to. The old law of settlement had its evils, but it
had its merits too. In sweeping it away in the
rough-and-tumble fashion you did, you turned the
vagrant from being a criminal into a pauper; you
turned the poor man who had worked as long as he
could hold a plough or use a flail, from a pauper into
a criminal. You take his very clothes from him
when you admit him in the " house," you dress him
in the pauper uniform, and you tell him that because
he has sunk so low he is not even fit to be admitted
into an almshouse.

These are the kind of assumptions which are at the bottom of too many of those schemes which have of late years been launched among us by authority. Just at the moment when we are told that centralisation is to be minimised, and that counties and cities and country parishes have arrived at a level of such high intelligence that they ought to be left to manage their own affairs, here you have the Charity Commissioners, dwelling in mysterious isolation—the veiled prophets whose sentences go forth irreversible from their chamber of horrors—saying to many a community of 100,000 citizens, " You blundering, ignorant jobbery-mongers, you narrow-minded, pig-headed Tories. You are permitted to manage your own schools, and highways, and libraries, and police, your sanitary arrangements, your water, your gas, and your paupers. But as to your charitable endowments, those endowments which your own citizens have in days gone by expressly given you for the benefit of those needy and stricken and sore broken, who were born and bred and grew up and toiled and struggled and dropped out of it under your very eyes, and whose needs and struggles and characters and sorrows you know, and you only can know—these funds you are not fit to deal with or to administer. These funds are to be taken out of your control, you are not to be trusted with them. In all that concerns your charitable endowments, you will have to do as we tell you. It is for us to order, for you to obey!"

In this new scheme, one of the latest which the Commissioners have put forth, it seems that any one who has ever been in the receipt of parish relief is for ever disqualified from admission to any of the existing almshouses or hospitals.

Oh! these dragons of routine, who go up and down seeking whom they may devour. Some of us remember the glorious hopes that they raised among us when they first were introduced to a too sanguine nation, eager for reforms, and believing in the need of them. We were all going to have the old trammels and fetters knocked off, and the governors, and trustees, and feoffees of the old charities were to be left with free hands! What has it all come to? Left with free hands! Nay, our hands are to be tied behind our backs!

The new Poor Law has done much good during the last fifty years in educating the nation; and the reform of our social organisation has been carried on earnestly and intelligently wherever we turn our eyes. What we need now is not restriction, but liberty of action. We want to be educated now into a belief in great *Principles*. You will never educate men by giving them mere *Rules* to go by, and telling them to hold their tongues when they ask the reason why. The red tape needs no tightening, it wants cutting, and there is some red tape that will have to be cut—is bound to be cut some day.

I have said that the new Poor Law has done a great deal for us in the way of educating the masses —educating them in certain sentiments of independence, helping them to the conviction that we are all bound to try and help ourselves. But there is a growing belief among some thoughtful philanthropists that the new Poor Law has almost done its work, that the abuses which it swept away are gone for ever, and can never be tolerated again; and that the time has come for starting upon a new departure. To begin with, there is one very mischievous doctrine which the new Poor Law has been the means of inculcating among us. It admits of being stated very simply; it is held unblushingly by many, and preached loudly by not a few. It stands thus.

The inhabitants of this world are divided into two classes. The first class includes all who are possessed of, or who have the power of earning the means of living without anybody's help except their own. The second class are they who have no means and no power of earning a livelihood. The first class are more than respectable; they are virtuous, estimable, exemplary persons. They are good citizens ; they are householders—compound or simple ; they have votes ; they have spotless souls and bodies —white as the driven snow ; some of them pay taxes, almost all of them pay rates. The second class are they who have no means of livelihood. These are beasts of prey feeding upon the members of the first class. Some of them are professional beggars, some are cadgers, some are tramps, some are receivers of outdoor relief, some are dwellers in the Union workhouse, and some are nondescripts. But be they what they may, as the first class are all white and glistering, so the second class are all black as soot—every one of them. This being so, why should you attempt to make out that the blacka- moors are anything else than blackamoors ? Why set up such a preposterous theory as that there are shades in black—light black and dark black ? That is undeniable rank heresy. Away with it !

Men and brethren, take note of it. There is nothing so catching as talking nonsense—pompous nonsense. Given the requisite mental constitution for the due development of the germ, and the period of efflorescence is almost instantaneously followed by immense fertility of reproduction. I've known a man described as a dazzlingly clever fellow, for no other reason than because he solemnly asserted that to eat a ham sandwich was a sin. He began with that, but he ended by founding a sect, and a large one.

Granted that all who have no means of livelihood are—as some of my severe friends tell me they are— all blacks, I really cannot see why some of them should *not* be a great deal blacker than others, and some in fact be little more than grey.

Looking along the sleeve of my well-worn coat as I write, I notice that there are very decided differences of shade in the texture of that venerable garment. Black? Yes! It's black, but observe the seams. And yet, alas! there's many a poor creature who would accept the gift of this old coat of mine with pathetic gratitude, and count himself a *beau* if he had it upon his lean shoulders.   .

It is just as false to assert that among the " Have nots " there are no grades as it is to maintain that among the *Masses* there are no *Classes ;* and how false that assumption is I will not stop to illustrate. Poverty has its aristocracy, such as it is, as well as its dreadful *residuum,* and between the two extremes of lonely shabbiness—where men and women suffer so patiently, so silently, so piteously—and semi-nakedness, where poor wretches have lost all decency and all semblance of self-respect, there are almost infinite shadings off.

Was it any fault of yours, sweet Lady Maud

mavourneen! that all your means of livelihood were
swept away, you scarce can tell us how, and no rent
came from those broad lands in county Kerry which
had given you an ample income, spent in good works
for the most part, even to the time when old age had
come upon you, and the sunny glow that once was as
a crown upon that noble brow had changed to winter's
rime ? Poor gentlewoman! You too have come to
feel the pinch of penury at last, come to accept the
scanty gifts of others and to bow to the sad inevitable. Were you to blame, Celsus, of the quick eye
and the iron nerve, because at the outset of a career
that promised so well a frenzied patient sprang upon
you from behind and left you a palsied man, with
your private resources exhausted almost to the last
pound ? Or when my worthy friend John Balls, in
his seventieth year—with a sickly wife for ever ailing
—found himself one morning out of place by the
bankruptcy of the firm which he had served as a
copying clerk for more than half a century ? Or
when blindness, sudden and incurable, came upon
that promising young schoolmaster who married
only a year ago ? Or that lone widow whose trustee
appropriated her little all and then vanished ? Or
those others whom the wise and prudent advised to
invest their savings in Dock shares which paid so
well for a time and now pay nothing? Were each

and all of these *criminals,* who got no more than they
deserved when they found themselves face to face
with want, not knowing where to turn for the daily
bread ? Are you going to lump them all together,
ticket them as paupers, and shut them up with
broken-down harlots and tramps and inebriates in
the same ward of a Union workhouse ? Are you
prepared to do this and assure us with a simper
that " It can't be helped. We are bound to dis-
courage improvidence, and if we once begin to make
class distinctions and differences and to indulge in
sentiment, the consequences will be disastrous and
dreadful to contemplate." My good man ! Are not
the consequences of *your* cruel and heartless *modus
operandi* dreadful to contemplate ?

*   *   *   *   *

There are some men who are born drudges, and
nothing on earth can make them fit for anything else.
As the poet says :

> Some men are born for great things,
>   Some are born for small,
> Some—it is not recorded
>   Why they were born at all.

These last may be content and thankful if they have
drudgery to do. They are the Gibeonites. The
hewers of wood and drawers of water for others,

they can have nothing to expect but bare existence. Without brains, without physique, without character, without anything that they can call their own except a rickety carcass, scrofulous and feebly puffy, commonly designated a human body, they flopped into the world somehow, and there they are. Of course they cannot be allowed to starve, nor will they be ; but they never can make the running in the fierce competition of our time, and the less ambition they have the better for themselves. They are below the average. But for the average man, and for him who is only a little above the average, let such be taught early and late that they are bound to have a reasonable ambition. For he who lacks the stimulus of any future, in this life or the next, must needs wither. Why should he live at all ?

The question is, What may fairly be called a reasonable ambition ? Leave the *residuum* out of account, and come to the working man in the widest acceptation of the term ; and is it too much to say that every man who plays the part of a good citizen may reasonably set before himself the hope of repose in his old age, when he has ceased to be the man he was, and when others can do his work better than he and with less effort ? In some form or another we all do look forward to " retire "—as the phrase is— in our old age. Some have a chance of earning their retirement and make the most of it, some have no chance, and some throw their chances away.

As to those who have thrown away their chances, the people who have earned good wages and spent them as they came, the reckless and the improvident, the workhouse is the place for them.

As to those who have never had a chance of doing more than earn a bare subsistence—the Gibeonites, the physically and mentally incompetent—in their case too I am inclined to think no special favour should be shown them. All gentle kindness, food and shelter and raiment should be assured to them, but more than that it is difficult to see why they should be encouraged to expect.

As to those who have used their opportunities, and made provision for their old age in time, they are the last people in the world to " come upon the rates." The joy and pride of their declining years is that they want no man to help them, that they are possessed of an independence, or, as we say in Norfolk, that they " live upright and walk with a stick."

But there still remain those who have lived all their lives at a comparative disadvantage. Circumstances have been against them, or that mysterious factor which is for ever baffling our most careful calculations which scientists with praiseworthy circumlocution deal with as " the personal equation," while the vulgar brutally call it *luck*. There is the peasant who has had a large family dragging at him for the last twenty years of his life and longer. There is the man who suffered from an accident in his prime, reducing him to something just a trifle less than an able-bodied workman. There is the man who with all his economies and frugality only managed to scrape together a little hoard of some three or four score pounds, and had lived too long and come to the end of it.

There is the man who has invested his all in a row of cottages, and somehow got into the hands of a rogue of an attorney, and finds himself just nowhere when the pinch comes. What need to multiply the instances? Observe! I am not thinking of the men of the streets. They have their champions and their friends, God bless them! who are not likely to forsake their clients and by no means likely to lack support. They have rich and earnest philanthropists at their backs who are not idle just now. I speak of the men and women in the wilderness. I speak as I do know.

And this is what I know: that during the last twenty years or so the agricultural labourer in Norfolk has become a *saving* animal. Yes! Since drinking has gone out of fashion and drunkenness has got to be looked upon as disgraceful, the agricultural labourer has begun to hoard. The mischief is, that he is afraid of doing anything more than hoard. He is afraid of the savings-banks. He is almost equally afraid of buying little bits of property near his home, afraid of letting any one know that he has money laid by, afraid to talk of it, afraid to whisper it, afraid of your suspecting it. How has this come about?

The explanation is plain and evident enough to those who know anything about the facts; and here it is. As long as a man is known to possess a shilling that he can call his own, he is debarred from receiving any relief from the rates for the barest necessaries of life. If a poor fellow has hidden away say £20 or £50 or £100—and again, I say, *I speak as I do know*—he will hardly let his own flesh and blood suspect the fact. Be seen in the post-office with a bank-book? What! that he may be called upon to produce it before the Board? Not he! Buy the house he lives in, though he could get it cheap? Why, he'd have to pay the rates on it, and when he wanted to put himself upon these same rates, " I mean to say as that there chairman would laugh at me ! " What does he do with his savings, then? What *can* he do with them? He *hides* them until such time as they have grown to inconvenient bulk, and then he slinks about and seeks for an investment. In point of fact, he starts as a money-lender on a small scale, under the secret guidance of Mr. Oily Gammon. I am not going to betray confidences, and so I will not stop to explain the methods pursued. It will perhaps be enough to assure my more knowing readers that I could point to one case where, when fourteen acres of land were sold some six years ago, there were *seven mortgagees to pay off*, each of whom, by a composition, received under eleven shillings in the pound.

Think of the surroundings of an agricultural labourer, and how he *must* be at the mercy of sharpers who can talk of things he cannot understand. You will never be able to protect poor Hodge from quacks and herbalists, who promise to cure all his aches and pains and sores; from touts who tempt him to take shares in a peripatetic provident society; from deputations who "stand forth, sir! before all the world," as the labourer's friend; from his own credulity and cunning, his own suspicion and self-conceit; from his ignorance of the world and his ignorance of the swindler's wiles and ways. No! you will never be able to do this, but you may do something else for him. You have no right to educate our peasantry into the belief that all their little savings are looked upon by the well-

18

to-do as mere pickings and stealings, which they
will have to answer for, when they are past work,
before a board of inquisitors, who will tempt them to
lie and shuffle lest they should suffer for their frugality. If, in his old age, the agricultural labourer
has the audacity to come before the guardians asking
for just a little *relief*, as distinct from *support*, he is
told, almost in so many words, that he is not starv-
ing yet, and it will be time enough to help him when
it comes to that. But the sot who has lived all his
life spending half his earnings at the pot-house, when
he breaks down at last is treated precisely as the
decent labourer; and is it to be wondered at that
this latter soon learns the needful lesson, to sham
indigence, to pretend that he is penniless, to protest
before God and man he has never laid by a pound
and that he hasn't a shilling in the world? It is an
odious and demoralising system and has lasted too
long.

     *   *   *   *

Frightful as have been the confiscations of our
charitable endowments during the last thirty years,
and amazing as is the bigoted idolatry of that grisly
phantom, yclept Education, which men have been
making such huge sacrifices to during the same
period, there still remains some funds here and there
in our country villages which have not yet been

taken from the poor. There are still some doles
and coals, still some blankets and cloaks, still some
loaves and flannel distributed in our country parishes.
I am told that it is only a question of time how long
these things shall be allowed to be distributed. I
am told that they will all, sooner or later, be absorbed into educational endowments. For myself, I
hope I shall not live to see that day, and I will say
more—I hope nobody else will live to see it. I do
hope, however, that these funds will, at no distant
day, be turned to better account than they now are.
I am quite ready to admit that there is a foolish
waste in distributing even £20 a year in actual
loaves given out to the "poor" of a parish of 700
inhabitants, with the vaguest possible notion of
who the "poor" are. I see, as plainly as any one
else, that in an "open" parish, with fifty or sixty
small owners of land and cottages, the annual gift
of fifty pounds' worth of coal means so much money
into the pockets of the creatures who own those
cottages. The evils of such a state of things are
patent, but the remedy hitherto in vogue has been
almost the clumsiest conceivable. It is a remedy
which has proceeded according to the old plan of
making a desert and calling it peace.

Again and again let it be said: These emoluments
were meant for the poor; to the poor they belong;

they are their birthright. They were left to lighten the hard lot of the poor; to take off, if ever so little, the *pinch* of poverty; to shed here and there some beam of the light of joy even upon the poor man's life; to lessen its burden; to cheer its dreariness. Here are resources which you actually possess, and which you say you know not how to use except by taking them away from those for whom they were meant. Some of us hear talk like this with indignation, and a burning blush at the shameful confession of helplessness which it is almost impossible to believe to be sincere. What difficulty can there be in applying such funds as those referred to to the building and maintaining of houses for the poor and needy, who are not, and never have been, of the lowest and most reckless? Throw the endowments of half a dozen parishes into a common fund, and let it be used partly to build almshouses for those parishes, and the maintenance of those who may be chosen to dwell in them. Let these live rent free— with their little gardens to make gay, their little chambers to keep clean, their little household gods not all confiscated. There is no need of any very great weekly allowance. Give the aged couple five or six shillings a week, and they will manage to live in comfort after their fashion. Let there be nothing grand about it all—no largeness, for that frightens our rustics ; no grand architectural "features," only some humble homeliness—a resting-place for him or her, and if it may be so, the house of prayer not far off, for the end is drawing nigh.

* * * * *

It is characteristic of all the great schemes put forth by idealists of past times for the reconstruction or amelioration of society that they postulate a human nature other than it is, and aim at the unattainable. We of the nineteenth century have grown to be intolerant of the idealists. We are proud of being realistic—very! We demand first and foremost, " How can this or that be *carried out ?* Show us how it can be *done.*" The present writer is no idealist, only a plain man—a *practical* man. He is humble in his aims ; he despiseth not the day of small things ; he does not even dream of being original ; he contemplates no more than that which is easily possible ; he starts with a single IF ; grant him his *if*, and this is what he means to do.

* * * * *

If God should ever grant me five thousand pounds, which I may without injustice to others spend in a lump during my own lifetime, I hereby promise and vow that I will indulge myself to the extent of the aforesaid five thousand pounds in giving shape and form to an old whim or dream.

I will buy half an acre of land, and in it I will build a humble row of five little houses, each with its own little garden, and each with its own little patch of land. There shall be ornamental trees planted, and there shall be a good fence all round, and there shall be a frontage to the road, and there shall be at least one well of water, and there shall be the best possible drainage. To the occupants of each house there shall be allowed six shillings a week, and there shall be a surplus income set apart for repairs and contingencies. There shall be a board—or a bench—of governors, or managers, or trustees, to whom the oversight or management of the said houses shall be entrusted, who shall be tied and bound by as few hard and fast rules as possible, consistent with providing for the absolutely necessary requirements of health, decency, and cleanliness. The area from which the governors shall be chosen shall be wider than any single parish, and so shall the area be from which the inmates of the houses may be elected, and no one shall have the right to claim priority of election over any one else. As I will allow of no disqualification for admission except such as [the managers may from time to time lay down for their own guidance, so I will allow no one to be irremovable from his or her house in cases where it shall seem necessary for the managers to exercise their right and power of dismissal. I will set down my houses at least three miles from any market town, and, if it may be so, not more than a quarter of a mile from the parish church, whither the old folk may resort if and when they can and are so disposed.

When I think of my model almshouses—as I often do—I really quite envy those dear old people hobbling in and out of one another's houses, and gossiping, and peeping, and sunning themselves, and telling stories—dreadful stories—and squabbling to their hearts' content; of course they will—and be all the better and happier for their little tiffs. And then I think, too, of other scenes; of how the light will fade and fade in the old eyes, and of the peaceful sleep in which the spirit will return to God who gave it, and the little house left empty for a while till it is made sweet and neat and smiling for the next comer. And I cannot help saying to myself, as I think of all this and a great deal more, " Oh, my dear old Biddy! we'll always do what we can for you in our small way : we will try and smooth your pillow, and come and speak of the great hope, and make the best of what we have for you, and you won't doubt us? But I wish—yes, I do so very much wish—you were in an almshouse such as we talk of and dream of sometimes. Such a one as should not be very far off, you know, where we could come and look at you, as we do now, and have our little talks and little secret communings, but a little home that might be just a trifle more bright and smiling than the one we wot of now, Biddy ! "

In the churchyard of the parish of Scarning there stands a little hooded cross of oak—how vain to try and make our monuments imperishable !—on which is inscribed in plain. letters that any one can read :

" Here rests all that was mortal of Mary Wright, who died Jan. 6, 1892, aged 95."

This is our Biddy's epitaph.

UNWIN BROTHERS, THE GRESHAM PRESS, CHILWORTH AND LONDON.

A

Complete
Catalogue
OF
BOOKS

Published by

MR. T. FISHER UNWIN.

London:

11, PATERNOSTER BUILDINGS,
PATERNOSTER SQUARE.

1893-94.

*_** *Reference to this Catalogue is facilitated by the Duplicate List at the end, which contains the titles of the books in the order of price.*

A Complete Catalogue

OF

Mr. T. Fisher Unwin's

PUBLICATIONS

A D A M S (*Francis*). — **AUS-TRALIANS (The)**: A Social Sketch. By FRANCIS ADAMS. Crown 8vo, cloth, 10s. 6d.

——— **NEW EGYPT (The)**. By FRANCIS ADAMS. Large crown 8vo, cloth, 5s.

——— (*Henry*).—**HISTORICAL ESSAYS**. By HENRY ADAMS. Large crown 8vo, cloth, 7s. 6d.

ADAMSON.—**MUMFORD MANOR**: A Novel. By JOHN ADAMSON. Crown 8vo, cloth, 6s.

ADULTERATIONS OF FOOD (How to Detect the). Illustrated. Crown 8vo, sewed, 9d.

ADVENTURE SERIES (The). Each Volume is large crown 8vo in size and fully Illustrated. Volumes 1 to 14 are bound in red cloth, price 5s. each, and Vols. 15 to 17 are elegantly bound in cloth extra, gilt, ·gilt tops, 7s. 6d. each.

1. **The Adventures of a Younger Son.** By EDWARD JOHN TRELAWNY. With an Introduction by EDWARD GARNETT.

ADVENTURE SERIES--*contd.*

2. **Madagascar** ; or, Robert Drury's Journal during Fifteen Years' Captivity on that Island. With Preface and Notes by Captain S. P. OLIVER, Author of 'Madagascar.'

3. **Memoirs of the Extraordinary Military Career of John Shipp.** Written by Himself. With Introduction by H. MANNERS CHICHESTER.

4. **Pellow's Adventures and Sufferings during his Twenty-three Years' Captivity in Morocco.** Edited, with an Introduction and Copious Notes, by ROBERT BROWN, Ph.D.

5. **The Buccaneers and Marooners of America :** Being an Account of the Famous Adventures and Daring Deeds of certain Notorious Freebooters of the Spanish Main. Edited and Illustrated by HOWARD PYLE.

6. **The Log of a Jack Tar :** Being Passages from the Adventurous Life of James Choyce, Master Mariner. Edited, from the Original Manuscript, by Commander V. LOVETT CAMERON.

ADVENTURE SERIES—*contd.*

7. The Travels of Ferdinand Mendez Pinto, the Portuguese Adventurer. A new Abridged Edition, annotated by Professor ARMINIUS VAMBÉRY.

8. The Story of the Filibusters. By JAMES JEFFREY ROCHE. To which is added THE LIFE OF COLONEL DAVID CROCKETT.

9. A Master Mariner: Being the Life and Adventures of Captain Robert William Eastwick. Edited by HERBERT COMPTON.

10. Kolokotrones : Klepht and Warrior. Translated from the Greek, and Prefaced with an Account of the Klephts, by Mrs. EDMONDS. With an Introduction by M. J. GENNADIUS.

11. Hard Life in the Colonies. Edited by C. CARLYON-JENKINS.

12. The Escapes of Latude and Casanova from Prison. Edited, with Introduction, by P. VILLARS.

13. Adventures of a Blockade Runner; or, Trade in Time of War. By WILLIAM WATSON, Author of 'Life in the Confederate Army.' Illustrated by ARTHUR BYNG, R.N.

14. Missing Friends; or, The Adventures of a Danish Emigrant in Queensland.

15. Women Adventurers : The Lives of Madam Velasquez, Hannah Snell, Mary Anne Talbot, and Mrs Christian Davies. Edited by MENIE MURIEL DOWIE, Author of 'A Girl in the Karpathians.' Seven Portraits. 7s. 6d.

16. The Life and Adventures of James P. Beckwourth. Mountaineer, Scout, Pioneer, and Chief of the Crow Nation of Indians. Written from his own dictation by T. D. BONNER. New Edition. Edited, and with Preface by, CHARLES G. LELAND . (' Hans Breitmann '). 7s. 6d.

ADVENTURE SERIES—*Contd.*

17. The Memoirs and Travels of Mauritius Augustus Count De Benyowsky in Siberia, Kamtchatka, Japan, the Linkui Islands, and Formosa. From the Translation of his Original Manuscript (1741-1771), by WILLIAM NICHOLSON, F.R.S., 1790. Edited by Captain PASFIELD OLIVER, R.A. 7s. 6d.

ALLARDYCE.—STOPS; or, How to Punctuate. With Instructions for Correcting Proofs, etc. By PAUL ALLARDYCE. Sixth, Revised and Cheaper Edition. Demy 16mo, sewed, 6d. ; cloth, 1s.

AMERICAN DISHES, and How to Cook them. By an American Lady. Crown 8vo, cloth extra, 2s. 6d.

ANDERTON. — BALDUR : A Lyrical Drama. By H. ORSMOND ANDERTON. Demy 8vo, paper, 2s.

ARGENT.—SETTLING DAY : A Sketch from Life. By SOPHIE ARGENT. Cr. 8vo, cloth, 3s. 6d.

ASHTON. — DAWN OF THE NINETEENTH CENTURY IN ENGLAND (The): A Social Sketch of the Times. By JOHN ASHTON. Third Edition. Illustrated. Large crown 8vo, cloth, 7s. 6d.

——— FLEET (The) : Its River, Prison, and Marriages. With 70 Drawings by the Author from Original Pictures. By JOHN ASHTON. Large crown 8vo, cloth, 7s. 6d.

——— LEGENDARY HISTORY OF THE CROSS (The): A Series of 64 Woodcuts, from a Dutch Book published by VELDENER, A.D. 1483. With an Introduction, written and illustrated by JOHN ASHTON, and a Preface by the Rev. S. BARING-GOULD, M.A. Square 8vo, bound in parchment, old style, brass clasps, 10s. 6d.

ASHTON.—**ROMANCES OF CHIVALRY.** By JOHN ASHTON. 46 fac-simile Illustrations by the Author. New and Cheaper Edition. Crown 8vo, cloth, 7s. 6d.

ATKINS. — **KELT OR GAEL** (The) : His Ethnography, Geography and Philology. By T. DE COURCY ATKINS, B.A., Lond., Barrister-at-Law. Demy 8vo, 5s.

BAILDON. — **MERRY MONTH** (The), and other Prose Pieces. By HENRY BELLYSE BAILDON, Author of 'The Spirit of Nature,' etc. Crown 8vo, cloth, 5s.

—— **RESCUE (The),** and other Poems. By H. BELLYSE BAILDON. Foolscap 8vo, cloth, 3s. 6d.

BARLOW. — **BOGLAND STUDIES :** Poems. By JANE BARLOW. Crown 8vo, cloth, 3s. 6d.

BEHNKE.—**STAMMERING : Its Nature and Treatment.** By EMIL BEHNKE. Second and Revised Edition. Demy 16mo, paper, 6d. ; cloth, 1s.

BESANT. — **ANNIE BESANT :** An Autobiography. With 12 Illustrations, 3 being Photogravure Portraits. Demy 8vo, cloth, 16s.

BIGELOW.— **PRINCIPLES OF STRATEGY (The).** By JOHN BIGELOW, 1st Lieut. U.S. Army. Illustrated mainly from American Campaigns. Fcap. folio, 32 Maps, cloth, £1 1s.

BOULGER.—**CENTRAL ASIAN QUESTIONS :** Essays on Afghanistan, China, and Central Asia. By DEMETRIUS C. BOULGER. Portrait and Maps. Demy 8vo, cloth, 18s.

BOURDILLON.—**SURSUM CORDA.** By F. W. BOURDILLON. Imperial 16mo, with Etching, cloth, 3s. 6d.—Also, a Fine, Large Paper Edition, numbered, limited to fifty copies. *Price on application.*

BOWEN. — **LAYMAN'S STUDY OF THE ENGLISH BIBLE** (A), considered in Its Literary and Secular Aspects. By F. BOWEN. LL.D. Crown 8vo, cloth, 4s. 6d.

BOWER (A.)—**ASSERTED, BUT NOT PROVED ;** or, Struggles to Live. By A. BOWER. Crown 8vo, cloth, 4s. 6d.

BOWER (Marian). — **PAYNTON JACKS, GENTLEMAN.** By MARIAN BOWER. Large crown 8vo, cloth extra, 6s.

BOYESEN.—**ESSAYS ON GERMAN LITERATURE.** By HJALMAR HJORTH BOYESEN. Large crown 8vo, cloth, 6s.

BRADBY. — **BOOKS OF THE BIBLE DATED (The) :** A Handbook of a New Order of the Several Books according to the Results of Biblical Criticism, with Brief Notices, where required, on the Authorship and Character of each Book. By Rev. E. H. BRADBY, D.D. Crown 8vo, cloth, 1s.

BRIGHT CELESTIALS : The Chinaman at Home and Abroad. By JOHN COMING CHINAMAN. Crown 8vo, cloth, 6s.

BRIGHTWEN.—**MORE ABOUT WILD NATURE.** By Mrs BRIGHTWEN. With Portrait of the Author and many other full-page Illustrations. Small crown 8vo, cloth, 3s. 6d.

—— **WILD NATURE WON BY KINDNESS.** By Mrs BRIGHTWEN. Fifth and Revised Edition, with additional Illustrations. Crown 8vo, imitation leather, gilt lettered, gilt edges, in box, 5s.

BROOKE.—**NEED AND USE OF GETTING IRISH LITERATURE INTO THE ENGLISH TONGUE (The) :** An Address by the Rev. STOPFORD A. BROOKE at the Inaugural Meeting of the Irish Literary Society in London. Small 8vo, paper covers, 1s.

BROOKFIELD (*Mrs Arthur*).—
ÆSOP'S FABLES FOR
LITTLE READERS. By Mrs
ARTHUR BROOKFIELD. Twenty-
five Illustrations by HENRY J. FORD.
Second Edition. Small 4to, cloth,
3s. 6d.

BROOKFIELD (*Colonel*).—
SPEAKER'S A B C (The): By
COLONEL BROOKFIELD, M.P. Demy
16mo, cloth, 2s.

BROOKS. — PERFECT FREE-
DOM. Addresses by PHILLIPS
BROOKS, with an Introduction by
Rev. JULIUS H. WARD, and an
Etched Portrait Frontispiece. Crown
8vo, cloth, 5s.

BROWN (*Rev. J. B.*).—RISEN
CHRIST (The): The King of
Men. By the Rev. J. BALDWIN
BROWN, M.A. Second and Cheaper
Edition. Crown 8vo, cloth 3s. 6d.

BROWNE.—NELSON: The Public and Private Life of Horatio
Viscount Nelson, as Told by Himself, His Comrades, and His Friends.
By G. LATHOM BROWNE. Dedicated to the Queen, by Her Majesty's
special permission. With Heliogravure Frontispiece Portrait, 13 full-
page Illustrations, and 4 Maps.
Demy 8vo, cloth, gilt tops, 18s.

BUCKLEY.—FAITH-HEALING:
Christian Science and Kindred
Phenomena. By Rev. J. M. BUCK-
LEY, I.L.D. Large crown 8vo,
cloth, 6s.

BUDDENSIEG. — JOHN WIC-
LIF, PATRIOT AND REFOR-
MER: His Life and Writings. By
RUDOLF BUDDENSIEG. Foolscap
12mo, antique paper, parchment
boards, 2s. ; paper covers, 1s.

BYLES.—BOY AND THE
ANGEL (The): Discourses for
Children. By Rev. JOHN BYLES.
Crown 8vo, cloth, 3s. 6d.

BYLES.—SPRING BLOSSOMS
AND SUMMER FRUIT ; or,
Sunday Talks for the Children. By
the Rev. JOHN BYLES. Crown 8vo,
cloth, 2s. 6d.

BYNG.—'93 ; or, THE RE-
VOLUTION AMONG THE
FLOWERS. By FLORENCE BYNG.
Profusely illustrated by HILDA FAIR-
BAIRN and others. Small 4to, paper
boards, 2s.

BYNG & STEPHENS.—AUTO-
BIOGRAPHY (THE) OF AN
ENGLISH GAMEKEEPER —
John Wilkins, of Stanstead, Essex.
Edited by ARTHUR H. BYNG, R.N.,
and STEPHEN M. STEPHENS. Illus-
trated by SIDNEY STARR and
ARTHUR H. BYNG, R.N. Second
Edition. Crown 8vo, cloth, 6s.

CAHON.—WHAT ONE WOMAN
THINKS: Essays by HARYOT
HOLT CAHON. Edited by CYNTHIA
M. WESTOVER. Crown 8vo, cloth,
3s. 6d.

CAMEO SERIES (The). Fcap.
8vo, half-bound, paper boards, price
3s. 6d. each.—Also, an Edition de
Luxe, limited to 30 copies, printed
on Japan paper. *Prices on application.*

1. The Lady from the Sea. By
HENRIK IBSEN. Translated
by ELEANOR MARX - AVELING.
Second Edition. Portrait.

2. A London Plane Tree, and other
Poems. , By AMY LEVY. Illustrated.

4. Iphigenia in Delphi, with some
Translations from the Greek. By
RICHARD GARNETT, LL.D.
Frontispiece.

5. Mireio : A Provençal Poem. By
FREDERIC MISTRAL. Translated
by H. W. PRESTON. Frontispiece
by JOSEPH PENNELL.

CAMEO SERIES (The)—*contd.*

6. **Lyrics.** Selected from the Works of A. MARY F. ROBINSON (Mme. JAMES DARMESTETER). Frontispiece.

7. **A Minor Poet.** By AMY LEVY. With Portrait. Second Edition.

8. **Concerning Cats :** A Book of Verses by many Authors. Edited by Mrs GRAHAM TOMSON. Illustrated.

9. **A Chaplet from the Greek Anthology.** By RICHARD GARNETT, LL.D.

10. **The Countess Kathleen :** A Dramatic Poem. By W. B. YEATS. Frontispiece by J. T. NETTLESHIP.

11. **The Love Songs of Robert Burns.** Selected and Edited, with Introduction, by SIR GEORGE DOUGLAS, Bart. With Front. Portrait.

12. **Love Songs of Ireland.** Collected and Edited by KATHARINE TYNAN.

13. **Retrospect,** and other Poems. By A. MARY F. ROBINSON (Mme. DARMESTETER), Author of 'An Italian Garden,' etc.

CARMEN SYLVA.—**PILGRIM SORROW.** By CARMEN SYLVA (the Queen of Roumania). Translated by HELEN ZIMMERN, Author of 'The Epic of Kings.' Portrait-etching by LALAUZE. Square crown 8vo, cloth extra, 5s.

CARPENTER.—**TOWARDS DEMOCRACY.** By EDWARD CARPENTER. New Edition, 1892, with numerous added Poems. Large crown 8vo, cloth, 5s.

CARR.—**HEART OF MONTROSE (The), and other Stories.** By ESTHER CARR (Mrs WILLIAM HARTOPP), Author of 'The Secret of Wrexford,' 'Fleur de Lis,' etc. Crown 8vo, cloth, 3s. 6d.

CATHERWOOD. — **ROMANCE OF DOLLARD (The).** By MARY HARTWELL CATHERWOOD. Illustrated. Crown 8vo, cloth, 6s.

——— **WHITE ISLANDER (The).** By MARY HARTWELL CATHERWOOD, Author of 'The Romance of Dollard,' etc. Illustrated by FRANCIS DAY. Crown 8vo, cloth, 6s.

CENTURY DICTIONARY (The): An Encyclopædic Lexicon of the English Language. Edited by Prof. W. D. WHITNEY, Ph.D., LL.D. (Yale University). Profusely and Artistically Illustrated. In 6 vols., cloth, gilt lettered, sprinkled edges, £2 2s. each ; or, in half-morocco, cloth sides, marbled edges, £2 16s. each. Also in 24 parts, cloth boards, 10s. 6d. each.—A Bookcase, for holding the Dictionary, price £3 3s.

CENTURY ILLUSTRATED MONTHLY MAGAZINE (The). A High-Class Literary and Artistic Publication. Price 1s. 4d. monthly, or 16s. for one year ; half - yearly volumes, price 10s. 6d. each. Cloth cases for binding the parts, price 1s. 4d. each.

CESARESCO.—**ITALIAN CHARACTERS IN THE EPOCH OF UNIFICATION.** By the Countess EVELYN MARTINENGO CESARESCO. Demy 8vo, cloth, 16s.

CHAPMAN. — **NEW PURGATORY (The),** and other Poems. By ELIZABETH RACHEL CHAPMAN. Crown 8vo, cloth, 4s. 6d.

CHATTERJEE. — **POISON TREE (The) :** A Tale of Hindu Life in Bengal. By BANKIM CHANDER CHATTERJEE. Translated by Mrs KNIGHT. Introduction by Sir E. ARNOLD, C.S.I. Cr. 8vo, cloth, 6s.

8   *Mr. T. Fisher Unwin's*

CHEYNE.—AIDS TO THE DEVOUT STUDY OF CRITICISM. Part I., The David Narratives. Part II., The Book of Psalms. · By Rev. T. K. CHEYNE, M.A., D.D., Oriel Professor of the Interpretation of Holy Scriptures at Oxford, Canon of Rochester. Large crown 8vo, cloth, 7s. 6d.

CHILDREN'S BOUQUET (The) OF VERSE AND HYMN. 32mo, red edges, cloth elegant, or wood, 1s.

CHILDREN'S LIBRARY (The). Illustrated, post 8vo, Pinafore cloth binding, floral edges, 2s. 6d. each.

1. **The Brown Owl.** By FORD H. HUEFFER. Illustrated by MADOX BROWN.

2. **The China Cup.** By FELIX VOLKHOVSKY. Illustrated by MALISCHEFF.

3. **Stories from Fairyland.** By GEORGES DROSINES. Illustrated by THOS. RILEY.

4. **The Story of a Puppet.** By C. COLLODI. Illustrated by C. MAZZANTI.

5. **The Little Princess.** By LINA ECKENSTEIN. Illustrated by DUDLEY HEATH.

6. **Tales from the Mabinogion.** By META WILLIAMS.

7. **Irish Fairy Tales.** Edited by W. B. YEATS. Illustrated by JACK B. YEATS.

8. **An Enchanted Garden.** By Mrs MOLESWORTH. Illustrated by J. W. HENNESSY.

9. **La Belle Nivernaise.** By ALPHONSE DAUDET. Illustrated by MONTEGUT.

10. **The Feather.** By FORD H. HUEFFER. Front. by MADOX BROWN.

11. **Finn and His Companions..** By STANDISH O'GRADY, Author of 'Red Hugh's Captivity,' etc. Illustrated by J. B. YEATS.

CHILDREN'S LIBRARY—*contd.*

12. **Nutcracker and Mouse King,** and other Stories. By E. T. A. HOFFMAN. Translated from the German by ASCOTT R. HOPE.

13. **Once upon a Time :** Fairy Tales. Translated from the Italian of LUIGI CAPUANA. With Illustrations by MAZZANTI.

14. **The Pentamerone;** or, The Story of Stories. By GIAMBATTISTA BASILE. Translated from the Neapolitan by JOHN EDWARD TAYLOR. New Edition, revised and edited by HELEN ZIMMERN. Illustrated by GEO. CRUIKSHANK.

15. **Finnish Legends.** Adapted by R. EIVIND. Illustrated from the Finnish text.

16. **The Pope's Mule,** and other Stories. By ALPHONSE DAUDET. Translated by A. D. BEAVINGTON-ATKINSON and D. HAVERS. Illustrated by ETHEL K. MARTYN.

17. **The Little Glass Man,** and other Stories. Translated from the German of WILHELM HAUFF, Illustrated by JAMES PRYDE.

CHRISTY.—PROVERBS, MAXIMS, AND PHRASES OF ALL AGES. By ROBERT CHRISTY. Classified subjectively and arranged alphabetically. Two vols. Large crown 8vo, half-cloth, gilt tops, 21s.

CLARK.—TWELVE MONTHS IN PERU. By E. B. CLARK. With 8 Illustrations. Crown 8vo, cloth, 5s.

CLAYDEN. — ENGLAND UNDER LORD BEACONSFIELD: A History of Political Events from the End of 1873 to the Fall of the Tory Ministry in 1880. By P. W. CLAYDEN. Third and Popular Edition. Crown 8vo, cloth, 6s.

CLAYDEN. — ENGLAND UNDER THE COALITION: The Political History of England and Ireland from the General Election of 1885 to the General Election of 1892. By P. W. CLAYDEN. Second, Revised and Enlarged Edition. Small demy 8vo, cloth, 12s. *N.B.*—The New Chapter, etc., to this edition may be obtained separately, price 1s. 6d.

COBBE. — MISS FRANCES POWER COBBE'S WORKS. —Popular re-issue. Each crown 8vo, cloth, 3s. 6d.

1. Religious Duty.
2. Peak in Darien.
3. Dawning Lights.
4. Alone.
5. Hopes of the Human Race.
6. Duties of Women.
7. Faithless World.

** Mr T. FISHER UNWIN holds a stock of all Miss COBBE's other Publications. *List on application.*

COLBECK. — SUMMER'S CRUISE IN THE WATERS OF GREECE, TURKEY, AND RUSSIA (A). By the Rev. ALFRED COLBECK. Frontispiece. Crown 8vo, cloth, 10s. 6d.

COLLIER.—PRINCE PEERLESS: A Fairy-Folk Story Book. By the Hon. MARGARET COLLIER. Illustrated by the Hon. JOHN COLLIER. Square imperial 16mo, cloth, 5s.

COLLINGWOOD.—BIBLE AND THE AGE (The); or, An Elucidation of the Principles of a Consistent and Verifiable Interpretation of Scripture. By CUTHBERT COLLINGWOOD, M.A. Demy 8vo, cloth, 10s. 6d.

COLLINS. — HADASSEH; or, From Captivity to the Persian Throne. By E. LEUTY COLLINS (EMILIE LANCASTER). Illustrated. Crown 8vo, cloth, 6s.

COMPTON.—PARTICULAR ACCOUNT OF THE EUROPEAN MILITARY ADVENTURERS OF HINDUSTAN (A), from 1784 to 1803. Compiled by HERBERT COMPTON, Editor of 'A Master Mariner,' etc. Map and Illustrations. Demy 8vo, cloth, 16s.

CONWAY AND COOLIDGE'S CLIMBERS' GUIDES. Edited by W. M. CONWAY and W. A. B. COOLIDGE. 32mo, limp cloth, gilt lettered, with pocket, flap, and pencil, price 10s. each.—Also, a Series of SIX COLOURED MAPS of the ALPS OF THE DAUPHINY, mounted on linen, and strongly bound in cloth case, price 4s. 6d. the set.

1. The Central Pennine Alps. By WILLIAM MARTIN CONWAY.
2. The Eastern Pennine Alps. By WILLIAM MARTIN CONWAY.
3. The Lepontine Alps (Simplon and Gothard). By W. A. B. COOLIDGE and W. M. CONWAY.
4. The Central Alps of the Dauphiny. By W. A. B. COOLIDGE, H. DUHAMEL and F. PERRIN.
5. The Chain of Mont Blanc. By LOUIS KURZ.
6. The Adula Alps of the Lepontine Range. By W. A. B. COOLIDGE.
7. The Mountains of Cogne. By GEORGE YELD and W. A. B. COOLIDGE. With Map.

COUPLAND.—GAIN OF LIFE (The), and other Essays. By WM. CHATTERTON COUPLAND, D.Sc., M.A. Crown 8vo, cloth, 6s.

COX (*Palmer*). — BROWNIES (The): Their Book. By PALMER COX. Fourth and Cheaper Edition. Med. 4to, paper boards, 3s. 6d.

COX (*Palmer*). — **ANOTHER BROWNIE BOOK.** By PALMER Cox. With many quaint Pictures by the Author. Second Edition. Medium 4to, cloth, 3s. 6d.

—— **BROWNIES AT HOME** (The). By PALMER Cox. Illustrated. Medium 4to, cloth, 6s.

COX (*Rev. S.*).—**BIRD'S NEST** (The), and other Sermons for Children of all Ages. By the Rev. SAMUEL Cox, D.D. Third and Cheaper Edition. Imperial 16mo, cloth, 3s. 6d.

—— **'EXPOSITIONS.'** By the Rev. SAMUEL Cox, D.D. In 4 vols. Each demy 8vo, cloth, 7s. 6d.

—— **HEBREW TWINS** (The): A Vindication of God's Ways with Jacob and Esau. By the late Rev. SAMUEL Cox, D.D., Author of 'Expositions,' etc. With Memorial Introduction of the Author. Crown 8vo, cloth, 6s.

—— **HOUSE AND ITS BUILDER** (The), with other Discourses: A Book for the Doubtful. By the Rev. SAMUEL Cox, D.D. Third Edition. Small crown 8vo, paper, 2s. 6d. ; cloth, 3s.

CRESSWELL. — **ALEXIS AND HIS FLOWERS.** By BEATRIX CRESSWELL. With Drawings from Flowers by HENRIETTA CRESSWELL. Crown 8vo, cloth gilt, bevelled boards, 3s. 6d.

CROCKETT.—**STICKIT MINISTER** (The), and some Common Men. By S. R. CROCKETT. Third Edition. Crown 8vo, cloth extra, 5s.

CROMMELIN.—**POETS IN THE GARDEN.** By MAY CROMMELIN. Cheap and Popular Edition, with Coloured Frontispiece. Square Pott 16mo, cloth binding, 6s.

CRYSTAL AGE (A). Crown 8vo, cloth, 4s. 6d.

CURRY. — **BOOK OF THOUGHTS (A).** Linked with Memories of the late JOHN BRIGHT. Selected and Edited by MARY B. CURRY. 24mo, cloth, 6s.

CURTIS.—**GEOMETRICAL DRAWING:** Containing General Hints to Candidates, Former Papers set at the Preliminary and Further Examinations. For Army Examination. By C. H. OCTAVIUS CURTIS. Illustrated. Crown 8vo, cloth, 2s. 6d.

CURTOIS. — **ROMANCE OF A COUNTRY** (The): A Masque. By M. A. CURTOIS, Author of 'Jenny,' 'My Best Pupil,' etc. 2 vols. Crown 8vo, cloth, 21s.

DANTE.—**ILLUSTRATIONS TO THE 'DIVINE COMEDY'** OF DANTE, Executed by the Flemish Artist JOH. STRADANUS, 1587, and reproduced in Phototype (facsimile in size and colour) from the originals existing in the Medicio-Laurenzian Library of Florence. Edited, with Essay, by Dr GUIDO BIAGI, of Florence, and with Preface by JOHN ADDINGTON SYMONDS. Limited Edition of 300 copies, 100 of which are reserved for sale in Italy. The work, in a Florentine binding, size 20 in. by 14 in., price £6 6s. nett.

DAUDET.—**FIG AND THE IDLER** (The): An Algerian Legend; and other Stories. By ALPHONSE DAUDET. With Illustrations by MONTEGUT. Demy 12mo, illustrated paper covers, 1s.

—— **ROSE AND NINETTE:** A Story of the Manners and Morals of the Day. By ALPHONSE DAUDET. New and Cheaper Edition. Crown 8vo, cloth, 2s. 6d.; paper boards, 2s.

DAVIDSON. — **SCARAMOUCH IN NAXOS, A PANTOMIME;** and other Plays. By JOHN DAVIDSON. Second Edition. Cloth, gilt tops, 5s.

DEFOE. — ADVENTURES OF ROBINSON CRUSOE (The). By DANIEL DEFOE. Newly Edited after the Original Editions. Nineteen full-page Illustrations. Large crown 8vo, cloth extra, gilt edges, 5s.

DEITERS. — JOHANNES BRAHMS: A Musical Biography. By Dr HERMAN DEITERS. Edited, with a Preface, by J. A. FULLER MAITLAND. Portrait. Small crown 8vo, cloth, 6s.

DE LAVELEYE.—LETTERS FROM ITALY. By EMILE DE LAVELEYE. Translated by Mrs THORPE. With Portrait. Crown 8vo, cloth, 3s. 6d.

DO THE DEAD RETURN? By a CLERGYMAN OF THE CHURCH OF ENGLAND. With Specimens of Spirit-writing. Crown 8vo, cloth, 2s. 6d.

DOLBY.—CHARLES DICKENS AS I KNEW HIM: The Story of the Reading Tours in Great Britain and America. By GEORGE DOLBY. *New Edition in Preparation.*

DUNN. — ART OF SINGING (The). By SINCLAIR DUNN, Certificated Teacher, R.A.M. With Diagrams. Demy 16mo, cloth, 2s.

EDWARDES. — THUMB-NAIL SKETCHES IN HOLLAND. By GEO. WHARTON EDWARDES. 12mo, bound in sheep, 3s. 6d.

EDWARDS (H. S.).—TWO RUN-AWAYS and other Stories. By HARRY STILWELL EDWARDS. Illustrated by KEMBLE. Crown 8vo, cloth, 6s.

——— (*M. B.*). — STARRY BLOSSOM (The), and other Stories. By M. BETHAM EDWARDS. Illustrated. Small 8vo, cloth extra, 1s. 6d.

ELLIS. — NATIONALISATION OF HEALTH (The). By HAVE-LOCK ELLIS, Editor of 'The Contemporary Science' Series. Crown 8vo, cloth, 3s. 6d.

ENGLISH GRAMMAR FOR SCHOOLS. Adapted to the requirements of the Revised Code. In Three Parts, 2d. each; or, complete in one cover, 6d.

ETHICAL SONGS. With Music. Crown 8vo, cloth, 2s. 6d.

FARIS. — DECLINE OF BRITISH PRESTIGE IN THE EAST (The). By SELIM FARIS. Crown 8vo, cloth, 5s.

FERGUSON. — OUR EARTH: Night to Twilight. By GEORGE FERGUSON. Two vols. Crown 8vo, cloth, gilt tops, 3s. each.

FINCK.—CHOPIN, and other Musical Essays. By HENRY T. FINCK. Small crown, 8vo, cloth, 6s.

FIRST NATURAL HISTORY READER. For Standard II. In accordance with the requirements of the Revised Code. Illustrated. Crown 8vo, cloth, 9d.

FISCHER. — DESECATES AND HIS SCHOOL. By KUNO FISCHER. Translated from the Third and Revised German Edition by J. P. GORDY, Ph.D. Edited by NOAH PORTER, D.D., LL.D. Demy 8vo, cloth, 16s.

FISHER.—NATURE AND METHOD OF REVELATION (The). By Rev. GEORGE PARK FISHER, D.D., LL.D. Crown 8vo, cloth, 4s. 6d.

FITZROY.—WAS HE THE OTHER? By ISOBEL FITZROY. Crown 8vo, cloth, bevelled boards, 3s. 6d.

FRANCIS.—CHEERFUL CATS, and other Animals. By J. G. FRANCIS. With numerous Illustrations. Super royal 12mo, coloured boards, 5s.

FREDERIC.—**THE YOUNG EMPEROR** (William II. of Germany): A Study of Character Development on a Throne. By HAROLD FREDERIC. Second Edition. Five Portraits. Crown 8vo, cloth, 3s. 6d.

GARLAND.—**LITTLE NORSK** (A); or, Ol' Pap's Flaxen. By HAMLIN GARLAND, Author of 'Main-Travelled Roads,' etc. Small crown 8vo, paper boards, 2s.

————— **MAIN - TRAVELLED ROADS**: Six Mississippi Valley Stories. By HAMLIN GARLAND. Second Edition. Crown 8vo, paper boards, 2s. ; cloth, 3s. 6d.

GARNETT (E.).— **LIGHT AND SHADOW**: A Novel. By EDWARD GARNETT. Crown 8vo, cloth, 6s.

————— **PARADOX CLUB** (The). By EDWARD GARNETT. With Frontispiece Portrait. Second Edition. Crown 8vo, cloth, 2s. 6d.

GARNETT (R.). — **TWILIGHT OF THE GODS** (The). By RICHARD GARNETT, LL.D. Crown 8vo, cloth, 6s.

GARRETT.—**HOUSE BY THE WORKS** (The). By EDWARD GARRETT. Third Edition. Frontispiece. Crown 8vo, cloth, 3s. 6d. '

GARRISON.—**LIFE AND TIMES** (The) **OF WILLIAM LLOYD GARRISON**, 1815-79. By his Sons. In 4 vols. Portraits and Illustrations. Demy 8vo, cloth, £3.

GIBB.—**GUDRUN, BEOWULF, AND ROLAND.** By Prof. JOHN GIBB. Illustrated. Second Edition. Crown 8vo, cloth extra, 3s. 6d.

—————**TABLE TALK OF DR MARTIN LUTHER**(The). By Prof. JOHN GIBB. Fcap. 12mo, antique paper, parchment boards, 2s.

GIDUMAL.—**BEHRAMJI M. MALABARI**: A Biographical Sketch. By DAYARAM GIDUMAL, LL.B., C.S. With Introduction by FLORENCE NIGHTINGALE. Crown 8vo, cloth, 6s.

GILCHRIST.—**ANNE GILCHRIST**: Her Life and Writings. By HERBERT H. GILCHRIST. Prefatory Notice by WM. M. ROSSETTI. Second Edition. Twelve Illustrations. Demy 8vo, cloth, 16s.

GILDER.—**TWO WORLDS,** and other Poems. By RICHARD WATSON GILDER. Fcap. 8vo, cloth gilt, gilt tops, 6s.

GOLF IN THE YEAR 2,000; or, What we are Coming To. By J. A. C. K. 8vo, paper, 1s. 6d.

GORDON. — **FOLKS O' CARGLEN** (The): A Story. By ALEXANDER GORDON. Frontispiece. Second and Cheaper Edition. Crown 8vo, cloth, 3s. 6d.

GOSSE.—**ROBERT BROWNING**: Personal Notes. By EDMUND GOSSE. Frontispiece. Small crown 8vo, parchment, 4s. 6d.

GREAT FRENCH WRITERS (The): Studies of the Lives, the Works and the Influence of the Principal Authors of French Literature. Edited by J. J. JUSSERAND. Heliogravure Frontispiece. Crown 8vo, cloth, 3s. 6d. each.—Also, an Edition on large paper, numbered, and limited to 30 copies, half parchment, price 10s. 6d. each.

1. **Madame de Stael.** By ALBERT SOREL.

2. **A. Thiers.** By P. DE REMUSAT.

3. **Bernardin de St. Pierre** (Author of 'Paul and Virginia'). By ARVEDE BARINE. With Preface by AUGUSTINE BIRRELL.

4. **Theophile Gautier.** By MAXIME DU CAMP. Translated by J. E. GORDON. Preface by ANDREW LANG.

GRINDROD.—**TALES IN THE SPEECH-HOUSE.** By CHARLES GRINDROD. Illustrated. Crown 8vo, cloth, 6s.

HALF-HOLIDAY HAND-BOOKS:—Guides to Rambles round London. With Maps, Illustrations, and Bicycle Routes. Crown 8vo, sewed, 9d. ; cloth, 1s. I. Kingston - on - Thames and District. II. Round Reigate. III. Dorking and District. IV. Round Richmond. V. Geological Rambles Round London. VI. Round Tunbridge Wells. VII. Greenwich and District. VIII. From Croydon to the North Downs. IX. Bromley, Keston and District X. Round Sydenham and Norwood. XI. Wimbledon, Putney and District.

HAMILTON.—**FEDERALIST** (The) ; A Commentary in the Form of Essays on the United States Constitution. By ALEXANDER HAMILTON and Others. Edited by HENRY CABOT LODGE. Demy 8vo, Roxburgh binding, 10s. 6d.

HANKIN.— **YEAR BY YEAR :** Poems. By MARY L. HANKIN. Crown 8vo, cloth, 2s. 6d.

HARDING.—**BO'S'UN OF THE 'PSYCHE'** (The). By CLAUD HARDING, R.N. Three Vols. Crown 8vo, cloth, 31s. 6d.

HARDY.—**BUSINESS OF LIFE** (The) : A Book for Everyone. By the Rev. E. J. HARDY, M.A. Square imperial 16mo, cloth, 6s.—Presentation Edition, bevelled boards, gilt edges, in box, 7s. 6d.

———— **FAINT, YET PURSUING.** By the Rev. E. J. HARDY, M.A. Square imperial 16mo, cloth, 6s. Popular Edition, small square 8vo, cloth, 3s. 6d.

———— **FIVE TALENTS OF WOMAN** (The) : A Book for Girls and Young Women. By the Rev.

E. J. HARDY, M.A. Popular Edition, small crown 8vo, cloth, 3s. 6d. —Square imperial 16mo, cloth, 6s.— Presentation Edition, bevelled boards, gilt edges, in box, 7s. 6d.

HARDY.—**HOW TO BE HAPPY THOUGH MARRIED:** Being a Handbook to Marriage. By the Rev. E. J. HARDY, M.A. Presentation Edition, imperial 16mo, white vellum, cloth, extra gilt, bevelled boards, gilt edges, in box, 7s. 6d. —Popular Edition, 26th Thousand, crown 8vo, gilt edges, cloth, bevelled boards, 3s. 6d.

———— **'MANNERS MAKYTH MAN.'** By the Rev. E. J. HARDY, M.A. Presentation Edition, imperial 16mo, cloth, bevelled edges, in box, 7s. 6d.—Cloth, 6s.—Popular Edition, small square 8vo, cloth, 3s. 6d.

———— **SUNNY DAYS OF YOUTH** (The) : A Book for Boys and Young Men. Square imperial 16mo, cloth, 6s.—Also, a fine Edition, elegantly bound, bevelled boards, gilt edges, 7s. 6d.

HARRIS.—**DADDY JAKE, THE RUNAWAY ;** and other Stories told after Dark. By JOEL CHANDLER HARRIS ('Uncle Remus'). New Edition. Medium 4to, cloth, 3s. 6d.

HARRISON (B.).—**CROW'S NEST, AND BELHAVEN TALES.** By Mrs BURTON HARRISON, Author of ' The Anglo-Maniacs,' etc. Illustrated. Large crown 8vo, cloth boards, 5s.

———— **SWEET BELLS OUT OF TUNE.** By Mrs BURTON HARRISON. Crown 8vo, cloth, 6s.

HARRISON (J. E.)—**INTRODUCTORY STUDIES IN GREEK ART ;** Delivered in the British Museum. By JANE E. HARRISON. Second Edition. Map and 10 Illustrations. Square imperial 16mo, cloth, 7s. 6d.

C

HARRISON AND MACCOLL.—
GREEK VASE PAINTINGS:
Select Examples. With an Introduction and Notes by JANE E. HAR-
RISON and D. S. MACCOLL. Size of
the book, 18 by 14 inches, bound in
strong cloth, price 31s. 6d.—Also, a
fine edition on Japan paper, limited
to 30 copies, 10 of which contain
coloured plates. *Prices on application.*

*HARTE.—***BIANCA:** A Novel. By
Mrs BAGOT HARTE. 2 vols., crown
8vo, cloth, 21s.

*HARTSHORNE.—***HANGING IN
CHAINS.** By ALBERT HARTS-
HORNE, F.S.A. With 11 Illustrations. Demy 12mo, parchment boards,
gilt tops, 4s. 6d.

HEALE. — **MARKHAM HOW-
ARD:** A Novel. By J. HEALE.
3 vols., 8vo, cloth, 31s. 6d.

HENDERSON. — **OLD - WORLD
SCOTLAND:** Essays on Old
Scotch Customs. By T. F. HENDER-
SON. Crown 8vo, cloth, 6s.

HERBERT. — **THE TEMPLE;**
Sacred Poems and Private Ejacu-
lations. By GEORGE HERBERT.
With Introductory Essay by J.
HENRY SHORTHOUSE. Fifth Edition. Small crown 8vo, half-bound,
old style, paper boards, 5s. ; or, real
sheep sprinkled, red edges, 5s. This
is a *fac-simile* reprint of the Original
Edition of 1633.

HERRICK. — LETTERS (The)
**OF THE DUKE OF WEL-
LINGTON TO MISS J.**
Edited, with Extracts from the
Diary of the latter. By CHRISTINE
TERHUNE HERRICK, Crown 8vo,
cloth, 6s.

*HEWITT.—***HEART OF SHEBA**
(The). As told in the Parchment of
Arnath, the Queen's Brother. By
ETHEL MAY HEWITT. Crown 8vo,
cloth, 3s. 6d.

*HILL (G.).—***WITH THE
BEDUINS;** A Narrative of
Journeys to the East of Jordan, Dead
Sea, Palmyra, etc. By GRAY HILL.
Numerous Illustrations and Map.
Demy 8vo, cloth, 15s.

*HILL (G. B.).—***WRITERS AND
READERS:** Educational Essays.
By GEORGE BIRKBECK HILL, D.C.L.
New and Cheaper Edition. Crown
8vo, cloth, 2s. 6d.

*HODGETTS.—***IN THE TRACK
OF THE RUSSIAN FAMINE.**
By E. A. BRAYLEY HODGETTS.
Frontispiece. Crown 8vo, cloth,
2s. 6d.

*HODSON.—***THE MEETING
HOUSE AND THE MANSE:**
or, The Story of the Independents of
Sudbury. By WILLIAM WALTER
HODSON, F.R.H.S. Crown 8vo,
cloth, 3s. 6d.

*HOLYOAKE.—***SIXTY YEARS
OF AN AGITATOR'S LIFE:**
The Autobiography of GEORGE
JACOB HOLYOAKE. In two volumes,
with Photogravure Frontispiece Por-
trait to each. Demy 8vo, cloth, 21s.
See, also, the REFORMER'S BOOK-
SHELF.

*HOPE (A. R.)—***BOY'S OWN
STORIES.** By ASCOTT R. HOPE.
Fourth Edition. Eight Illustrations.
Crown 8vo, cloth, gilt edges, 5s.

——— **ROYAL YOUTHS:** A
Book of Princehoods. By ASCOTT
R. HOPE. Illustrated. Crown 8vo,
cloth, 5s.

*HOPE (N.)—***MILLIARA:** An Australian Romance. By NOEL HOPE.
2 vols. Crown 8vo, cloth 21s.

*HORTON.—***INSPIRATION
AND THE BIBLE:** An Inquiry.
By R. F. HORTON, M.A., D.D.
Fifth Edition. Crown 8vo, cloth,
3s. 6d.

HORTON.—REVELATION AND THE BIBLE. Large crown 8vo, cloth, 7s. 6d.

———— VERBUM DEI: Being the Yale Lectures on Preaching for 1893. Large crown 8vo, cloth, 5s.

HOUSSAYE.—MANUAL OF FRENCH GRAMMAR (A), For Army Examination. By LE COMPTE DE LA HOUSSAYE. Crown 8vo, cloth, 2s 6d.

HUMPHREY.—QUEEN AT BALMORAL (The): By FRANK POPE HUMPHREY, Author of 'A New England Cactus,' etc. 14 full-page Illustrations. Large crown 8vo, cloth gilt, 6s.

HUTCHINSON.—MORE THAN HE BARGAINED FOR: An Indian Novel. By J. R. HUTCHINSON. Crown 8vo, cloth, 6s.

HUTTON.—LITERARY LANDMARKS OF LONDON. By LAURENCE HUTTON. Fifth, Revised, and Cheaper Edition. Crown 8vo, Illustrated cover, 2s. 6d.; half-bound cloth, gilt top, 3s. 6d.

YDE.—LOVE SONGS OF CONNACHT. Being the Fourth Chapter of the 'Songs of Connacht.' Now for the first time Collected, Edited and Translated. By DOUGLAS HYDE, LL.D., M.R.I.A., Author of 'Beside the Fire,' etc. Crown 8vo, paper, sewed, 2s. 6d. nett.

ILLUSTRATED POETRY BOOK (The) FOR YOUNG READERS. Crown 8vo, cloth, gilt edges, 2s. 6d.

INAGAKI.—JAPAN AND THE PACIFIC, and A JAPANESE VIEW OF THE EASTERN QUESTION. By MANJURO INAGAKI, B.A. Five Maps. Crown 8vo, cloth, 7s. 6d.

INDEPENDENT NOVEL SERIES (The). Demy 12mo, cloth, price 3s. 6d. each.

1. The Shifting of the Fire. By FORD H. HUEFFER, Author of 'The Brown Owl,' etc.

2. A Phantom from the East. By PIERRE LOTI. Translated by J. E. GORDON.

3. Jean de Kerdren. By PHILIPPE SAINT HILAIRE, Author of 'Colette.' Transl. by Mrs WAUGH.

4. Poor Lady Massey. By H. RUTHERFURD RUSSELL.

5. A Constant Lover. Translated from the German of WILHELM HAUFF.

6. Stories from Garshin. Translated by ALICE VOYNICH. With Critical Introduction by SERGIUS STEPNIAK.

7. Tiari: A Tahitian Romance. By DORA HORT, Author of 'Tahiti: The Garden of the Pacific,' etc.

8. Hugh Darville. By E. L. ST GERMAINE.

INDUSTRIAL RIVERS OF THE UNITED KINGDOM. By Various well-known Experts. Illustrated. Second and Cheaper Edition. Crown 8vo, cloth, 3s. 6d.

JANVIER.—AN EMBASSY TO PROVENCE. By THOS. A. JANVIER. Fully Illustrated. 12mo, cloth, 4s. 6d.

JAPP.—INDUSTRIAL CURIOSITIES. By ALEX. H. JAPP, LL.D., F.R.S.E. Sixth Edition. Crown 8vo, cloth, 3s. 6d.

JEANS.—ENGLISH FACTORY ACT LEGISLATION: Being the Cobden Club Prize Essay for 1891. By VICTORINE JEANS. Crown 8vo, cloth, 3s. 6d.

JEFFERSON.—AUTOBIOGRAPHY OF JOSEPH JEFFERSON ('Rip Van Winkle'). With many full-page Portraits and other Illustrations. Royal 8vo, cloth, gilt tops, 16s.

JESSOPP.—ARCADY : for Better, for Worse. By Rev. AUGUSTUS JESSOPP, D.D. Fourth Edition. Crown 8vo, cloth, 3s. 6d.

——— COMING OF THE FRIARS (The), and other Mediæval Sketches. By Rev. AUGUSTUS JESSOPP, D.D. Sixth Edition. Crown 8vo, cloth, 3s. 6d.

——— STUDIES BY A RECLUSE : In Cloister, Town, and Country. By Rev. AUGUSTUS JESSOPP, D.D. Illustrated. Crown 8vo, cloth, 7s. 6d.

——— TRIALS OF A COUNTRY PARSON (The): Some Fugitive Papers. By Rev. AUGUSTUS JESSOPP, D.D. Crown 8vo, cloth, 7s. 6d.

JEWETT.—BUNNY STORIES FOR YOUNG PEOPLE (The). By JOHN HOWARD JEWETT. 78 Illustrations by CULMER BARNES. Small 4to, cloth, 5s.

JOHNSTON. — THE WINTER HOUR. By R. UNDERWOOD JOHNSTON. Crown 8vo, cloth, 5s.

JOHNSON & BUEL.—BATTLES AND LEADERS OF THE AMERICAN CIVAL WAR. By ROBERT U. JOHNSON and CLARENCE C. BUEL. An Authoratative History written by Distinguished Participants on both sides, and edited by the above. Four volumes, royal 8vo, elegantly bound, £5 5s.

JONES.—MITHAZAN : A Secret of Nature. A Novel. By W. BRAUNSTON JONES. Three vols. Crown 8vo, cloth, 31s. 6d.

JUSSERAND.—ENGLISH NOVEL (The) IN THE TIME OF SHAKESPEARE. By J. J. JUSSERAND, Conseiller d'Ambassade. Translated by ELIZABETH LEE. Revised and Enlarged by the Author. Illustrated by six Heliogravures by DUJARDIN, and 21 full-page and many smaller Illustrations in fac-simile. Demy 8vo, cloth, gilt tops, 21s.

JUSSERAND.—ENGLISH WAYFARING LIFE IN THE MIDDLE AGES (XIVth CENTURY). By J. J. JUSSERAND, Conseiller d'Ambassade. Translated from the French by LUCY A. TOULMIN SMITH. Illustrated. Third and Revised Edition. Large crown 8vo, cloth, 7s. 6d.

——— FRENCH AMBASSADOR (A) AT THE COURT OF CHARLES II., Le Comte de Cominges. From his unpublished Correspondence. By J. J. JUSSERAND, Conseiller d'Ambassade. With Ten Illustrations, five being photogravures. Demy 8vo, cloth, gilt, 12s.

KEAN.—AMONG THE HOLY PLACES : Travels in Palestine. By Rev JAMES KEAN, M.A., B.D. Third Edition. Illustrated. Demy 8vo, cloth, 7s. 6d.

KEARY.—VIKINGS IN WESTERN CHRISTENDOM (The). A.D. 789-888. By C. F. KEARY. With Map and Tables. Demy 8vo, cloth, 16s.

KEELING. — IN THOUGHTLAND AND IN DREAMLAND. By ELSA D'ESTERRE KEELING. Square imperial 16mo, cloth, 6s. — Presentation Edition, cloth elegant, bevelled boards, gilt edges, in box, 7s. 6d.

——— ORCHARDS CROFT: The Story of a Artist. By ELSA D'ESTERRE KEELING. Crown 8vo, cloth, 6s.

KENN. — DOWN IN THE FLATS ; or, Party before Fitness. By CLEVEDEN KENN. Demy 12mo, cloth, 3s. 6d.

KENNEDY.—LIFE AND WORK IN BENARES AND KUMAON, 1839-77. By JAMES KENNEDY, M.A. Introduction by Sir WILLIAM MUIR. Illustrated. Cr. 8vo, cloth, 6s.

KETTLE.—**FURZE BLOS- SOMS**: Stories and Poems for all Seasons. By ROSA MACKENZIE KETTLE. Second Edition. Crown 8vo, cloth, 6s.

———— **ROSE, SHAMROCK AND THISTLE**: A Story. Large crown 8vo, cloth extra, 6s.

———— **MAGIC OF THE PINEWOODS** (The): A Novel. Crown 8vo, cloth, 6s.

———— **MEMOIRS OF CHARLES BONER** (The). Two vols. Crown 8vo, cloth, 4s. each.

———— **OLD HALL AMONG THE WATER MEADOWS** (The). Crown 8vo, cloth, 6s.

———— **SISTERS OF OM- BERSLEIGH** (The). Crown 8vo, cloth, 3s. 6d.

———— Also 'The Wreckers,' 'Lew- ell Pastures,' 'On Leithay's Banks,' 'La Belle Marie,' 'The Sea and the Moor,' 'The Mistress of Langdale Hall,' 'Under the Grand Old Hills,' 'The Falls of the Loder,' 'The Last Mackenzie of Redcastle,' 'The Ten- ants of Beldornie.' Crown 8vo, cloth, 4s. each.

KING.—**LIONEL VILLIERS**; or, True and Steadfast. By A. FIELDER KING. Crown 8vo, cloth, 6s.

KNOX.—**UNITED STATES NOTES**: A History of the Various Issues of Paper Money, by the U.S. Government. By JOHN T. KNOX. Royal 8vo, cloth, 12s.

KOSTROMITIN. — **THE LAST DAY OF THE CARNIVAL**: A Life Sketch. By T. KOSTROMITIN Translated from the Russian. 12mo, paper, 1s. 6d.

KROEKER. — **FAIRY TALES FROM BRENTANO.** Told in English by KATE FREILIGRATH KROEKER. Twenty-two Illustra-

tions by F. CARRUTHERS GOULD. Third and Popular Edition. Square imperial 16mo, cloth gilt, gilt edges, 3s. 6d.

KROEKER.—**GOTTFRIED KELLER**: A Selection of his Tales, Translated with a Memoir, by KATE FREILIGRATH KROEKER. With Portrait. Crown 8vo, cloth, 6s.

———— **NEW FAIRY TALES FROM BRENTANO.** Told in English by KATE FREILI- GRATH KROEKER. Pictured by F. CARRUTHERS GOULD. Eight full- page Coloured Illustrations. Square 8vo, illustrated, paper boards, cloth back, 5s.; cloth, gilt edges, 6s.

LADD.—**INTRODUCTION TO PHILOSOPHY**: An Inquiry after a Rational System of Scientific Principles in their Relation to Ulti- mate Reality. By Professor GEORGE TRUMBALL LADD, D.D. Demy 8vo, cloth, 12s.

LEADER & MARCOTTI.—**SIR JOHN HAWKWOOD (L'ACUTO)**: The Story of a Condottiere. By — JOHN TEMPLE LEADER and GUISEPPE MARCOTTI. Translated from the Italian by LEADER SCOTT. Illustrated. Limited Edition of 500, numbered and signed. *Terms on application.*

LEE. (Rev. F. G.).—**SINLESS CONCEPTION OF THE MOTHER OF GOD** (The): A Theological Essay. By Rev. FRED- ERICK GEORGE LEE, D.C.L. Demy 8vo, 7s. 6d.

LEE (V.). — **BALDWIN**: Being Dialogues on Views and Aspirations. By VERNON LEE. Demy 8vo, cloth, 12s.

———— **BELCARO**: Being Essays on Sundry Æsthetical Questions. By VERNON LEE. Crown 8vo, cloth, 5s.

LEE (V.).—EUPHORION: Studies of the Antique and the Mediæval in the Renaissance. By VERNON LEE. Cheap Edition. Demy 8vo, cloth, 7s. 6d.

―――― JUVENILIA: Essays on Sundry Æsthetical Questions. By VERNON LEE. Two vols. Small crown 8vo, cloth, 12s.

―――― OTTILIE: An 18th Century Idyl. By VERNON LEE. Square 8vo, cloth extra, 3s. 6d.

―――― PRINCE (The) of the Hundred Soups. With Preface by VERNON LEE Cheaper Edition. Square 8vo, cloth, 3s. 6d.

―――― STUDIES OF THE EIGHTEENTH CENTURY IN ITALY. By VERNON LEE. Demy 8vo, cloth, 7s. 6d.

LEGGE.—SUNNY MANITOBA: Its People and its Industries. By ALFRED O. LEGGE, Author of 'The Unpopular King,' etc. Eight Illustrations and Map. Crown 8vo, cloth, 7s. 6d.

LELAND.—BOOK (The) OF THE HUNDRED RIDDLES OF THE FAIRY BELLARIA. By CHARLES GODFREY LELAND ('Hans Breitmann'). Profusely Illustrated. . Demy 16mo, paper, 1s. ; cloth, 2s.—Also, a Fine Edition, limited to 100 copies, with an Original Illustration to each, bound in cloth, price 7s. 6d. nett.

―――― ETRUSCAN ROMAN REMAINS IN POPULAR TRADITION. By CHARLES GODFREY LELAND, Hon. F.R.L.S., President of the Gypsy-Lore Society, &c. With many Illustrations, and copiously decorated with head- and tailpieces by the Author, illustrative of Etruscan Art. (Uniform with 'Gypsy Sorcery.') Small 4to, cloth, 21s.—Also, an Edition de Luxe, limited to 100 copies, with an Original Drawing by Mr LELAND, numbered and signed, price £1 11s. 6d. nett.

LELAND.—GIPSY SORCERY AND FORTUNE TELLING. By CHARLES GODFREY LELAND ('Hans Breitmann'), President of the Gypsy-Lore Society, etc., etc. Illustrated by numerous Incantations, Specimens of Medical Magic, Anecdotes and Tales, by the Author. With numerous Illustrations and Initial Letters drawn by the Author. Small 4to, cloth, 16s.—Limited Edition of 150 .copies, numbered and signed, price £1 11s. 6d. nett.

LE ROW.—ENGLISH AS SHE IS TAUGHT. Genuine Answers to Examination Questions. Collected by CATHERINE B. LE ROW, and with Commentary by MARK TWAIN. Third Edition. Demy 16mo, sewed, 6d. ; cloth, 1s.

LEVY.—ROMANCE OF A SHOP (The). By AMY LEVY, Author of 'Reuben Sachs,' etc. Crown 8vo, cloth, 6s.

LINSKILL. — LOST SON (A), and THE GLOVER'S DAUGHTER. By MARY LINSKILL. Crown 8vo, cloth, 4s. 6d.

'LIVES WORTH LIVING' SERIES (The) OF POPULAR BIOGRAPHIES. Illustrated. Crown 8vo, cloth extra, 3s. 6d. Six vols. in handsome box, 21s.

1. Leaders of Men : A Book of Biographies specially written for Young Men. By H. A. PAGE, Author of 'Golden Lives.' Sixth Edition.

2. Wise Words and Loving Deeds : A Book of Biographies for Girls. By E. CONDER GRAY. Sixth Edition.

3. Master Missionaries : Studies in Heroic Pioneer Work. By A. H. JAPP, LL.D., F.R.S.E. Fourth Edition.

'LIVES WORTH LIVING'
SERIES (The)—*continued.*

4. **Labour and Victory.** By A. H.
JAPP, LL.D. Memoirs of those
who Deserved Success and Won
it. Third Edition.

5. **Heroic Adventure :** Chapters in
Recent Explorations and Discovery. Illustrated. Fourth Edition.

6. **Great Minds in Art :** With a
Chapter on Art and Artists. By
WILLIAM TIREBUCK. Second
Edition. Many Portraits.

7. **Good Men and True.** By ALEX.
H. JAPP, LL.D. Second Edition.

8. **The Lives of Robert and Mary
Moffat.** By JOHN SMITH MOF-
FAT. Ninth Edition.

9. **Famous Musical Composers :**
Biographies of Eminent Musicians.
By LYDIA J. MORRIS. Second
Edition.

LLOYD. — JOAN TRACEY : A
Story. By SIDNEY LLOYD. Crown
8vo, cloth, 2s.

LOVEJOY.—FRANCIS BACON
(Lord Verulam). A Critical Re-
view of His Life and Character, with
Selections from His Writings. By
B. G. LOVEJOY, A.M., LL.B.
Crown 8vo, half-bound cloth, gilt
top, 6s.

LOWE (C.).—FOUR NATIONAL
EXHIBITIONS IN LONDON,
and their Organiser, JOHN R. WHIT-
LEY By CHARLES LOWE, M.A.
With many Portraits and full-page
Illustrations. Demy 8vo, cloth, 7s. 6d.
—Also, an Edition de Luxe on hand-
made paper, price 12s.

LOWE (J.). — MEDICAL MIS-
SIONS : Their Place and Power.
By JOHN LOWE, F.R.C.S.E. In-
troduction by Sir WILLIAM
MUIR. Frontispiece. Second Edi-
tion. Crown 8vo, cloth, 5s.

LUSHINGTON, — MARGARET
THE MOONBEAM : A Tale
for the Young. By CECILIA LUSH-
INGTON. With Illustrations by M.
E. EDWARDS. · Second Edition.
Small 8vo, cloth extra, gilt edges,
2s. 6d.

LYNCH.— THE BOY GOD :
Troublesome and Vengeful. An
Ethical Romance. By E. M. LYNCH.
Illustrated. 12mo, cloth, 6s.

LYSTER.— WITH GORDON IN
CHINA : Letters from Lieut. T.
LYSTER, R.E. Edited by E. A.
LYSTER. With Portrait. Large
crown 8vo, cloth, 6s.

MACAULAY.—DOCTOR JOHN-
SON : His Life, Works, and Table
Talk. By Dr MACAULAY. Fcap.
12mo, antique paper, parchment
boards, 2s. ; paper covers, 1s.

MACDONALD.—D I A R Y O F
THE PARNELL COMMIS-
SION (The). By JOHN MAC-
DONALD, M.A. Revised, with Ad-
ditions, from the *Daily News.* Large
crown 8vo, cloth, 6s.

MACGREGOR. — T O I L A N D
TRAVEL : Being a True Story of
Roving and Ranging, when on a
Voyage Round the World. By JOHN
MACGREGOR (' Ralph '), Author of
' The Girdle of the Globe,' etc. Six
full-page Illustrations. Demy 8vo,
cloth, 16s.

MACGUIRE. — A M A B E L : A
Military Romance. By CATHAL
MACGUIRE. 3 vols. Crown 8vo,
cloth, 31s. 6d.

MAGNUS. — J E W I S H P O R-
TRAITS. By Lady MAGNUS.
With Frontispiece by HARRY FUR-
NISS. Small crown 8vo, cloth, 5s.

MARJORIE AND HER PAPA :
How they Wrote a Story and Made
Pictures for It. A Book for Child-
ren. 4to, bevelled boards, 3s. 6d.

MARTIN.—OLD CHELSEA: A
Summer-day's Stroll. By BENJAMIN
ELLIS MARTIN. Illustrated by
JOSEPH PENNELL. Third and
Cheaper Edition. Square imperial
16mo, cloth, 3s. 6d.

MASON.—WOMEN OF THE
FRENCH SALONS (The): A
Series of Articles on the French
Salons of the Seventeenth and Eight-
eenth Centuries. By AMELIA G.
MASON. Profusely Illustrated.
Fcap. folio, cloth, £1 5s.

MASSON.—MY POOR NIECE,
and other Stories. By ROSALINE
MASSON. Square 8vo, paper, 1s. 6d.

MATSON.—ST. GEORGE AND
THE DRAGON. By SARAH
ANN MATSON. Illustrated by
CLAUDIA MAY SOUTHBY. Crown
8vo, cloth, 6s.

MATTHEWS.—LAST MEET-
ING (The): A Story. By
BRANDER MATTHEWS. Crown 8vo,
cloth, 4s. 6d.

MAXWELL. — NEGRO QUES-
TION (The); or, Hints for the
Physical Improvement of the Negro
Race. By JOSEPH RENNER MAX-
WELL, M.A., B.C.L. Crown 8vo,
cloth, 6s.

MERMAID SERIES (The): The
Best Plays of the Old Dramatists.
Literal Reproductions of the Old
Text. Post 8vo, each Volume con-
taining about 500 pages, and an
etched Frontispiece, cloth, 2s. 6d.
*After Jan. 1st, 1894, the price will be
raised to 3s. 6d. per volume.*

1. The Best Plays of Christopher
Marlowe. Edited by HAVELOCK
ELLIS, and containing a General
Introduction to the Series by JOHN
ADDINGTON SYMONDS.

2. The Best Plays of Thomas
Otway. Introduction by the Hon.
- RODEN NOEL.

3. The Best Plays of John Ford.
Edited by HAVELOCK ELLIS.

MERMAID SERIES (The)—*contd.*
4 and 5. The Best Plays of
Thomas Massinger. Essay and
Notes by ARTHUR SYMONS.

6. The Best Plays of Thomas
Heywood. Edited by A. W.
VERITY. Introduction by J. A.
SYMONDS.

7. The Complete Plays of William
Wycherley. Edited by W. C.
WARD.

8. Nero, and other Plays. Edited
by H. P. HORNE, ARTHUR
SYMONS, A. W. VERITY and H.
ELLIS.

9 and 10. The Best Plays of
Beaumont and Fletcher. Introduction by J. ST LOE STRACHEY.

11. The Complete Plays of William
Congreve. Edited by ALEX. C.
EWALD.

12. The Best Plays of Webster and
Tourneur. Introduction by JOHN
ADDINGTON SYMONDS.

13 and 14. The Best Plays of
Thomas Middleton. Introduc-
tion by ALGERNON CHARLES
SWINBURNE.

15. The Best Plays of James
Shirley. Introduction by ED-
MUND GOSSE.

16. The Best Plays of Thomas
Dekker. Notes by ERNEST
RHYS.

17. The Best Plays of Ben Jonson
(Vol. 1). Edited, with Introduction
and Notes, by BRINSLEY NICHOL-
SON and C. H. HERFORD.

MOFFAT.—LIVES OF ROBERT
AND MARY MOFFAT (The).
By their Son, JOHN SMITH MOFFAT.
Sixth Edition. Portraits, Illustrations and Maps. Crown 8vo, cloth,
7s. 6d.—Presentation Edition, full
gilt elegant, bevelled boards, gilt
edges, in box, 10s. 6d.

MONTEIRO.—LEGENDS AND
POPULAR TALES OF THE
BASQUE PEOPLE. By
MARIANA MONTEIRO. With full-

page Illustrations in Photogravure by HAROLD COPPING. Third and Popular Edition. Imp. 8vo, cloth, gilt edges, 3s. 6d.

MORRIS.—FAMOUS MUSICAL COMPOSERS. Being Biographies of Eminent Musicians. By LYDIA J. MORRIS. Numerous Portraits. 8vo, cloth, gilt edges, 6s.

NATIONAL LIFE AND THOUGHT; or, Lectures on Various Nations of the World. Delivered at South Place Institute by Professor THOROLD ROGERS, J. S. COTTON MINCHIN, W. R. MORFILL, F. H. GROOME, J. THEODORE BENT, Professor A. PULSZKY, EIRIKE MAGNUSSON, and other Specialists. Demy 8vo, cloth, 10s. 6d.

NEUMAN. — INTERPRETER'S HOUSE (The): A Book of Parables. By B. PAUL NEUMAN. 8vo, cloth, 5s.

———— RAYMOND'S FOLLY. By B. PAUL NEUMAN. 8vo, cloth, 5s.

NEW IRISH LIBRARY (The). Edited by Sir CHARLES GAVAN DUFFY, K.C.M.G., Assisted by DOUGLAS HYDE, LL.D., and T. W. ROLLESTON. Small crown 8vo, paper covers, 1s. each; cloth, 2s. each.

1. The Patriot Parliament of 1689, with its Statutes, Votes and Proceedings. By THOMAS DAVIS. Edited, and with Introduction, by Sir C. G. DUFFY, K.C.M.G.

2. The Bog of Stars, and other Stories of Elizabethan Ireland. By STANDISH O'GRADY, Author of 'Finn and His Companions,' etc. *Other volumes in preparation.*

NEWMAN. — BIRD SKINNING AND BIRD STUFFING: A Complete Description of the Nests and Eggs of Birds which Breed in Britain. By EDWARD NEWMAN. Revised and Re-written, with Directions for their Collection and Preservation, and a Chapter on Bird Stuffing, by MILLER CHRISTY. Crown 8vo, 1s.

NICOLAY & HAY.—ABRAHAM LINCOLN: A History. JOHN G. NICOLAY and Colonel JOHN HAY. With many full - page Illustrations, Portraits, and Maps. Royal 8vo, complete in 10 vols., bound in cloth, price £6 nett.

NORMAN.—REAL JAPAN (The): Studies of Contemporary Japanese Manners, Morals, Administration, and Politics. By HENRY NORMAN. With about 40 Illustrations, chiefly from Photographs taken by the Author. Cheaper Edition. Crown 8vo, cloth, 3s. 6d.

O'CONNOR.—PARNELL MOVEMENT (The): Being the History of the Irish Question from the Death of O'Connell to the Suicide of Pigott. By T. P. O'CONNOR, M.P. Crown 8vo, paper covers, 1s.; cloth boards, 2s.

OGLE.—THE MARQUIS D'ARGENSON: A Study in Criticism. Being the Stanhope Prize Essay for 1893. By ARTHUR OGLE, Exhibitioner of Magdalen College. Crown 8vo, cloth, 6s.

OMAN (Prof. J. C.).—INDIAN LIFE: Religious and Social. By Professor JOHN CAMPBELL OMAN. Crown 8vo, cloth, 6s.

ORME.—TREASURE BOOK OF CONSOLATION (The): For All in Sorrow or Suffering. By BENJAMIN ORME, M.A. Popular Edition. Crown 8vo, cloth extra, gilt edges, 3s. 6d.

OWEN. — OLD RABBIT, THE VOODOO, and other Sorcerers. Edited by MARY ALICIA OWEN. With Introduction by CHARLES GODFREY LELAND. Over 50 Illustrations by JULIETTE A. OWEN and LOUIS WAIN. Large crown 8vo, cloth, 6s.

OXFORD. — BERWICK HYMNAL (The). Edited by the Rev. A. W. OXFORD, M.A. Imperial 32mo, cloth, 2s. 6d.

OXFORD.—**CHILDREN'S SER-
VICES**, with Hymns and Songs.
By the Rev. A. W. OXFORD, M.A.
Second Edition. 16mo, cloth, 9d.

——— **SHORT INTRODUC-
TION TO THE STUDY OF
ANCIENT ISRAEL (A).** By
the Rev. A. W. OXFORD, M.A.
Crown 8vo, cloth, 2s. 6d.

PAGE (T. N.).—**TWO LITTLE
CONFEDERATES.** By THOMAS
NELSON PAGE. Illustrated. Sq.
8vo, cloth, gilt edges, 6s.

PASQUEIR.—**REVOLUTION
AND THE EMPIRE (The):**
Being the Memoirs of Chancellor
PASQUEIR. 3 vols. Large Demy
8vo, cloth, 16s.

PEARCE.—**ESTHER PENT-
REATH, THE MILLER'S
DAUGHTER:** A Cornish Ro-
mance. By J. H. PEARCE, Author
of 'Bernice,' etc. Crown 8vo, cloth, 6s.

PEARSON.—**ETHIC OF FREE-
THOUGHT (The):** A Selection
of Essays and Lectures. By Professor KARL PEARSON, M.A.
Demy 8vo, cloth, 12s.

——— **NEW UNIVERSITY
FOR LONDON (The):** A
Guide to Its History, and a Criticism
of Its Defects. By KARL PEARSON,
M.A. Crown 8vo, cloth 2s.

PENNELL.—**OUR JOURNEY
TO THE HEBRIDES.** By
JOSEPH and ELIZABETH ROBINS
PENNELL. Forty-three Illustrations
by JOSEPH PENNELL. Crown 8vo,
cloth, half-bound, gilt top, 7s. 6d.

——— **OUR SENTIMENTAL
JOURNEY,** through France and
Italy. By JOSEPH and ELIZABETH
ROBINS PENNELL. Second Edition,
with Appendix. Map and Illustra-
tions. Crown 8vo, cloth, 3s. 6d.

PENNELL.—**PLAY IN PRO-
VENCE.** By JOSEPH and ELIZA-
BETH ROBINS PENNELL. With
nearly 100 Illustrations by JOSEPH
PENNELL. Crown 8vo, cloth gilt, 6s.

——— **STREAM OF PLEA-
SURE (The):** A Narrative of a
Journey on the Thames from Oxford to London. By ELIZABETH
ROBINS PENNELL. Profusely Illustrated by JOSEPH PENNELL. Small
crown 4to, cloth, 5s.

——— **TO GIPSYLAND.** By
JOSEPH and ELIZABETH ROBINS
PENNELL. Illustrated by JOSEPH
PENNELL. 12mo, cloth, 6s.

PENTREATH.—**IN A COR-
NISH TOWNSHIP WITH
OLD VOGUE FOLK.** By DOLLY
PENTREATH. Photogravure Frontis-
piece, and 18 other Illustrations by
PERCY B. CRAFT. Large crown
8vo, cloth, 7s. 6d.

PETISCUS.—**GODS OF OLYM-
POS (The);** or, Mythology of the
Greeks and Romans. Translated
and Edited from the 20th Edition of
A. H. PETISCUS by KATHERINE
A. RALEIGH. Preface by JANE
E. HARRISON. Eight full-page and
numerous smaller Illustrations. Demy
8vo, cloth, 7s. 6d.

PHELPS.—**MY NOTE-BOOK:**
Fragmentary Studies in Theology,
and Subjects adjacent thereto. By
Professor AUSTIN PHELPS, D.D.
With Portrait. Crown 8vo, cloth, 6s.

PIATT.—**AN IRISH WILD-
FLOWER,** and other Poems. By
SARAH M. B. PIATT. Crown 8vo,
half-bound, 2s. 6d.

PITT.—**TRAGEDY OF THE
NORSE GODS (The).** By RUTH
J. PITT. Illustrated by G. P.
JACOMB-HOOD and J. A. J. BRIND-
LEY. Large crown 8vo, cloth, 6s.

POLLARD.—**EVERY-DAY
MIRACLES.** By BEDFORD
POLLARD. Illustrated. Small crown
8vo, cloth, 3s. 6d.

PRESCOTT.—**REFORM IN EDUCATION**: Showing the Improvements possible in the Present Methods. By the Rev. PETER PRESCOTT. Cr. 8vo, paper, 6d. ; cloth, 1s.

PRESTON.—**A YEAR IN EDEN.** By HARRIET WATERS PRESTON. Two vols. Crown 8vo, cloth, 21s.

PRINCESS HELIOTROPE; or, Peter Stummel and the Magic Cherries. By PYNX GRYPII. With 34 Illustrations by GERTRUDE TROTTER. Large crown 8vo, cloth, 3s. 6d.

PSEUDONYM LIBRARY (The). 24mo, paper covers, 1s. 6d. each; cloth, 2s. each.

1. Mademoiselle Ixe. By LANOE FALCONER. 10th Edition.

2. The Story of Eleanor Lambert. By MAGDALEN BROOKE. 3rd Edit.

3. A Mystery of the Campagna, &c. By VON DEGEN. 3rd Edit.

4. The School of Art. By ISABEL SNOW. 3rd Edition.

5. Amaryllis. By ΓΕΩΡΓΙΟΣ ΔΡΟΣΙΝΗΣ. 3rd Edition.

6. The Hotel d'Angleterre. By LANOE FALCONER. 3rd Edition.

7. A Russian Priest. By ΠΟΤΑΠΕΗΚΟ. 4th Edition.

8. Some Emotions and a Moral. By JOHN OLIVER HOBBES. 3rd Edition.

9. European Relations. By TALMAGE DALIN. 2nd Edition.

10. John Sherman, and Dhoya. By GANCONAGH. 3rd Edition.

11. Through the Red-Litten Windows. By THEODOR HERTZ-GARTEN.

12. Green Tea: A Love Story. By V. SCHALLENBERGER. 2nd Edit.

13. Heavy Laden, and Old-Fashioned Folk. By ILSE FRAPAN.

PSEUDONYM LIBRARY—*contd.*

14. Makar's Dream, etc. By B. A. KOPOAEHKO, etc.

15. A New England Cactus, etc. By FRANK POPE HUMPHREY.

16. The Herb of Love. By ΓΕΩΡΓΙΟΣ ΔΡΟΣΙΝΗΣ.

17. The General's Daughter. By ΠΟΤΑΠΕΗΚΟ.

18. The Saghalien Convict, etc. By B.A. KOPOAEHKO, etc.

19. Gentleman Upcot's Daughter. By TOM COBBLEIGH.

20. A Splendid Cousin. By Mrs. ANDREW DEAN.

21. Colette. By PHILLIPPE SAINT HILAIRE.

22. Ottilie. By VERNON LEE. 2nd Edition.

23. A Study in Temptations. By JOHN OLIVER HOBBES. 3rd Edition.

24. The Cruise of the 'Wild Duck,' and other Tales from the Danish of HOLGER DRACHMANN.

25. Squire Hellman. Translated from the Finnish of JUHANI AHO.

26. A Father of Six, and An Occasional Holiday. By J. POTAPENKO.

27. The Two Countesses. Translated from the German of MARIE VON ESCHENBACH, by Mrs. WAUGH.

28. The Sinner's Comedy. By JOHN OLIVER HOBBES, Author of 'Some Emotions and a Moral. 3rd Edition.

29. Cavalleria Rusticana, and other Tales of Sicilian Peasant Life. By GIOVANNI VERGA.

30. The Passing of a Mood, and other Stories. By V., O., C. S. 2nd Edition.

31. God's Will, and other Stories. By ILSE FRAPAN, Author of 'Heavy Laden,' etc.

PSEUDONYM LIBRARY—*contd.*

32. **Dream Life and Real Life.** By RALPH IRON, Author of 'Dreams,' 'The Story of an African Farm,' etc.

33. **The Home of the Dragon: A Tonquinese Idyll.** BY ANNA CATHARINA.

34. **A Bundle of Life.** By JOHN OLIVER HOBBES, Author of 'The Sinner's Comedy,' etc.

35. **Mimi's Marriage: A Sketch.** By V. MIKOULITCH.

36. **The Rousing of Mrs Potter, and other Stories.** By JANE NELSON.

37. **A Study in Colour.** By ALICE SPINNER.

38. **The Hon. Stanbury, and Others.** By TWO.

PULSZKY.—**THEORY OF LAW AND CIVIL SOCIETY** (The). By AUG. PULSZKY (Dr JURIS). Demy 8vo, cloth, 18s.

PURNELL.—**LONDON AND ELSEWHERE.** By THOMAS PURNELL. Foolscap 8vo, paper, 1s.

QUEVEDO. — **PABLO DE SEGOVIA:** The Adventures of a Spanish Sharper. By FRANCISCO DE QUEVEDO. Illustrated with over 100 Drawings by DANIEL VIERGE. With an Introduction on 'Vierge and his Art,' by JOSEPH PENNELL; and 'A Critical Essay on Quevedo, and his Writings,' by H. E. WATTS. Super royal 4to, bound in parchment, old style (limited edition only), £3 13s. 6d. nett.—Also 10 copies, numbered and signed, with India proof Illustrations, £15 15s. each.

RADCLIFFE.—**OUT OF IT: A** Story for Children. By A. F. RADCLIFFE. Crown 8vo, cloth, 3s. 6d.

RAIKES.—**VIOLIN CHAT FOR BEGINNERS.** By A. H. RAIKES, M.A. Small crown 8vo, cloth, 3s. 6d.

RAMAKRISHNA.—**LIFE IN AN INDIAN VILLAGE.** By T. RAMAKRISHNA, B.A. With Introduction by the Right Hon. Sir M. E. GRANT DUFF, G.C.S.I. Crown 8vo, cloth, 6s.

RAY. — **BIRTH - RIGHTS:** A Novel. By EDGAR RAY. Crown 8vo, cloth, 6s.

REAL COOKERY. By 'Grid.' Demy 16mo, cloth, 2s.

RECIPES FOR THE MILLION: A Handy-Book for the Household. 2nd Edition. Crown 8vo, cloth, 2s. 6d.

REID.—**GLADYS FANE:** The Story of Two Lives. By T. WEMYSS REID. Popular Edition. Crown 8vo, cloth, 6s.

REFORMER'S BOOK-SHELF (The). Large crown 8vo, cloth, 3s. 6d. each.

1. **The English Peasant: His Past and Present.** By RICHARD HEATH.

2. **The Labour Movement.** By L. T. HOBHOUSE, M.A. Preface by R. B. HALDANE, M.P.

3. **Sixty Years of an Agitator's Life:** The Third and Cheaper Edition of Geo. JACOB HOLYOAKE'S Autobiography. 2 vols. With Portrait by WALTER SICKERT.

4. **Bamford's Passages in the Life of a Radical.** Edited, and with an Introduction, by HENRY DUNCKLEY ('VERAX'). 2 vols.

RENSSELAER.—**ART OUT OF DOORS:** Hints on Good Taste in Gardening. By Mrs SCHUYLER VAN RENSSELAER, Author of 'English Cathedrals,' etc. 8vo, cloth, 5s.

RENSSELAER.—DEVIL'S PIC-TURE BOOKS (The): A History of Playing Cards. By Mrs JOHN KING VAN RENSSELAER. Many full-page Coloured and Plain Illustrations. Royal 8vo, handsome cloth, 25s.

—— ENGLISH CATHE-DRALS. Described by Mrs VAN RENSSELAER, and Illustrated by JOSEPH PENNELL. Royal 8vo, cloth elegant, 25s.—Also, an Edition de Luxe, in two vols., 20 sets only being for sale in England; size, 10 in. by 14 in. ; Printed on fine plate paper ; the Illustrations from the original wood-blocks, the full-page ones and the seals of the Cathedrals (printed in appropriate colours) on separate sheets; each copy signed. Price £6 6s. nett.

—— HAND-BOOK OF ENGLISH CATHEDRALS. By Mrs VAN RENSSELAER. Fully Illustrated. Crown 8vo, cloth, 10s. 6d.

RENTON.—THE SONGS OF WILLIAM RENTON. Foolscap 8vo, cloth, 6s.

RHYS.—THE GREAT COCK-NEY TRAGEDY: Told in Sonnets. By ERNEST RHYS. With seven Illustrations by J. YEATS. 4to, paper covers, 2s.

RICHTER.—MELITA : A Turkish Love Story. By LOUISE M. RICH-TER. Crown 8vo, cloth, 6s.

RIDOUT. — TEN YEARS OF UPPER CANADA, IN PEACE AND WAR, 1805-1815. By THOMAS RIDOUT. Being the Rid-out Letters, with Annotations by MATILDA EDGAR. Also an Appen-dix of the Narrative of THOMAS RIDOUT's Captivity among the Shaw-anese Indians. Frontispiece Portrait and Maps. Royal 8vo, cloth, bevelled edges, 10s. 6d.

ROBERTS.—GERMAN EM-PEROR AND EMPRESS (The) (Frederick III. and Victoria). By DOROTHEA ROBERTS. Sixth and Popular Edition of 'Two Royal Lives.' Crown 8vo, cloth gilt, 2s. 6d.

ROBERTSON.—ESSAYS TO-WARDS A CRITICAL METHOD. By JOHN M. ROBERT-SON. Crown 8vo, cloth, 7s. 6d.

ROBINSON (A. M. F.).—AN ITALIAN GARDEN. By A. MARY F. ROBINSON (Mme. JAMES DARMESTETER). Foolscap 8vo, parchment, 3s. 6d.

—— END OF THE MIDDLE AGES (The) : Essays and Ques-tions in History. By A. MARY F. ROBINSON (Mme. JAMES DARMES-TETER). Demy 8vo, cloth, 10s. 6d.

—— NEW ARCADIA (The). Being Idylls of Country Life, with Other Poems. By A. MARY F. ROBINSON (Mme. JAMES DARMES-TETER. Crown 8vo, paper cover, 3s. 6d.

—— SONGS, BALLADS, AND A GARDEN PLAY. By A. MARY F. ROBINSON (Mme. JAMES DARMESTETER). With Frontispiece of Durer's 'Melan-cholia.' Small crown 8vo, half-bound, Japanese vellum, 5s.

ROBINSON (C. S.).—PHARAOHS OF THE BONDAGE (The) AND THE EXODUS. By the Rev. CHARLES S. ROBINSON, D.D., LL.D. Eighth Edition. Large crown 8vo, cloth, 5s.

ROBINSON (Phil).—SOME COUNTRY SIGHTS AND SOUNDS. By PHIL ROBINSON. Crown 8vo, cloth, bevelled boards, gilt edges, 6s.

ROCHE.—LIFE OF JOHN BOYLE O'REILLY. Together with his Complete Poems and Speeches. By JAMES JEFFREY ROCHE. Edited by Mrs JOHN BOYLE O'REILLY. ◆ With Introduction by H. E. JAMES Cardinal GIBBONS, Archbishop of Baltimore. Portraits and Illustrations. Royal 8vo, cloth, £1 1s.

ROGERS (Prof. J. E. T.).—ECO-NOMIC INTERPRETATION OF HISTORY (The). Lectures on Political Economy and Its History, delivered at Oxford, 1887-88. By Professor J. E. THOROLD ROGERS. New and Cheaper Edition. Demy 8vo, cloth, 7s. 6d.

—— INDUSTRIAL AND COMMERCIAL HISTORY OF ENGLAND (The). Lectures delivered to the University of Oxford. By Professor J. E. THOROLD ROGERS. Edited by his Son, ARTHUR G. L. ROGERS. Demy 8vo, cloth, 16s.

ROGERS (Dr J.). — REMINIS-CENCES OF A WORK-HOUSE MEDICAL OFFI-CER. By JOSEPH ROGERS, M.D. Edited, with a Preface, by Professor J. E. THOROLD ROGERS. Large crown 8vo, cloth, 7s. 6d.

ROMAN STUDENTS (The); or, On the Wings of the Morning. A Tale of the Renaissance. Illustrated. Cheaper Edition. Imp. 8vo, cloth, 3s. 6d.

ROSS.—THREE GENERA-TIONS OF ENGLISH-WOMEN: Memoirs and Correspondence of Mrs JOHN TAYLOR, Mrs SARAH AUSTIN and LADY DUFF GORDON. By JANET ROSS. New Edition, revised and augmented. With Portraits. Small demy 8vo, cloth, 7s. 6d.

ROWLANDS.—FISH-GUARD INVASION by the FRENCH IN 1797 (The). Some pass-ages taken from the Diary of the Reverend DANIEL ROWLANDS, some-time Vicar of Llanfiangelpenybont. Illustrated. Dedicated, by permission, to the Right Honourable the Earl of CAWDOR. Crown 8vo, cloth, 5s.

RUNCIMAN. — SIDE - LIGHTS. By the late JAMES RUNCIMAN. With Memoir by GRANT ALLEN, and an Introduction by W. T. STEAD. Large crown 8vo, cloth, 5s.

RUSSELL (Hon. R.). — THE BREAK OF DAY, and other Poems. By the Hon. ROLLO RUSSELL. Foolscap 8vo, buckram, 3s. 6d.

RUSSELL (Rev. J. S.). — THE PAROUSIA: A Critical Inquiry into the New Testament Doctrine of Our Lord's Second Coming. By the Rev. J. S. RUSSELL, M.A., D.D. New and Cheaper Edition. Demy 8vo, cloth, 7s. 6d.

RUTHERFORD.—THE AUTO-BIOGRAPHY OF MARK RUTHERFORD. Edited by his Friend, REUBEN SHAPCOTT. Fifth Edition, corrected, and with additions. Post 8vo, cloth, 3s. 6d.

—— MARK RUTHER-FORD'S DELIVERANCE. Edited by his Friend, REUBEN SHAPCOTT. New Edition. Post 8vo, cloth, 3s. 6d.

—— MIRIAM'S SCHOOL-ING, and other Papers. By MARK RUTHERFORD. Edited by his Friend, REUBEN SHAPCOTT. With Frontispiece by WALTER CRANE. Second Edition. Post 8vo, cloth, 3s. 6d.

—— THE REVOLUTION IN TANNER'S LANE. By MARK RUTHERFORD. Edited by his Friend, REUBEN SHAPCOTT. Post 8vo, cloth, 3s. 6d.

RYLANDS.—CRIME: ITS CAUSES AND REMEDY. By L. GORDON RYLANDS, B.A. Crown 8vo, cloth, 6s.

ST NICHOLAS MAGAZINE FOR YOUNG FOLKS. Conducted by Mrs MARY MAPES DODGE. Price 1s. monthly; or 12s. per year, post free; half-yearly volumes, price 8s. each. Cases for binding the parts, price 2s. each.

SALVINI.—THE AUTO-BIOGRAPHY OF THOMAS SALVINI. Containing Full-page and smaller Illustrations. Demy 8vo, cloth, 6s.

SAMSON · HIMMELSTIERNA.—RUSSIA UNDER ALEXANDER III., and in the Preceding Period. Translated from the German of H. VON SAMSON-HIMMELSTIERNA by J. MORRISON, M.A., and Edited, with Explanatory Notes and Introduction, by FELIX VOLKHOVSKY. Frontispiece. Large crown 8vo, cloth, 16s.

SANBORN AND HARRIS.—A. BRONSON ALCOTT: His Life and Philosophy. By F. B. SANBORN and WILLIAM T. HARRIS. In 2 vols. 12mo, cloth, 16s.

SCANNELL.—IN THE TIME OF ROSES: A Tale of Two Summers. By FLORENCE & EDITH SCANNELL. Thirty-two Illustrations. Square imperial 16mo, cloth, 5s.

SCHREINER. — DREAMS: A Collection of Tales. By OLIVE SCHREINER, Author of 'The Story of an African Farm,' &c. With Portrait. Fourth and Cheaper Edition. Fcap. 8vo, cloth, 2s. 6d.

SCOTT.—TUSCAN STUDIES AND SKETCHES. By LEADER SCOTT. Many full-page and smaller Illustrations. Square imperial 16mo, cloth, 10s. 6d.

SCOTT.—VINCIGLIATA AND MAIANO. By LEADER SCOTT. (Uniform with 'Sir John Hawkwood.') With 2 Illustrations. Large 4to, cloth, 25s. nett. Only 85 copies for sale.

SCRIVENER. — OUR FIELDS AND CITIES; or, Misdirected Energy in Our Towns and Cities. By SCRIVENER C. SCRIVENER. Second Edition. Two Plans. Cr. 8vo. cloth, 1s.

SCULLY.—POEMS. By WILLIAM CHARLES SCULLY. Foolscap 8vo, cloth, 4s. 6d.

SERGEANT.— THE GOVERNMENT HAND-BOOK: A Permanent Record of the Forms and Methods of Government in Great Britain, her Colonies, and Foreign Countries. With an Introduction on the diffusion of Popular Government over the Surface of the Globe, and on the Nature and Extent of International Jurisdictions. Edited by LEWIS SERGEANT. Large crown 8vo, half-bound, Roxburgh, 10s 6d.

SEVENTY YEARS OF LIFE IN THE VICTORIAN ERA: Embracing a Travelling Record in Australia, New Zealand, and America, etc. By a Physician. Illustrated. Crown 8vo, cloth, 5s.

SIDGWICK. — CAROLINE SCHLEGEL AND HER FRIENDS. By Mrs ALFRED SIDGWICK. With Steel Portrait. Crown 8vo, cloth, 7s. 6d.

SIMPSON. — JEANIE O' BIGGERSDALE, and other Yorkshire Stories. By KATHARINE SIMPSON. With Preface by the Rev. J. C. ATKINSON, Canon of York and Vicar of Danby-in-Cleveland. Large crown 8vo, cloth, 6s.

SMITH (F. H.). — **AMERICAN ILLUSTRATORS.** By F. HOP-KINSON SMITH. Fifteen Plates, printed in Colour on Japan paper, and 100 Sketches, Portraits and Drawings in the text. The text is printed on heavy-coated paper. The cover is from a design by W. L. METCALF. In handsome portfolio, with etched design on cover, £3 12s. 6d. nett. 100 copies only for sale in England, each being numbered.

SMITH(H.).—**THROUGH ABYS-SINIA**: An Envoy's Ride to the King of Zion. By Lieut. HARRISON SMITH, R.N. Maps and Illustrations. Crown 8vo, cloth, 7s. 6d.

SMITH (R. M.).—**EMIGRATION AND IMMIGRATION**: A Study in Social Science. By RICHARD M. SMITH. Square imperial 16mo, cloth, 7s. 6d.

SMYTH.—**CHRISTIAN FACTS AND FORCES.** By Rev. NEW-MAN SMYTH. Crown 8vo, cloth, 4s. 6d.

————— **PERSONAL CREEDS**: or, How to Form a Working Theory of Life. By Rev. NEWMAN SMYTH. Crown 8vo, cloth, 2s. 6d.

————— **REALITY OF FAITH** (The). By Rev. NEWMAN SMYTH. Fourth and Cheaper Edition. Crown 8vo, cloth, 4s. 6d.

SOUL-SHAPES. Crown 4to, with 4 Lithographic Plates of Souls. Bound in parchment, 3s. 6d.

SOVEREIGNS AND COURTS OF EUROPE (The). Being full descriptions of the Home and Court Life of the Reigning Families of Europe. By 'POLITIKOS.' With many Portraits. Crown 8vo, cloth, 10s. 6d.

SPALDING.—**HOUSE OF LORDS (The)**: A Retrospect and Forecast. By THOMAS ALFRED SPALDING, LL.B., Barrister-at-Law. Small demy 8vo, cloth, 10s. 6d.

SPENDER. — **STORY OF THE HOME RULE SESSION.** Written by HAROLD SPENDER and Sketched by F. CARRUTHERS GOULD. With many Portraits and Cartoons. Crown 4to, with specially designed cover, cloth, 2s.

SPINOZA.—**ETHIC**: Demonstrated in Geometrical Order, and Divided into Five Parts, which treat (1) Of God; (2) Of the Nature and Origin of the Mind; (3) Of the Nature and Origin of the Affects; (4) Of Human Bondage, or of the Strength of the Affects; (5) Of the Power of the Intellect, or of Human Liberty. By BENEDICT DE SPINOZA. Translated from the Latin by AMELIA HUT-CHINSON STIRLING and W. HALE WHITE. Second Edition, revised and corrected, with New Preface. Demy 8vo, cloth, 7s. 6d.

STEP. — **EASY LESSONS IN BOTANY.** By EDWARD STEP. 120 Illustrations by Author. Third Edition. Linen covers, 7d.; in two parts, paper covers, each 3d.

————— **PLANT LIFE**: Popular Papers on the Phenomena of Botany. By EDWARD STEP. 148 Illustrations by the Author. Third Edition. Crown 8vo, cloth extra, 3s. 6d.

STERRY. — **LAZY MINSTREL** (The). By J. ASHBY STERRY, Author of 'Cucumber Chronicles,' etc. With Frontispiece by E. A. ABBEY. Fifth and Popular Edition, foolscap 8vo, parchment, 2s. 6d.; also a Cheap Edition, in paper, 1s.

STEVENS.—**HOW MEN PRO-POSE**: The Fateful Question and its Answer. Love Scenes collected from Popular Works of Fiction. Edited by AGNES STEVENS. Square imperial 16mo, cloth, 6s.; Presentation Edition, cloth elegant, bevelled boards, gilt edges, in box, 7s. 6d.; Popular Edition, small square 8vo, cloth, 3s. 6d.

STILLMAN. — OLD ITALIAN MASTERS. By W. J. STILLMAN. Engravings and notes by T. COLE. Royal 8vo, cloth elegant, price £2 2s. —Also, an Edition de Luxe, in two portfolios. *Price on application.*

STINDE. — WOODLAND TALES. By Dr JULIUS STINDE, Author of 'The Buchholz Family.' Crown 8vo, cloth, 3s. 6d.

STOCKTON. — AMOS KIL- BRIGHT: His Adscititious Ad- ventures; with other Stories. By FRANK R. STOCKTON, Author of 'The Lady and the Tiger,' etc. 8vo, cloth, 3s. 6d.

STORY OF THE NATIONS (The). Each Volume is Furnished with Maps, Illustrations and Index. Large crown 8vo, fancy cloth, gold lettered, 5s. each.—Or may be had in the following special bindings: half Persian, cloth sides, gilt tops; full calf, half extra, marbled edges; Tree calf, gilt edges, gold roll inside, full gilt back. *Prices on application.*

1. Rome. By ARTHUR GILMAN, M.A.
2. The Jews. By Professor J. K. HOSMER.
3. Germany. By the Rev. S. BARING-GOULD.
4. Carthage. By Prof. ALFRED J. CHURCH.
5. Alexander's Empire. By Prof. J. P. MAHAFFY.
6. The Moors in Spain. By STANLEY LANE POOLE.
7. Ancient Egypt. By Prof. GEORGE RAWLINSON.
8. Hungary. By Prof. ARMINIUS VAMBÉRY.
9. The Saracens. By ARTHUR GILMAN, M.A.
10. Ireland. By the Hon. EMILY LAWLESS.
11. Chaldea. By ZÉNAIDE A. RAGOZIN.

STORY OF THE NATIONS (The)—*continued.*

12. The Goths. By HENRY BRAD-LEY.
13. Assyria. By ZENAIDE A. RAGOZIN.
14. Turkey. By STANLEY LANE-POOLE.
15. Holland. By Prof. J. E. THOROLD ROGERS.
16. Mediæval France. By GUSTAVE MASSON.
17. Persia. By S. G. W. BENJAMIN.
18. Phœnicia. By Prof. GEORGE RAWLINSON.
19. Media. By ZENAIDE A. RAGOZIN.
20. The Hansa Towns. By HELEN ZIMMERN.
21. Early Britain. By Prof. ALFRED J. CHURCH.
22. The Barbary Corsairs. By STANLEY LANE-POOLE.
23. Russia. By W. R. MORFILL.
24. The Jews under the Roman Empire. By W. DOUGLAS MORRISON, M.A.
25. Scotland. By JOHN MACKINTOSH, LL.D.
26. Switzerland. By R. STEAD and LINA HUG.
27. Mexico. By SUSAN HALE.
28. Portugal. By H. MORSE STEPHENS.
29. The Normans. By SARAH ORNE JEWITT.
30. The Byzantine Empire. By C. W. C. OMAN, M.A.
31. Sicily: Phœnician, Greek and Roman. By the late E. A. FREEMAN.
32. The Tuscan and Genoa Republics. By BELLA DUFFY.
33. Poland. By W. R. MORFILL.

STORY OF THE NATIONS (The)—*continued.*

34. **Parthia.** By Prof. GEORGE RAWLINSON, Author of 'Ancient Egypt,' etc.

35. **The Australian Commonwealth** (New South Wales, Tasmania, Western Australia, South Australia, Victoria, Queensland, New Zealand). By GREVILLE TREGARTHEN.

36. **Spain:** A Summary of Spanish History from the Moorish Conquest to the Fall of Granada (711-1492). By H. E. WATTS.

37. **South Africa.** By GEORGE M. THEAL. [*In preparation.*

38. **The Crusades:** The Story of the Latin Kingdom of Jerusalem. [*In preparation.*

STOWE. — UNDER SUSPICION. By EDITH STOWE. Crown 8vo, cloth, 6s.

STRETTELL.—TENERIFFE: Personal Experiences of the Island as a Health Resort. By GEORGE W. STRETTELL. Crown 8vo, paper, 1s.

STUBBS.—GOD AND THE PEOPLE: The Religious Creed of a Democrat. Being Selections from the Writings of JOSEPH MAZZINI. Large crown 8vo, cloth, 5s.

STUTTARD.—BUTTERFLY (The): Its Nature, Development. and Attributes. By JOHN STUTTARD. Illustrated. Foolscap 8vo, limp cloth, 1s.

SWINTON.—CHESS FOR BEGINNERS; and, The Beginnings of Chess. By R. B. SWINTON. Illustrations by the Author and from Ancient Sources. Fourth Edition. Crown 8vo, cloth, 2s.

SYMONDS.—DAYS SPENT ON A DOGE'S FARM. By MARGARET SYMONDS. Photogravure Frontispiece and 50 other Illustrations. Demy 8vo, cloth, 12s.

TALKS WITH SOCRATES ABOUT LIFE. Translations from the Georgias and the Republic of Plato. 12mo, cloth, 3s. 6d.

TENGER. — RECOLLECTIONS OF THE COUNTESS THERESE OF BRUNSWICK. By MARIAM TENGER. Translated by the Hon. Mrs RUSSELL. Two Portraits. Crown 8vo, cloth, 3s. 6d.

TENNYSON (LORD) AND HIS FRIENDS. A Series of Twenty-five Portraits. With Essay by Mrs THACKERAY RITCHIE, and Introduction by H. H. HAY CAMERON. 400 only printed, of which 350 are for sale (150 of this number in America). All copies numbered. Columbier folio, price £6 6s. nett —Also, an Edition of the Proofs, on India paper, limited to 16 sets, 10 of which are for sale, each copy numbered and signed. *Prices on application.*

THEORIES. By A. N. T. A. P. Demy 12mo, cloth, 3s. 6d.

THEURIET.—JULES BASTIEN-LEPAGE AND HIS ART: A Memoir. By ANDRE THEURIET. With which is included 'Bastien Lepage as Artist,' by GEORGE CLAUSEN, A.R.W.S.; 'Modern Realism in Painting,' by WALTER SICKERT; and 'A Study of Marie Bashkirtseff,' by MATHILDE BLIND. Illustrated by Reproductions of Bastien-Lepage's and Marie Bashkirtseff's Works. Royal 8vo, cloth, gilt tops, 10s. 6d.

THOMAS.—ICHABOD: A Portrait. By BERTHA THOMAS. Two vols. Crown 8vo, cloth, 21s.

THRING.—ADDRESSES. By Rev. EDWARD THRING, M.A. With Portrait. Second Edition. Small crown 8vo, cloth, 5s.

THRING.—**POEMS AND TRANSLATIONS.** By Rev. EDWARD THRING, M.A. Small crown 8vo, cloth, 2s.

—————— **UPPINGHAM SCHOOL SONGS AND BORTH LYRICS.** By Rev. EDWARD THRING, M.A. Small crown 8vo, cloth, 2s.

TONE (Wolfe). — **THE AUTOBIOGRAPHY OF THEOBALD WOLFE TONE:** A Chapter from Irish History, 1790-1798. Edited, with an Introduction, by R. BARRY O'BRIEN, of the Middle Temple, Barrister-at-Law, Author of 'Fifty Years of Concessions to Ireland,' 'Thomas Drummond,' etc. 2 vols., with Photogravure Frontispiece to each. 4 Steel-Plates, and a Letter in facsimile. Royal 8vo, cloth, 32s.

TOPSYS AND TURVYS. An Amusing Book for the Nursery. Coloured Illustrations, oblong size (9 in. by 7 in.) Paper boards, 5s.

TOUSSAINT.—**MAJOR FRANK.** By BOSBOOM TOUSSAINT. Translated by JAS. AKEROYD. Crown 8vo, cloth, 6s.

TOWNDROW.—**A GARDEN,** and other Poems. By RICHARD FRANCIS TOWNDROW. Crown 8vo, cloth, 3s. 6d.

TUNSTALL.—**HOUSEHOLD NURSING.** By JOHN OGLE TUNSTALL, M.D., Lond., M.R.C.S., late Senior Resident Medical Officer at Birmingham Infirmary. Demy 16mo, cloth, 2s.

TWO SPHERES; or, Mind and Instinct. By 'T.E.S.T.,' Revised and Enlarged. Demy 8vo, cloth, 5s.

TYLOR.—**CHESS:** A Christmas Masque. By LOUIS TYLOR. Fcap. 8vo, parchment, 3s. 6d.

TYTLER.—**BEAUTIES AND FRIGHTS,** with THE STORY OF BOBINETTE. By SARAH TYTLER. Illustrated by M. E. EDWARDS. Second Edition. Small 8vo, cloth, 2s. 6d.

—————— **FOOTPRINTS:** Nature seen on its Human Side. By SARAH TYTLER. Illustrated. Fourth Edition. Imperial 16mo, cloth, gilt edges, 3s. 6d.

UNWIN'S NOVEL SERIES. About 300 pages each, clearly printed. Pocket size, 6½ by 4½ ins., in stiff paper wrapper, price 1s. 6d. each.

1. **Gladys Fane.** By T. WEMYSS REID.
2. **Isaac Eller's Money.** By Mrs ANDREW DEAN.
3. **Concerning Oliver Knox.** By G. COLMORE.
4. **A Mariage de Convenance.** By C. F. KEARY. Second Edition.
5. **Chronicles of a Health Resort:** A Novel. By A. HELDER.
6. **Tarantella.** By MATHILDE BLIND.

URWICK. — **BIBLE TRUTHS AND CHURCH ERRORS.** By the Rev. WILLIAM URWICK, M.A. 8vo, cloth, 6s.

VAMBERY.—**ARMINIUS VAMBERY:** His Life and Adventures. By Himself. With Portrait and 14 Illustrations. Seventh and Popular Edition. Square imperial 16mo, cloth extra, 6s.—Boys' Edition, with Introductory Chapter dedicated to the Boys of England. Portrait and 17 Illustrations. Crown 8vo, cloth gilt, gilt edges, 5s.

VAN DYKE. — **REALITY OF RELIGION (The).** By HENRY J. VAN DYKE, D.D. Second Edition. Crown 8vo, cloth, 4s. 6d.

*VERO.—*FRANCIS: A Socialistic Romance. By M. DAL VERO. Crown 8vo, cloth, 4s. 6d.

*VILLARI (L.).—*CAMILLA'S GIRLHOOD. By LINDA VILLARI. Two vols. Crown 8vo, cloth, 21s.

—— ON TUSCAN HILLS AND VENETIAN WATERS. By LINDA VILLARI. Illustrated. Square imperial 16mo, 7s. 6d.

—— WHEN I WAS A CHILD: or, Left Behind. By LINDA VILLARI. Illustrated. Square 8vo, cloth, gilt edges, 3s. 6d.

*VILLARI (Prof. P.).—*LIFE AND TIMES OF GIROLAMO SAVONAROLA. By Prof. PASQUALE VILLARI. Translated by LINDA VILLARI. Third and Cheaper Edition. Portraits and Illustrations. Two vols. Large crown 8vo, cloth, 21s.

—— LIFE AND TIMES OF NICCOLO MACHIAVELLI. By Professor PASQUALE VILLARI. Translated by LINDA VILLARI. New, Revised, and Complete Edition, containing New Preface and Two New Chapters. In Two volumes. Four copperplate and 29 other Illustrations. Demy 8vo, cloth, 32s.

VOSMAER. — AMAZON (The): An Art Novel. By CARL VOSMAER. Preface by Professor GEORG EBERS, and Frontispiece drawn specially by L. ALMA TADEMA, R.A. Crown 8vo, cloth, 6s.

WAGNER.—NAMES; AND THEIR MEANING: A Book for the Curious. By LEOPOLD WAGNER. Second and Revised Edition. Large crown 8vo, cloth, 3s. 6d.

—— MORE ABOUT NAMES. Large crown 8vo, cloth, 7s. 6d.

WALKLEY.—PLAYHOUSE IMPRESSIONS. By A. B. WALKLEY. Small cr. 8vo, cloth, 5s.

WARNER.—STUDIES IN THE SOUTH AND WEST, with Comments on Canada. By CHARLES DUDLEY WARNER. Crown 8vo, cloth, 10s. 6d.

WATSON. — SYLVAN FOLK: Sketches of Bird and Animal Life in Britain. By JOHN WATSON. Crown 8vo, cloth, 3s. 6d.

WATTS.—PRINCIPLES TO START WITH. By ISAAC WATTS, D.D. Seventh Thousand. 32mo, red edges, 1s.

WAY TO FORTUNE (The): A Series of Short Essays with Illustrative Proverbs and Anecdotes from many Sources. Ninth Thousand. Small 8vo, 1s.; cloth 2s. 6d.

WESTON.—DICK'S HOLIDAYS, AND WHAT HE DID WITH THEM. By JAMES WESTON. Illustrated. New and Cheaper Edition. Imperial 16mo, cloth extra, gilt edges, 3s. 6d.

WHITE.—THE HEART AND SONGS OF THE SPANISH SIERRAS. By GEORGE WHIT WHITE. Seven Illustrations. Large crown 8vo, cloth, 6s.

WIDER HOPE (The). Essays and Strictures on the Doctrine and Literature of the Future. By numerous Writers, Lay and Clerical: Canon FARRAR, the late Principal TULLOCH, the late Rev. J. BALDWIN BROWN, the Very Rev. E. H. PLUMPTRE, D.D., Rev. WILLIAM ARTHUR, Rev. JAMES H. RIGG, the late Rev. HENRY ALLON, D.D. With a Paper by THOMAS DE QUINCEY, and a Bibliography of Recent Eschatology as contained in the British Museum. Crown 8vo, cloth, 7s. 6d.

WILKINS.—DAILY LIFE AND WORK IN INDIA. By Rev. W. J. WILKINS. Fifty-nine full-page and other Illustrations. Second Edition. Crown 8vo, cloth, 3s. 6d.

——— MODERN HINDUISM Being an Account of the Religion and Life of the Hindus in Northern India. By Rev. W. J. WILKINS. Demy 8vo, cloth, 16s.

WILLIAMS(R.)—PSALMS AND LITANIES, COUNSELS AND COLLECTS FOR DEVOUT PERSONS. By ROWLAND WILLIAMS, D.D., late Vicar of Broadchalke, sometime Senior Fellow and Tutor of King's College, Cambridge. Edited by his Widow. New Edition. Crown 8vo, cloth, 3s. 6d.

——— STRAY THOUGHTS FROM THE NOTE-BOOKS OF ROWLAND WILLIAMS, D.D. Edited by his Widow. New Edition. Crown 8vo, cloth, 3s. 6d.

WOLLSTONECRAFT.— VINDICATION (A) OF THE RIGHTS OF WOMAN : With Strictures on Political and other Subjects. By MARY WOLLSTONECRAFT. New Edition, with Introduction by Mrs HENRY FAWCETT. Demy 8vo, cloth, 7s. 6d.

WRIGHT (A.). — BABOO ENGLISH AS 'TIS WRIT : Being Curiosities of Indian Journalism. By ARNOLD WRIGHT. Second Edition. Demy 16mo, paper, 6d. ; cloth, 1s.

WRIGHT (C.). — OFF DUTY : Stories of a Parson on Leave. By CHARLES WRIGHT. Crown 8vo, cloth, 2s. 6d.

WRIGHT (H.C.).—CHILDREN'S STORIES IN ENGLISH LITERATURE, from Shakespeare to Tennyson. By H. C. WRIGHT. Crown 8vo, cloth, 5s.

WRIGHT (T.).-- THE LIFE OF WILLIAM COWPER. By THOMAS WRIGHT, Principal of Cowper School, Olney, Author of 'The Town of Cowper,' etc. With 21 full-page Illustrations. Demy 8vo, cloth, 21s.—Also, an Edition de Luxe (the number of which is strictly limited), printed on Dutch handmade paper, and bound in parchment, price 30s. nett.

YEATS.—THE WANDERINGS OF OISIN, and other Poems. By W. B. YEATS. Large crown 8vo, cloth, 5s.

YORKE.—WHEN MOTHER WAS LITTLE. By S. P. YORKE. 13 Full-page Illustrations by HENRY J. FORD. Small square 8vo, cloth, gilt edges, 3s. 6d.

YOUNG (A.).—A SHORT HISTORY OF THE NETHERLANDS. By ALEXANDER YOUNG. 77 Illustrations. Demy 8vo, cloth, 7s. 6d.

YOUNG(R.)—LIGHT IN LANDS OF DARKNESS. By ROBERT YOUNG. Illustrated. Second Edition. Crown 8vo, cloth extra, 6s.

——— MODERN MISSIONS : Their Trials and Triumphs. By ROBERT YOUNG. Map and Illustrations. Third Edition. Crown 8vo, cloth extra, 5s.

ZIMMERN.—HEROIC TALES : Retold from Firdusi the Persian. By HELEN ZIMMERN. With Illustrations from Etchings by L. ALMA TADEMA, and Prefatory Poem by E. W. GOSSE. Popular Edition. Crown 8vo, cloth extra, gilt edges, 5s.

A LIST OF BOOKS
Arranged in Order of Price.

36   *Index.*

38   *Index.*

COLSTON AND COMPANY, PRINTERS, EDINBURGH.

www.ingramcontent.com/pod-product-compliance
Lightning Source LLC
Chambersburg PA
CBHW021214270326
41929CB00010B/1118